KB171458

Money and Society

A Societal Investigation into Class, Money, and Power

Geld und Gesellschaft
Versuch einer gesellschaftlichen Theorie des Geldes

By

Wilhelm Gerloff

Translation and Notes by

Hans DG Hyun

2023

Shoin House

Book Information:

Book Title: Money and Society - A Societal Investigation into Class, Money, and Power

Date of Publication: December 15, 2023

Editor in Chief: Keon Hee Han

Publisher: Bookk Co., Ltd.

Publisher License: 2014.07.15.(No. 2014-16)

Address: 119 Gasan digital 1-ro, Geumcheon-gu, Seoul, The Republic of Korea (08589)

Tel: 1670-8316

Email: info@bookk.co.kr

ISBN: 979-11-410-6040-4

www.bookk.co.kr

Original Title:

Wilhelm Gerloff, *Geld und Gesellschaft – Versuch einer gesellschaftlichen Theorie des Geldes,* Vittorio Kolstermann, Frankfrut am Main, 1952

Cover pictures:

Front: Tax Collectors (ca. 1525–30), Quinten Massys (1465-1530)

Back: Peasants at the Tax Collector (1539), Jan Massys (active 1531–1573).

MONEY & BANKING CLASSICS SERIES BY SHOIN HOUSE:

1. *Sacred Money – A Historical Investigation into the Sacred Origin of Money* (Bernhard Laum) (2023).
2. *Staatliche Theorie des Geldes* (Georg F. Knapp) (2023) (A version retyped in modern scripts from Fraktur). German version.
3. *The State Theory of Money – A New and Complete Translation* (Georg F. Knapp) (2023).
4. Theorie des Geldes – Allgemeine Lehre vom Gelde (Friedrich von Wieser) (2023).

About the Author:

Wilhelm Gerloff (1880-1954) was born in Krefeld, Germany in 1880 and had a multifaceted educational journey, starting as an elementary school teacher and eventually becoming a distinguished academic. He pursued studies in various disciplines including economics, political science, and finance. He held teaching positions in different universities, finally becoming a full professor at the University of Innsbruck, where his focus on finance became prominent.

His interest in finance was significant, advocating for its stronger representation in the academic landscape. He played a pivotal role in redefining financial studies, especially in the context of the challenges posed by World War I. He is known as the founding father of public finance in Germany, known as the editor of *Handbuch der Finanzwissenschaft* (1926).

Gerloff's contributions were not limited to finance; he ventured into socio-political and economic issues, often presenting views that contrasted with prevailing ideologies. He aimed to modernize the Historical School, integrating its traditions into contemporary economic theories. His works demonstrated a close connection to sociology, echoing the thoughts of Max Weber and Franz Oppenheimer. He integrated sociological understanding into his economic analyses, emphasizing the significance of social, historical, and cultural factors in shaping economic systems.

His tenure at the University of Frankfurt faced challenges due to his critical stance against National Socialism. He was eventually removed from office by Nazis and subjected to political scrutiny and restrictions on international activities.

Health issues affected his later career, leading to his early retirement in 1940. However, he remained connected to academia, contributing to the reconstruction of the Faculty of Economics and Social Sciences at the University of Frankfurt after World War II. He passed away in 1954, leaving a legacy of academic excellence and a significant impact on economic thought.

About the Translator:

Hans DG Hyun is a Post Keynesian economist with a specialization in money and banking. He has worked for over 30 years with major international banks as a senior management. He has translated several books, including "The State Theory of Money" by G. F. Knapp, "Sacred Money" by Bernhard Laum, "Money and Society" by W. Gerloff, and "Theory of Money" by Friedrich von Wieser. Additionally, he is the author of "Abenomics and Its Enemies from the Alice Wonderland" and has contributed numerous academic articles on money and banking to international journals.

Noes for Readers:

- "[tn]" in the footnotes indicates translator's notes.
- "[℗*]" references the page number in the original German text.
- Wording enclosed in square bracket "[ ]" represents translator's additions or comments.
- Bold typefaces and double quotation marks are those originally included in the text.
- Single quotation marks (') are utilised to demonstrate compounded meanings for longer phrases or words (e.g., 'power of disposal and control' – *Verfügungsmacht*) or to emphasise particular points as indicated by the translator.
- We employ *italics* to denote non-English languages or translator's emphases.
- We aimed for fidelity to the original German text, resulting in translation terms that might not be commonly used in English. Our priority was accuracy, aiming to convey the author's original intent even if it sacrifices the smoothness of the reading experience, possibly posing a risk of altering the author's message.
- Therefore, we frequently use hyphens to convey the distinctive German practice of forming compound words by linking more than two words, particularly when we want to emphasise that they constitute single concepts rather than individual, separate words. For example, gift-exchange (*Gabentausch*), gift-traffic (*Gabenverkehr*), goods-usage (*Gütergebrauch*), purpose-pursuit (*Zweckverfolgung*), and so on. This choice is inevitable albeit not quite aligned with common English usage, because of a need to reflect author's intention as closely as possible and not to lose German nuisance.

Table of Contents

Meiner Lieben Frau Helene

My Dear Lady Helene

Wer weiß, wie die Menschen zum Gelde stehen, der weiß, wie es um ihre Seele steht.

Das gilt nicht nur von den einzelnen, sondern auch von den Gesellschaftsklassen und von ganzen Zeitaltern und Völkern.

Who knows how people feel about money, knows how it stands with their soul.

This applies not only to individuals, but also to social classes, entire eras, and nations.

Foreword

In his biography, Herbert Spencer compares scientific work to mountain climbing. Who would this comparison appeal to more than someone who, like me, was allowed to spend eleven of the best years of his life at a university located in the Alps? Finally, as a paraphrase of Spencer's train of thought, the summit is reached. A broad and seemingly comprehensive view opens up. Yet, very soon, one notices higher mountain peaks veiled by mist in close proximity. The new task is set: those must also be conquered.

As described here, I experienced a similar situation when I brought my research on "The Emergence of Money and the Beginnings of the Monetary Framework" (*Die Entstehung des Geldes und die Anfänge des Geldwesens*) (Gerloff 1940) to its initial conclusion and for publication. Since the first edition of that book, a second and a third have followed. In the meantime, I attempted to conquer the next summit. This book reveals some of the difficulties of this mountain ascent. Above all, however, it should showcase the achieved height and the gained view, the new horizon. Whether it was the right summit and whether the view is worthwhile, let others decide. It is self-evident that further summits lie beyond. Even the one that I believe I conquered here will, I hope, see many other climbers who will enter themselves into the summit book that I started, and they will supplement and correct much-concerning access, path, altitude, and perspective.

The reason why I remained in the domain I entered with my investigation into the emergence of money is hereby explained.

To the superficial judge who merely reads the section headings, it might appear at times as if there are repetitions of what has been said in my previous book about the emergence of money (Gerloff 1940), but this is by no means the case. Just as in ancient Greek culture, it was considered the poet's supreme art to provide a new interpretation to an old narrative in a fresh form, genuine scientific research must also demonstrate its strength by generating new questions, new solutions, and new foundations from an old material.

Money is a cultural-good (*Kulturgut*) that immediately prompts the question: How did it come into existence? Once we have attempted to answer this question, the second one arises: What is the position (*Stellung*) and function of money in society, once it exists? This is also connected to the question of its transformations. The societal or social[1] function of money manifests itself within social relationships. Insofar as such relationships are expressed through money or are created through money-usage (*Geldgebrauch*),[2] they are the subject of this investigation. Our focus is not on the money-usage as economic events, but rather on its societal aspect, which is the object of our understanding.

As J. J. Bachofen[3] states in the famous preface to "Mother Right" (*Mutterrecht*; Bachofen 1861),

> The truly scientific understanding does not merely consist in answering the question of 'what.' Its completion is attained when it is able to discover the 'where from' and thereby knows how to

---

[1] [tn] See Translate Note on p. 354.

[2] [tn] We distinguish between '*Geldgebrauch*' (money-usage) and '*Geldverwendung*' (money-expending), with the latter emphasising the act of spending money, while the former encompasses the broader spectrum of money's application, extending beyond mere spending.

[3] [tn] Johann Jakob Bachofen (1815–1887) was a Swiss jurist, anthropologist, and cultural historian. He is known for his pioneering work in the fields of cultural anthropology and sociology, particularly for his studies on the history of human societies, family structures, and the role of women in ancient societies.

connect the 'where to.' Understanding elevates knowledge when it can encompass origin, progression, and conclusion.

No better than with these words can I describe the path I have attempted to take in my investigation.

Certainly, I am aware that I am by no means exhausting the problem and range of questions outlined in my topic. Who could possibly do that? I still have many concerns in this regard. I am no different from Jeremias Gotthelf,[4] the Sage of Lützelflüh,[5] who wrote to his friend Joseph Burkhalter on June 12, 1843:

> You know the fable[6] of the man who rolls a stone up the mountain and, once at the top, has to watch it roll back down and start over. I believe that man is me. When I have something at hand, I look forward to freedom, and make all kinds of plans; [p11] but once the thing is done, freedom is no longer on the table. Another task lies ahead, needs to be completed, and I start rolling the stone anew. Yet, despite many experiences, I find joy in the freedom once again.

Whether I will attempt to roll a stone once more, and which stone that will be, remains uncertain here.

I dedicate this book in deep gratitude to my dear wife, the guiding spirit of my life, the faithful companion of my journey, and my life's work.

Oberursel Taunus, Herbst 1951.

W. Gerloff.

---

[4] [tn] Jeremias Gotthelf is the pen name of the Swiss novelist, pastor, and social critic Albert Bitzius (1797–1854). He is best known for his works of fiction that offer vivid depictions of rural life in Switzerland and explore social and moral issues of his time.

[5] [tn] A municipality located in the Emmental region of the canton of Bern in Switzerland.

[6] [tn] The myth of Sisyphus in Greek mythology.

Money and Society

A Societal Investigation into Class, Money, and Power

2

I. Money as a Social Phenomenon

§1. The Task

[☙13] Money is a creation of 'social action' (*soziales Handeln*).[1][2] This insight, the result of my research on the emergence of money, is the starting point of the following investigations.[3] My investigations have as their object the task of acknowledgement of money as a social category. It is the task faced by every sociological inquiry to make social action understandable in an illuminating way. Regarding our subject of study, this means nothing other than understanding the phenomenon of money as a *social means of relationship* (*Beziehungsmittel*), which can be traced back to certain *original forces* (*ursprüngliche Kraft*) and *facts of societal life* as they exist within the nature of society, thus placing it within the broader cultural context. At the same time, this implies that it is not money itself, but the money-usage (*Geldgebrauch*), that needs explaining. However, the money-usage is the subject of our investigation only to the extent that it is determined by the essence of money (*Wesen des Geldes*) itself — what one might call the 'essential services of money' (*Wesensleistungen des Geldes*). Therefore, it is the question of the nature of money (*Natur des Geldes*) or the 'condition of being money' (*Wesenheit des Geldes*) as revealed through its usage that we pose initially and primarily. This question can only be answered if we are able to fathom money in its existence (*Dasein*), in money's life-sphere (*Lebensbereich*).

The realm of the existence of money is society. Society, as meant here without going into specifics, can provisionally be defined as a human community characterised in some way. It is the result of societalisation

---

[1] [tn] See Translation Note on p. 350.

[2] [tn] This sentence contrasts with G. F. Knapp's famous proposition, "money is the creation of legal-order" (Knapp 2023/1923:2).

[3] [tn] It is also a conclusion of this book. See p. 306.

(*Vergesellschaftung*),[4] that is, all those processes through which people enter into relationships with each other. It is the same fact seen from different perspectives that the concepts 'human' and 'society' express. [❡14] This means: the foundations of society rest in those forces that constitute human beings themselves. "*Unus homo nullus homo*" (One person is no person). This is what Gierke[5] expressed in the introduction to his "*Rechtsgeschichte der deutschen Genossenschaft*" (Legal History of the German Cooperative) with the words, "What a person is, they owe to the uniting (*Vereinigung*) from person to person." Societal existence is a necessary condition of humanity. There's no humanity without society.

Societal existence is based on mental ties. These connections create certain relationships that connect individuals and manifest in causally conditioned interactions (*Wechselwirkung*): the societal fact (*Tatbestand*). This becomes objective in specific manifestation-forms: culture, trade (*Verkehr*), law, custom, etc. Each of these manifestation-forms uses means of expression (*Ausdrucksmittel*) as a means of communication (*Mittel der Verständigung*). These are gestures and language; in addition, physical objects, certain items, come into play as a third category. Money is one of these means of expression. From this arises the task: interpreting money as a means of social communication (*soziale Verständigung)* or social activities (*sozialer Handlungen*).

The significance of the position that money holds among social categories is evident in the fact that the question has also been posed for money from the very beginnings of scientific inquiry about money

---

[4] [tn] See Translation Note on p. 354.

[5] [tn] Otto von Gierke (1841–1921), a German legal scholar and historian. He is well-known for his work on the history of German law, constitutional law, and political theory.

whether it arose by nature (*physei*[6]) or by agreement (*thesei*[7]), similar to some others for society itself such as the state and language. And just as opinions were divided into adherents of Stoic and Epicurean teachings, some of whom claimed that society had naturally evolved, while others argued that it had come about purposeful establishment by statute with regard to the emergence of society and the state, opinions about the emergence of money also diverged in the same manner right from the beginning. However, much like society, the state, or language was not invented, contrived, or established by people, and neither was money. Money is not a technical thing, or rather: it did not originate as a technical thing, even though it serves a technical purpose, which becomes increasingly refined. [p15] What money is, as already mentioned, can only be understood through its entire life-sphere. Its life-sphere, encompassing both the place of its origin and the stage of its operation, and potentially even the cause of its decline, is society. Therefore, it can only be comprehended through a societal theory of money (*gesellschaftliche Theorie des Geldes*).

The general theory of money addresses two problem areas as its subject matter. One is referred to as the qualitative problem of money, and the other as the quantitative problem of money. Naturally, there are other essential areas of inquiry within the theory of money, but they fall under the purview of specialised monetary theory or general monetary policy. This is true, for instance, of the question of currency standard (*Währung*). The subject of this book belongs to the realm of qualitative monetary theory. This declaration is made explicitly to preclude any misunderstandings or criticisms from arising. Such a statement and

---

[6] [tn] '*Physei*' (φύσει), meaning 'by nature,' from the root '*physis*' (φύσις), which means 'nature.'

[7] [tn] '*Thesei*' (θέσει), meaning 'by convention' or 'by agreement' is the dative form of the word '*thesis*' (θέσις), which means 'a placing,' 'a setting,' or 'a position.' It also refers to a point of view, an assertion, or the central idea of a written work.

assertion are entirely warranted. It has been believed, for instance, that the well-known State Theory of Money, presented in the succinct manner elucidated by Knapp,[8] could be dismissed by criticising its inability to address the issue of the quantity of money. This objection is entirely unwarranted. It is merely a lamentable indication of the confusion that still pervades monetary theory. Certainly, no physician would consider critiquing a theory about the quality of blood cells simply because it might not provide insights into quantitative changes in human blood volume. However, just as certain connections [between them] naturally exist in the medical context, the theory of money's quality is also not devoid of connections to the theory of monetary circulation.

As previously mentioned, the primary question we confront is that of the nature of money or the condition of being money. It can only be answered if we are capable of delving into money's becoming (*Werden*), its existence, and its life process. The method employed in this endeavour is simple: to examine social phenomena as *causally conditioned socio-psychological processes*, independent of the legal, ethical, or other types of external presentation or embellishments they may have acquired. [p16] For those processes are evidently the core of things, while the embellishments are merely the shell. The task, therefore, is to elucidate the functional interplay of money within the societal conduct-process (*Gehabensablauf*)[9] and trace it back to its *psychological root*.

---

[8] [tn] Knapp (2023/1923).

[9] [tn] '*Gehaben*' in German often signifies a more inherent or habitual manner of behaving, occasionally indicating an individual's overall demeanour or conduct rather than specific actions in a given situation. We render this as 'conduct.'

§2. The Meaning of the Societal Theory of Money

When we talk about a societal theory of money, the initial question that arises is: What is meant by such a theory of money? In other words, what is the societal aspect that the comprehensive description of money's subject matter should encompass in order to provide us with a scientific explanation of this phenomenon?

In addressing this question, we immediately encounter the difficulty that there is no unanimity among representatives of societal theory about what is *the social* or what is to be understood here as synonymous with the social. However, it is not the intention at this point to present the various, quite different opinions on this matter, nor to engage in a debate about their merits and drawbacks. Similarly, we do not intend to delve into the associated question about the concept and nature of society.[10] For the task at hand, it will suffice to state what is meant by 'societal' or 'social' in the context of phrasing like 'societal or social theory of money.'

Society, as we understand it, is a collective of individuals connected by purpose-conscious relationships that form an imagined unity. The nature of society is perceived either in its purposes and goals and the resulting interrelationships among its members, or (which is the same thing) in the psychological togetherness (*Gemeinsamkeit*) that exists among the members of society, in the psychological process that gives rise to societal life. [▶17] Society is thus not merely a coexistence or mere co-living (*Zusammenleben*), but a collective (*gemeinsam*) action — meaning a particular behaviour — primarily caused by the *inequality* of individuals, directed by certain drives, rooted in specific 'purpose-settings' (*Zwecksetzung*), and aimed at certain goals. The entirety of phenomena arising from this situation, constituting societal life as such, is what we

---

[10] A valuable guide in these contentious matters is provided by H. L. Stoltenberg in the annotations to his translation of Ellwood (1927), especially on p. 2, footnote 2, and p. 226, footnote 10.

refer to as *the societal*. This societal aspect, with regard to the institution (*Einrichtung*) commonly referred to as money, is the subject of this exposition. The societal, therefore, is a human purposive action (*Zweckhandel*) that arises from co-living, directed towards [an attitude] for, with or against each other. It is also often termed the social process. This generally encompasses the embodiment of interrelations among people in the service of human objectives. The *tensions* (*Spannung*) arising from the inequalities among individuals set in motion and sustain the social process. These tensions provide us with the key to understanding the social process.

The societal or social process encompasses all realms of human relationships, including economic domains, which include the economy itself. "The economy," as Heinz Sauermann once put it, "is a specific form of social action." It means, as he further explains in another context, "all economic events and occurrences are *a priori* societal."[11] [18] Therefore, it is reasonable to question whether, as is done here, it is even justified to speak of a societal theory of money in contrast to an economic theory of money, and what this juxtaposition implies. Addressing this question requires a brief exploration of the various meanings in which the terms 'societal' or 'social' are commonly used in academic discourse.[12] This topic is almost inexhaustible, but here, only what is essential to clarify the intent of this investigation will be discussed.[13]

---

[11] Sauermann et al. (1931: 381 and 379). A. von Navratil goes as far as to say: "The economy, economic life, is the most fundamental and often the most characteristic expression of social phenomena in general." In fact, he asserts that "economic life constitutes the content of individuals living in a social community" (Navratil 1906:14-15).

[12] [tn] See footnote 1 for the difference between 'societal' and 'social.'

[13] Regarding the various meanings of the term 'social,' see references such as Wasserrab (1903); Stammler (1914:634n64); Wiese (1921:12); also Jastrow (1902:17 ff. & 27). Illustrative of the fluctuating sense and prevailing confusion in the use of the term 'social' is also the observation made by Adolf Günther,

8

Both designations, 'societal' (*gesellschaftlich*) and 'social' (*sozial*), are used interchangeably in many expressions. This shall also be the case here. One speaks of 'societal or social harms' ('*societal*' or '*soziale*' *Schäden*), 'societal or social sciences' (*Gesellschafts- oder Sozialwissenschaften*), and so on. However, one commonly refers to 'society and economy' (*Gesellschaft und Wirtschaft*) and uses 'economic and social policy' (*Wirtschafts- und Sozialpolitik*), thus indicating that 'society' or the 'social' carries a different meaning than 'economy' or 'economic' (*wirtschaftlich*). The term 'social,' as Jastrow points out, was introduced in contrast to a purely political, and then purely economic, perspective. He further explains:

> Despite the considerable number of authors emphasising the contrast between the social perspective and the economic one, and despite the prominent thinkers among them, there has never been a moment when the reading and debating world reached a clear understanding that the same things can be perceived from either a purely economic or a societal standpoint.[14]

---

who in his book lists 13 different meanings of the term 'social policy' alone (Günther 1923:467). Albion Woodbury Small defined the concept of the 'social' as follows:

> The 'social,' then, is the interaction and the reciprocity between the persons that live and move and have their being as centres of reaction in a world filled with like centres. ... The social, then, is all the give-and-takeness ... It is attraction and it is repulsion. It is mutual aid, and it is mutual hindrance. It is consciousness of kind and it is consciousness of unkind. It is selection and it is rejection. It is adaptation and it is the tearing to pieces of adaptations (Small 1920: 511-512).

[14] J. Jastrow (1902), explains further:

> Since both the social perspective and the economic perspective emerged by breaking away from the purely governmental (legal) perspective, and since this emancipation engaged the educated classes of all nations to a great extent, and even the scholarly literature has not yet fully dealt with this stage, it is not surprising that the commonalities have sometimes had a stronger effect than the differences. Thus, the terms 'social' (*sozial*) and '

[p19] Upon closer examination, one will soon realise that society and economy are not mutually exclusive concepts. The economical aspect, or the economy itself, is a part of social phenomena, and indeed a significant part, but it by no means forms their exclusive content. "The forces driving towards societalisation," as von Zwiedineck states, "are of various natures. Especially in their beginnings, societalisation occurred under the influence of factors other than the need-satisfaction, which is now the goal of the economy."[15] This makes it clear that the societal encompasses more than just the economic. The concept of society is the broader concept, the genus concept; economy is the species concept. Both concepts relate to each other in a manner similar to the relation between the concepts of intercourse (*Verkehr*) and exchange-intercourse (*Tauschverkehr*). [16] Intercourse is any relationship-engagement (*Beziehungsnahme*) between people. Exchange-economic intercourses or economical intercourse is a relationship-engagement that involves giving and receiving economical goods, i.e., goods for fulfiling human demand for material things. Money can illustrate this comparison well: it serves as a means of intercourse (*Mittel des Verkehrs*) in the early stages of societalisation, but not necessarily as a means of strictly 'economical intercourse' (*ökonomisches Verkehr*),[17] both initially and subsequently.

The social or societal consideration in the broader sense always includes the economic realm; however, it views this as only a component of the

---

economic' (*wirtschaftlich*) are occasionally used interchangeably. However, since every social development is also an economic one, and vice versa, this blending is sometimes excused (although it can never be considered justified when 'social' is used where 'economic' is meant).

[15] Zwiedineck-Südenhorst (1911:3).

[16] [tn] For *Verkehr* and *Tausch*, Translation Note on p. 352.

[17] [tn]Refer to the Translation Note on p. 351 for clarification on the differentiation between 'economical' (*ökonomisch*) and 'economic' (*wirtschaftlich*) used in this translation.

societal process. [₱20] An economic monetary theory or an economic theory of money considers money solely as an economic phenomenon; in contrast, a societal doctrine of money aims to reveal the essential aspects of the monetary phenomenon within the entire social process. The latter extends in its scope beyond that of monetary economics, but in terms of content, the latter is less exhaustive than monetary economics within the latter's limited domain. Consequently, the social consideration includes the economic aspect of society in a broader sense while simultaneously excluding it in a narrower sense. Therefore, it is not contradictory to contrast the societal consideration with the economic one. Even legal life and the legal-order are societal facts, yet legal perspective is often distinguished from sociological ones without thereby failing to recognise the importance of a holistic view that encompasses both perspectives and without fundamentally renouncing it. This is exactly the point of view that is taken here towards the monetary phenomenon. Additionally, language usage sometimes equates the social with the economic, and at other times refers to something not covered by the concept of the economic. Following this language usage, which is unlikely to change and undoubtedly has its valid reasons, one must always diligently ensure that the intended meaning is clearly derived from the context.

We proceed with the understanding that while there is no society without economic relationships, these relations only express a portion of the forces, exertion (*Betätigung*), and overall life of the social whole. Just as the human environment is not solely economic, and the interpretations and values through which one relates to the environment are not purely economic, social relations also extend beyond the scope of economic interests. This holds true for our subject of investigation as well. Just as societal life is not solely filled with economic content, the monetary phenomenon cannot be characterised solely by unveiling its economical nature. According to our perspective, money originates from a social realm that transcends the economic domain. [₱21] It emanates from this realm into the sphere of the economic, exercising considerable influence, yet simultaneously extending beyond this circle into the general social. Money is not merely an economic instrument; rather, it is an expression of societal forms and ways of co-living. Consequently, its existence and essence can only be fully grasped when it is not seen solely within a specific context — such as the economic one — but when all its ties and relationship with the actual conditions of life are fundamentally illuminated. This is what we mean when we contrast a societal theory of money with an economic one.

12

§3. Socio-Psychological Foundation

The societal theory of money posits that money is a manifestation of the 'social lifepath' (*sozialer Lebensablauf*). 'Social lifepath' is understood as the interplay of human relationships in their emergence and impact on the participants, which arises among people from their purpose-settings and the pursuit of these purposes, along with the efforts to achieve them. To explain this lifepath, the so-called 'social process' (*sozialer Prozeß*), we resort to psychological facts as they are given in human nature understood as a unity (*Einheit*). All social phenomena are subject to psychological conditions and laws; that is, they are based on mental causes that we must try to uncover if we want to recognise those phenomena in their essence. Starting from the agreement on human essence, as assumed by both history and anthropology, we perceive certain innate drives (*Triebe*) as the primal forces (*Urkraft*) of the societal lifepath, which are effective, albeit with varying degrees of strength, and whose development is inhibited or promoted in different ways by different circumstances. [p22] Accordingly, all human purpose-settings and purpose-pursuits arise from certain motives, and establishing this array of motives as the motivations for human activities is both the starting point for elucidating the social lifepath itself and for understanding the creations and the conduct-forms (*Gehabensform*) arising from this lifepath, including the monetary framework (*Geldwesen*)[18] and money-usage.

The analysis of human motivations has been a subject of considerable effort in social psychology. However, there is by no means a consensus, neither in terms of the number and description of these motivations nor

---

[18] [tm] In this translation, we distinguish between *'Geldwesen'* (monetary framework) and *'Geldsystem'* (monetary system). *'Geldwesen'* encompasses all aspects related to money in a broader sense, while *'Geldsystem'* specifically denotes the system or structure regulating money within an economic or societal framework.

in their classification and evaluation regarding their primordial driving forces. Nevertheless, we are able to extract certain general foundations and concepts from social psychology. Accordingly, human conduct (*Gehaben*) is founded on certain innate or inherited drives (*Trieb*). From these drives, needs (*Bedürfnis*) emerge. The fulfilment of these needs leads to the experience of the suitability (*Tauglichkeit*) of certain things for specific purposes. This experience forms the basis for appreciation (*Wertschätzung*) of certain goods, precisely appreciation of them for their suitability. It will not be misleading if, as a result, we believe we can equally refer to needs as the foundation of the social process, instead of the drives.

Undoubtedly, there is a debate over whether and to what extent economics should address the study of needs. Nevertheless, it is a fact that significant insights have been gained from this starting point in economic theory. Indeed, the explanation of economic phenomena as a whole has only become possible through the 'Theory of Human Needs' [19] (*Bedürfnislehre*) and the understanding of the 'law of need-satisfaction' (*Gesetz der Bedürfnisbefriedigung*). Therefore, it also appears to me that a societal theory of money is impossible unless it takes those needs as its starting point, upon which societal relationships are built. These needs are of two kinds: first, those that lead people to societalisation, and second, those that are the result of society, meaning they arise within and from it.

[P23] Among the natural human drives that form the "raw material of societal institutions and individual habits" (Ellwood), thus giving rise to certain needs, the so-called 'herd instinct' (*Herdentrieb*), or what we can also refer to as the 'horde instinct' (*Hordeninstinkt*) [20] or 'drive for

---

[19] [tn] It may refer to the theory of human motivation by Abraham Maslow (Maslow 1943), which outlined a hierarchy of human needs, starting from basic physiological needs (food, shelter) and progressing to higher-level needs (self-esteem, self-actualisation). This theory suggests that individuals are motivated to fulfil these needs in a specific order.

[20] [tn] While 'herd' instinct and 'horde' instinct point to the instinctual

sociability' (*Geselligkeitstrieb, sec.* Vierkandt [21]), holds the foremost position. It is the 'impulsive inclination' (*triebhafte Neigung*) toward co-living in larger groups. The greater the number of people of co-living, the more perfect is the satisfaction of this instinct, the more effective are the drives that arise from coexistence, reinforced by habit, experience or the influence of the environment. This principle also applies, as we will see, to the emergence of money. Society must reach a certain size for the conditions for the emergence of money to be present. According to the doctrine known as social physics (*soziale Physik*), as advocated by Carey,[22] the power (*Macht*)[23] of associating (*Zusammenschluss*) and intercourse (*Verkehr*) between individuals is stronger the greater the differences among them. If this is accurate, and we do not doubt it despite certain reservations that can be made about this assertion, then this fact also holds significance for the emergence and usage of money. Money does not originate among equals but among those who are unequal, and as will be demonstrated, it serves as a means to solidify and outwardly express the disparities among individuals. The fact that all money, as we will see, originates as "class-money" (*Klassengeld*) does not contradict this observation. We should also add that even a class is by no means composed of perfectly equal individuals within it.

What the 'drive for sociability' means is clearly evident from the fact

---

tendencies of social animals, the former has a slightly stronger connotation of organised, cohesive group behaviour, while the latter might suggest a more loosely organised or even chaotic collective behaviour.

[21] [tn] Georg Vierkandt (1865-1953): a German sociologist and ethnologist known for his contributions to understanding social behaviour and the formation of societies based on shared instincts and behaviours.

[22] [tn] Henry Charles Carey (1793 –1879) was an American economist and advocate of protectionist economic policies known for his influential writings on social physics and economics.

[23] [tn] See Translation Note on p. 352.

that society itself has been referred to as a conduct-process resulting from co-living. As is known, the herd instinct is strongly developed in many animal species. What sets humans apart from animal associating (*Gesellung*) and thus turns the human group into a society is the purpose-conscious shaping (*Formung*) and formation of oneself, one's interpersonal relationships, as well as the things and institutions of one's environment, based on their inherent intellectual capacities – in other words, the creation of what we call culture. [▶24] This implies that society is indeed the carrier of culture, but it is not independent of culture, nor does it emerge and exist prior to culture. The societal conduct-process is nothing other than social action that brings forth those creations we term culture, whether those creations are mere behavioural patterns or psychological expressions like language and worship, or material means of existence such as weapons and tools. All of these phenomena – and this includes money to a significant extent – are prerequisites as well as products of society, and thereby, they are expression-forms of society (*Ausdrucksformen der Gesellschaft*) itself.

Perhaps the most socially significant drive that societal coexistence stimulates is the 'drive for distinction' (*Auszeichnungstrieb*), also known as the "drive for societal esteem" (*Trieb der gesellschaftlichen Hochgeltung*) (Franz Oppenheimer).

> All other drives that have been mentioned as the ultimate goal of historical social activity are only modal, striving only for intermediate goals, for means to the ultimate goals.[24]

The 'drive for distinction' has its roots in self-esteem (*Selbstgefühl*). Self-esteem is felt as an emotion (*Gefühl*) of demarcation (*Abhebung*) and accentuation (*Hervorhebung*) in comparison to others. This does not imply an emotion of independence from others, but quite the opposite: it makes a person's attitude dependent on the judgment of their fellow

---

[24] Oppenheimer (1922:272).

human beings. The opinions of others and, even more so, their behaviour, determine their behaviour. Hence arises a mental kinship and mutual interdependence among people, from which no one can entirely escape. This becomes evident in every act of social intercourse. The entirety of a person's actions and refrains (*Tun und Lassen*), it could be said, unfolds with a consideration of the behaviour of fellow individuals and with attentive ears to the judgments of others. The motivations for this are certainly not unequivocal; however, it is assured that the predominant role in this lies with the 'desire for acknowledgement' (*Wunsch nach Anerkennung*), 'desire for accentuation' (*Wunsch nach Hervorhebung*), and 'desire for distinction' (*Wunsch nach Auszeichnung*) — in short, everything that can satisfy the 'drive for societal esteem.' [p25] Consistently, this drive is referred to by modern sociology as the most significant of all social drives, the one whose fulfilment constitutes the true, ultimate goal of all social activity, for both individuals within society and societies themselves. What the Homeric verse expresses with the words, "always to be the first and to outdo the others,"[25] is not, as some admirers of classical Greece suppose, a "driving force unknown to other peoples" (as Jacob Burckhardt (1898:32 & 81) and many others similarly claim). Instead, the Greek state has, as Nietzsche rightly emphasises, "since the desire to conquer and excel is an unconquerable trait of nature," orderly arranged the gymnastic and musical competitions only in an exemplary way, "thus demarcating a playground where that drive could be discharged without endangering the political order"[26] (Nietzsche, 1886: 226). The "*agonal* nature,"[27] the competition among each other, however, is not only "a fundamental force of all Greek things" (J. Burckhardt), but the

---

[25] [tn] Homer's Iliad (Iliad VI 208): "ἀεὶ δὲ κριτέον καὶ ὑπεροχὴν ἔμμεναι ἄλλων."

[26] [tn] It means that the Greek state created a controlled outlet for that competitive drive without posing a threat to the overall political structure.

[27] [tn] From the Greek word '*agon*' (ἀγών), which means a contest, competition, or struggle.

'fundamental drive' (*Grundtrieb*) of human activities in general.

This 'fundamental drive' assumes various forms in its development (*Ausbildung*), and its exertion is therefore labelled with different terms in social psychology. It is this drive that provides individuals with the incentive to stand out from the group or the crowd. However, this accentuation – the distinction – is only possible through acknowledgement by others. So, if we consider the specific drive that leads to companionship in the herd or the 'drive for sociability,' we see in the 'drive for distinction' the strongest and most important drive that comes into existence within societalisation. For the development of human society from its earliest beginnings up to the present day, this drive has been of the utmost importance.

If the enthusiasts of ancient Greece interpret the entire life of the Greeks, both the political and artistic aspects, and the entire intellectual culture, through this 'drive to excel' (*Trieb nach aristeuein*[28]), the sociologist can only view it as a particularly striking example of the paramount importance of rivalry in the life of nations; [26] for he knows that every nation that has entered the realm of history possesses *agonal* characteristics.

Certainly, it must be added that this drive always appears in connection with a counterpart of the play. Social development is guided by two seemingly opposing fundamental forces. On one hand, there is the 'impulsive inclination' of individuals to stand out from the group, which is indeed a manifestation-form of the 'drive for distinction'; on the other hand, there is the inclination of the masses to recognise leadership and achievement — which naturally does not imply a judgment on their moral and cultural value — often to the point of blind, uncritical admiration. Connected to this is the inclination towards 'societal assimilation'

---

[28] [tn] *Aristeuein* (ἀριστεύειν) is derived from Ancient Greek and associated with the concept of 'excelling' or 'striving for the best.' It is related to the Greek word '*aristos*' (ἄριστος), which means 'best' or 'excellent.'

(*gesellschaftliche Angleichung*) and thus the imitation of those who are respected and leading within the group. Their conduct serves as a model and example for imitative activities (*Nachahmungshandlung*) by the masses. Kant recognised this to some extent. "Man has an inclination to associate," he says in the essay "The Idea for a Universal History with a Cosmopolitan Purpose" (*Idee zu einer allgemeinen Geschichte in weltbürgerlicher Absicht*) (Kant 1884). "However," he continues, "he also has a strong tendency to isolate himself, because within himself he also encounters the unsocial trait of wanting to direct everything according to his own inclination, and therefore he expects resistance (*Widerstand*) everywhere, just as he knows of himself that he is inclined to resist others in turn." This resistance is what awakens all of humanity's forces, driving him to overcome his inclination towards laziness and, propelled by lust for honour, dominance, or wealth, compels him to establish a rank among his fellow beings whom he may not tolerate well, yet he cannot refrain from. This implies that from inclination arises craving (*Sucht*). Thus, needs emerge: the 'need for recognition' (*Geltungsbedürfnis*),[29] the 'need for domination' (*Bedürfnis nach Herrschaft*), the 'need for possession' (*Bedürfnis nach Besitz*) and so on. And Kant adds after some further elaboration:

> So let us be grateful to nature for incompatibility (*Unvertragsamkeit*),[30] for enviously competitive vanity (*Eitelkeit*), for the unsatisfying desire to possess or to dominate. Without them, all excellent natural qualities within humanity would forever remain undeveloped.

[p27] The individual's 'drive for distinction' thus finds its necessary complement in the 'drive for acknowledgement' (*Anerkennungstrieb*) of

---

[29] [tn] See Translation Note on p. 352.

[30] [tn] It refers to the quality of not being able to coexist or interact harmoniously with someone else, i.e., the inherent conflicts and clashes that drive individuals to overcome challenges and strive for distinction.

the masses, and there is a confirming influence on its manifestation-form in their 'need for assimilation' (*Angleichungsbedürfnis*)[31] [32] Upon closer examination, it becomes clear that ultimately, even the 'inclination to assimilation' (*Neigung zur Angleichung*) to role models, and so forth, must indeed be considered as a manifestation-form of the 'drive for distinction.'

---

[31] [tn] It means that the 'need for assimilation' or conformity within a group reinforces or validates the way the individual expresses their 'need for distinction.' In other words, when individuals strive for distinction and seek to stand out, the fact that others in the group recognise and respond to these efforts provides validation and encouragement for that behaviour. When people strive to be different or excel in certain ways, and the group acknowledges or rewards these efforts, it reinforces their inclination to continue seeking distinction. The need to be recognised or acknowledged by the larger community acts as a confirming influence, affirming that their pursuit of standing out or being distinct is valuable within that social context.

[32] When speaking of a 'drive for recognition' here, it should be understood in a different sense than the usual one, namely as the 'impulsive inclination,' observable in all masses, to seek, acknowledge, and admire role models. In his review of the first edition of my book "The Emergence of Money" (Gerloff 1940), A. Günther referred to the 'impulsive inclination' toward 'societal assimilation' (*gesellschaftliche Angleichung*) as a 'drive for levelling' (*Niveautrieb*)* (1941: 101 ff.). Other sociologists speak of a 'drive for leadership' (*Führertrieb*) or 'drive for pioneering' (*Vorkämpfertrieb*) on the one hand and a 'drive for rivalry' (*Rivalitätstrieb*) or 'drive for imitation' (*Nachahmungstrieb*) on the other, although one could actually speak of a 'drive for following' (*Gefolgschaftstrieb*). In this context, terms like the 'drive for honor' (*Ehrtrieb*), and sometimes even the 'drive for mastery' (*Meistertrieb*) (Franz Oppenheimer), are frequently used. It seems quite questionable to me whether such designations, which give the impression that they are independent drives and not expressions of a 'fundamental drive,' in the current case, the 'drive for recognition,' are advisable. Of course, in this field, there is still much that is unclear, which makes the prevailing confusion regarding the main types of drives, their classification, delimitation, designation, etc., understandable.

[tn] *A drive to seek and recognise role models or standards, with the aim of aligning themselves with those standards or achieving a similar status.

Therefore, the mention of seemingly opposing forces may, in fact, be related to an underlying primal drive that can trigger various types of exertions (*Betätigung*). Viewed in this way, the 'drive for distinction' reveals itself as the gravitational force that directs and governs movements within the social grouping.

It is not the so-called economic nature of humans that gives content and direction to the social process, but rather the individual's aspiration to distinguish and excel among their peers. The world is not ruled by *homo oeconomicus* (economic man) but by *homo ambitiosus* (aspirant man)[33] or the person driven by *anthropos doxomanés* (opinionated human[34]). The *homo oeconomicus* is a fiction; *homo ambitiosus* is a living reality.

For a long time, it has been a mistake not only of many historians but especially of economists and social policymakers (and still is in many cases today) to view humans as *homo oeconomicus* and not, as I have called them, to understand them as *homo ambitiosus*. [P28] Only more recent American scholars in business studies have emphatically pointed out that the strongest motivator for willingness to work, and I add for the entire societal conduct-process, is not an economical advantage but rather the acknowledgement of service and personal accentuation and distinction. Hoard-good (*Hortgut*), treasures, and money are means for realising the

---

[33] [tn] The concept of '*homo ambitiosus*' as an alternative or contrasting idea to '*homo oeconomicus*' appears to have been introduced by the sociologist and philosopher Max Scheler. He explored the idea in his work (1928). Scheler's view was that human behaviour is driven not solely by economic rationality but also by ambitions, desires for recognition, and various non-economic factors.

[34] [tn] *Doxomanés* is a Greek term that can be broken down into two parts: '*doxo*' (δόξο) meaning 'opinion' or 'belief,' and '*manés*' (μανής) meaning 'mad' or 'insane.' Therefore, '*doxomanés*' could be understood as 'one who is mad for opinions' or 'one who is obsessed with beliefs.' It seems to convey the idea of a person who is fervently driven by their opinions, beliefs, or viewpoints.

desire "for personal individual significance."[35]

But there is yet another primordial driving force that played a role in the emergence of money. This is the 'drive for appropriation' (*Aneignungstrieb*) or the 'drive for amassing' (*Sammeltrieb*). It is a primal drive that humans have inherited as legacy from their ancestors. It belongs to those primitive instincts that, as A. Comte once put it, "will always remain the underlying foundation of human existence." The pre-societal roots of this drive, just like the origins of herd instinct and the 'drive for distinction,' reach into those depths where the psychological emerges from the unconscious biological. However, delving back into this stage is not within the scope of our task. Moreover, the processes that transformed anthropoids into humans are as inaccessible to us as the living conditions of early humans. This is not to say that the fundamental elements of the emergence of money are not to be sought in those distant times; just as the sound that accompanies a gesture, as a means of communication (*Verständigungsmittel*), has evolved into language, a certain goods-utilisation (*Güterverwendung*) as a means of communication of social intercourse turns those goods into money.

Not all original driving forces appear to be equally developed in both sexes. This is not entirely unimportant for our investigation. The 'drive for amassing' and the 'drive for possession' (*Besitztrieb*), similar to the 'drive for fight' (*Kampftrieb*), are particularly characteristic of the male sex, while the 'drive for adornment' (*Schmucktrieb*) is commonly attributed predominantly to the female sex. [p29] Certainly, we are dealing here with differences in degree, and we also do not venture to distinguish how much of it is inherent disposition and how much is acquired legacy (*Erbe*).

At this point, we shall not delve into a further discussion on the nature and functioning of these fundamental forces of social development.

---

[35] Cf. Heron (1949), cited in Gross (1949: 81).

Whether they are called drives or 'impulsive inclinations,' desires or needs, their decisive significance for the development of societal conduct and their crucial role in societal shaping are points of consensus among social researchers. While much remains to be scientifically clarified in this field, there is hardly any dispute about this fundamental aspect. It suffices to note here that the indicated interplay of social forces, as crucial for the emergence of other material cultural-goods, is also of essential importance for the emergence of money.

II. The Beginnings of the Money-Usage[36]

§4. The Emergence of Money

[⸮30] The previously customary explanation for the emergence of money is based on the assumption that money originated from the exchange-intercourse. Accordingly, the origin and meaning of money are seen in its service during exchange-intercourses. This perspective starts with the notion that originally every trade was a direct exchange, a natural-exchange (*Naturaltausch* – it is called 'barter' in English). If one assumes this, then it is easy to demonstrate the level of patience required in many cases to accomplish such exchanges and how the seemingly straightforward path is actually a laborious detour that often fails to lead to the desired outcome. The execution of direct exchange becomes more challenging in direct proportion to the increase in the number of exchange-goods. [37] The act of exchange always requires a double coincidence of the desires of the parties involved, and in addition, several other conditions must also be met for the smooth process of exchange. Some goods are poorly divisible or not divisible at all. One would like to exchange them but perhaps forced to do so for reasons of demand-fulfilment (*Bedarfsdeckung*), not for a single good, but only for various other goods that are in the hands of different owners. What is to be done in such a case? Furthermore, in many instances, there is a lack of a standardised measure for the exchange-ratio (*Tauschverhältnis*) between goods, as it is impossible to establish an exchange-ratio for each individual

---

[36] The content of this chapter is not an excerpt from my previous study (Gerloff 1940), but an independent presentation and extension of the fundamental idea developed in that book. It incorporates new evidence and explores new perspectives.

[37] [tn] If there are 'n' goods in the economy, the number of possible exchange-ratios is given by n*(n-1)/2. If there are 100 goods in a community, then the total number of ratios should be 4950, and no one can memorize all such ratios.

good against every other good that might potentially be exchanged. [p31] For someone who wants to exchange wheat, it is believed that they would need to know its exchange value compared to livestock, iron, wine, wool, and so on. To avoid these numerous inconveniences, the practice emerged of accepting a single type of good or a few items as payment, which could then be used in exchange. Thus, the belief is that intentionally, though not according to a preconceived plan, money came into existence.

This doctrine can be traced back to Plato and Aristotle, and possibly even further. In the renowned 8th and 9th chapters of the first book of "Politics," where Aristotle presents his economic theory, the Stagirite[38] demonstrates the necessity of goods-exchange (*Güteraustausch*). As he explains, this necessity extends to all things and naturally arises from the fact that "men had more than enough of some things and less than enough of others."[39] He explains that the goods of nature are available for everyone, but they are not conveniently situated, available, or abundant for each person to enjoy at the right place and time. Instead, they must be acquired through indirect means and the exchange of what is dispensable for what is essential. As needs evolve and the necessity for trade increases, the in-kind exchange, meaning the direct exchange of one good for another, proves inadequate. In its place emerges the artificial (*künstlich*) exchange of goods for money. Aristotle finds this development to be unavoidable. Let's hear his own words:

---

[38] [tn] A term used to refer to Aristotle, as he was born in the town of Stagira in northern Greece.

[39] [tn] Full text is

> And the same also holds good about the other articles of property; for all of them have a use in exchange related to them, which began in the first instance from the natural order of things, because men had more than enough of some things and less than enough of others (Aristotle 1932: 40, 1257a).

Out of it the art of money-making (*chrematistic*)[40] in the narrower sense is the monetary economy. For when they had come to supply themselves more from abroad by importing things in which they were deficient and exporting those of which they had a surplus, the employment of money necessarily came to be devised. For not every object of natural need is easily portable. Therefore, for the purpose of exchange,[41] it was agreed to give and take a certain value among each other, which, belonging to the coveted things themselves, would at the same time have the advantage of being easy to use in everyday life: iron for instance, silver and other metals, at the first stage defined merely by size and weight, but finally also by impressing on it a stamp in order that this might relieve them of having to measure it; [P32] for the stamp was put on as a token of the amount.[42]

In clarification of this, we learn from the *Nicomachean Ethics* (Book V, Chapter 8) that the purpose-designation (*Zweckbestimmung*) of money is

---

[40] [tn]In Greek, χρηματιστικῆς, from *chrematistiki* (χρηματιστικήή). The latter is derived from the Greek word '*chrēma*' (χρῆμα), which generally means 'money' or 'property' and the suffix '-τική' (-tikí), which is commonly used to form nouns related to a specific field or activity. Cf. In Aristotle (1932) it is translated as 'art of business.'

[41] [tn] The original text is '*allagi*' (αλλαγή), meaning exchange or barter. It is translated as 'barter' in Aristotle (1932:42; 1257a35).

[42] [tn] Aristotle (1932:42-42; 1257a35 & 1257a20-40). This quotation is followed by the sentence:

> Exchange on these lines therefore is not contrary to nature, nor is it any branch of the art of wealth-getting, for it existed for the replenishment of natural self-sufficiency.

The next sentence is:

> So when money had been now invented as an outcome of the necessary interchange of goods, there came into existence the other form of wealth-getting, trade, which at first no doubt went on in a simple form, but later became more highly organised as experience discovered the sources and methods of exchange that would cause most profit.

to serve as a value-measure (*Wertmesser*)[43] and a means of exchange. It is stated there:

> This is why all things that are exchanged must be somehow comparable. It is for this end that money has been introduced, and it becomes in a sense an intermediate; for it measures all things, and therefore the excess and the deficiency — how many shoes are equal to a house or a certain quantity of food. (...) For if this is not so, there will be no exchange and no community. (...) All goods must therefore be measured by some object that can be the measure of everything. Now this measure is in truth need, [missing quotations: which holds all things together (for if men did not need one another's goods at all, or did not need them equally, there would be either no exchange or not the same exchange)]; but money has become by convention a sort of representative of needs; and this is why it has the name 'money' (*nomisma*; νομισμα) — because it exists not by nature but by law (*nomos*; νομορ) and it is with us to change it and make it useless.[44]

Wilhelm Oncken, whose translation and explanations we have followed here[45] regarding the cited passages from Aristotle's "Politics," remarks on these discussions:

> The stages of trade and the emergence of money could not be portrayed more accurately in substance and more faithfully in historical terms than they have been done in these two chapters.

In another passage, he states:

---

[43] [tn] In this translation, we distinguish between 'value-standard' (*Wertmaß*) and 'value-measure' (*Wertmesser*). The former signifies the criteria or standard used to assess the value or worth of something, whereas the latter denotes the means or units employed to quantify or measure the value of goods or services.

[44] [tn] Aristotle (2009:88-9;1133a18-31). The words enclosed in square brackets have been inserted by the translator to provide a complete quotation from Aristotle.

[45] [tn] We have utilised the English translation referenced in earlier footnotes.

There is nothing more to add to the presentation provided here regarding the natural emergence of coined money. It captures the essence of the matter with utmost precision and conveys it in a classical brevity and definiteness.[46]

When a respected historian evaluates this theory of the emergence of money in such a manner, it should not surprise us that national economists and jurists have not expressed objections to this presentation for a long time, but rather passed it down through the centuries with only minor modifications. What further supported this theory, if ever such support was necessary, was that they could appeal not only to the authority of the Greek philosophical school but also to ancient Roman jurisprudence, [↯33] particularly to that famous passage from the Digests[47] "On the Contract of Sale" (L. 1 D. 18, 1.),[48] where it is stated that money was made from a useful substance by prior agreement.

Further elaboration on that older theory can be omitted here, as the adaptations it underwent over time in accordance with the evolution of the monetary economy do not fundamentally alter the essence of the matter. It is worth noting the response given by G. Tarde[49] to the question "How a currency could have been established" (*comment une monnaie a pu s'établir*)[50] among occasional alternative attempts at solutions. He suggests that one must bear in mind that human society initially consisted of small, closed groups with similar needs and inclinations. The childlike desire to possess certain things for reasons of utility and even more so for

---

[46] Oncken (1875:94 ff.).

[47] [tn] The Digests (*Digesta* or *Pandects*) is a compilation of Roman legal texts that were put together under the orders of the Byzantine Emperor Justinian I in the 6th century AD.

[48] [tn] *De Emptione Venditione.*

[49] [tn] Gabriel Tarde (1843-1904), a French sociologist, criminologist, and social psychologist.

[50] [tn] Tarde (1902:281).

aesthetic motives quickly became generalised and, 'through reciprocal influence' (*par la stimulation réciproque*), rose to a practically unlimited extent. This led to the idea of utilising these objects, which were valued continuously and infinitely, as a general value-standard (*Wertmaß*),[51] a means of exchange, and a means of wealth-aggregation (*Mittels der Reichtumsanhäufung*).[52] One can see that even this attempt to explain the emergence of money hardly delves deeper than the old peripatetic doctrine.[53]

What is fundamentally objectionable to these and similar views is this: an explanation of the emergence of money from its [already] proven (*erweislich*) purpose within a given economy is, like the explanations of other social facts based on final purpose, unacceptable.[54] The demonstration of the advantages of using money or, to provide another example, the benefits of division of labour based on their common execution of the process, can never be used to explain the emergence of these institutions; [⟨34] because these institutions, like most social institutions, originated independently of the process of purpose-adaptation or purpose-setting, to which they were eventually introduced. This also implies that the explanation of the emergence of money from peculiar (individualistic) purpose-settings (the clever leader!) is also misguided. Just as the nature of money can only be understood within the existing social conditions in which it plays a more or less significant role, its emergence can also only be illuminated by reference to those social

---

[51] [tn] See footnote 43.

[52] Tarde (1902:283).

[53] [tn] 'Peripatetic' refers to the philosophy of Aristotle and his followers, who used to walk around while teaching and discussing their ideas.

[54] [tn] It means an explanation that focuses solely on the purpose or benefits of money already proven within an existing economy is inadequate for explaining its origin.

conditions under which it becomes apparent in a given society.

A. Vierkandt formulated the principle of "continuity in cultural change" in one of his earliest works. This insight, which was indeed a new formulation for the position of anthropological cultural research at that time, also applies to the emergence of money.[55] The same applies to it, as Vierkandt generally states about the emergence of new cultural-goods or the modification of existing ones: "It has a long prehistory." Especially in the emergence of money, it is not a singular event or an original invention, a creation *ex nihilo*, but rather a gradual development spanning a longer period of time, intertwined with origins in entirely different contexts than those in which it appears to us today.

With the emergence of society or societies, the prerequisite for the emergence of money is established. Money does not originate within a community (*Gemeinschaft*), to apply the well-known distinction,[56] but

---

[55] Vierkandt (1908). Especially in reference to money, which Vierkandt does not mention among the numerous examples he provides, H. Schurtz had already written over ten years earlier:

> Ethnology has its laws that apply everywhere. The first and most well-known of these laws teaches us that a new custom or institution never arises suddenly, but that beginnings and seeds must be present and often work in secret for a long time before more complete forms emerge. Therefore, it can also be assumed that the concept of money has undergone a long development (Schurtz 1897:1 ff.).

[56] [tn] The distinction between '*Gemeinschaft*' (community) and '*Gesellschaft*' (society) is a concept often attributed to Ferdinand Tönnies in his famous book "*Gemeinschaft und Gesellschaft*" (Community and Society), first published in 1887. '*Gemeinschaft*' refers to a close-knit community characterised by strong personal relationships, shared values, and a sense of belonging. It is often associated with traditional, rural, or small-scale societies. On the other hand, '*Gesellschaft*' represents a more modern, complex society where interactions are often based on self-interest, formal contracts, and economic considerations. Tönnies' distinction emphasises that '*Gemeinschaft*' is rooted in genuine emotional bonds, while '*Gesellschaft*' is driven by more utilitarian and

rather within a society (*Gesellschaft*). Just as the latter is not based on contract or agreement, neither are its fundamental societal institutions. [p35] This also applies to money. It has emerged and been shaped from deeply rooted forces that extend back to the earliest human existence, and perhaps even beyond.

As shown in the preceding section, there are a few impulsive fundamental forces (*triebhafte Grundkraft*) to which we must attribute the emergence of culture in general, as well as the emergence of money. The 'drive for sociability' creates society and thereby lays the foundations for the societal conduct-process. The 'drive for distinction' and its counterparts, i.e., 'drive for following' (*Gefolgschaftstrieb*) and 'drive for assimilation' (*Angleichungstrieb*), are the forces that provide content and direction to the conduct-process. That is why these drives have also been referred to as the most important among all social drives, as the 'fundamental drives' of society. In any case, they belong to the strongest motives of human action and thus also to the forces that largely determine social events. Even in primitive society, the social conduct-process is determined not by the *homo oeconomicus*, but by the *anthropos philótimos* (recognition-seeking human).[57]

The 'drive for distinction' has numerous and often quite peculiar manifestation-forms, the task of illustrating which could be the rewarding endeavour of a history of human vanities. In almost all nations, we find that distinction and social differentiation (*soziale Unterscheidung*) are consistently sought in the acquisition of certain goods and seen in the

---

contractual relationships.

[57] [tn] '*Anthropos philótimos*' (Άνθρωπος φιλότιμος) is a Greek term that can be translated as 'honor-seeking human.' '*Philotimos*' is a Greek word that roughly means having a love of honour, reputation, or a sense of dignity. In this context, it refers to humans who are motivated by a 'need for recognition,' status, and honour in their actions and interactions within society, as opposed to being solely driven by economic considerations.

possession of such goods. Here it is evidently the **'drive for amassing'** (*Sammeltrieb*), which we encounter already in the animal world, and which, along with other 'impulsive inclinations,' guides the 'drive for distinction.'

The anthropological and cultural-historical literature is full of examples that demonstrate the role that **goods-stockpiling** (*Güteraufspeicherung*) has played and continues to play in the lives of both primitive and historical peoples. However, this stockpiling is by no means about sustenance (*Lebensfürsorge*), as one might interpret it rationally; because these are goods that often have no relevance to livelihood and are not even usable for obtaining food. [p36] We find such hoarding practices even among peoples who naturally have little to no concerns about sustenance. The role of these possessions is actually quite different from being an immediate purposeful good for sustenance. Such possessions serve as means of social differentiation, societal demarcation (*gesellschaftliche Abhebung*), and distinction.

As a result, such a possession holds significance and recognition (*Geltung*) only where it emerges within society, primarily during [social] congregations. Occasions of regular congregations are the festivals. Celebrating festivals and games are primordial social activities; they are means and ways of societalisation (*Vergesellschaftung*), of social associating (*Zusammenschluss*), and often enough, the two are intertwined. The festivities of primitives are almost always connected with a procession, dance, play, and the like. Just as the emergence of language has been seen in the expressions of emotional excitement during play and festivity, the beginnings of socially distinctive possessions may also be detected in such occurrences. Almost all original games are competitive and martial games, and as such, they are associated with a distinction of the winner, which is not only acknowledgement but also visible identification. The festivities of primitives are always a kind of cult as well, and the processions, dances, and feasts that accompany them carry an element of ritual solemnity. They are, along with play, the occasions where distinguishing marks

(*Kennzeichen*), which can easily become distinctions, are displayed and worn. Such occasions are therefore of great significance for the emergence of distinguishing possessions. At the same time, they are also the most important means of social intercourse, not only within the tribe (*Stamme*)[58] but also between individual tribes.

An example of how the 'need for recognition' (*Geltungsbedürfnis*) leads to the goods-accumulation (*Güterakkumulation*) as well as the goods-circulation (*Güterzirkulation*) and thus the emergence of a form of money is provided by the social system of the Kwakiutl Indians,[59] knowledge of which we owe to the excellent works of Franz Boas.[60] [P37] Gaining reputation (*Ansehen*)[61] and recognition (*Geltung*) through outdoing rivals is the overarching goal of their social ambition that dominates the entire life of the Kwakiutl. All events of social life, marriage and birth, coming of age and entry into the secret union (*Geheimbund*), death and burial, serve as occasions for them to engage in contests of rank. The main means are

---

[58] [tn] See Translation Note on p. 353.

[59] [tn] The Kwakiutl, also spelled Kwakwaka'wakw, is an Indigenous people in the northern part of Vancouver Island, Canada. The Kwakiutl society placed a strong emphasis on wealth, status, and ceremonial *potlatches* (a traditional ceremonial practice). *Potlatches* were elaborate social and ceremonial events where hosts would distribute gifts, display their wealth, and reinforce social hierarchies. These events were crucial for displaying prestige and accumulating social standing within the community.

[60] Source: "The social organisation and secret societies of the Kwakiutl Indians," *Report of the U. S. National Museum for 1895*, Washington 1897, p. 311 ff. "Ethnology of the Kwakiutl," 2 vol. 35. *Annual Report, American Ethnology*, Washington 1921. [tn] Franz Boas (1858-1942) was a pioneering anthropologist whose extensive research and contributions greatly enriched the understanding of diverse cultures and shaped the modern field of anthropology.

[61] [tn] '*Ansehen*' encompasses elements of esteem, prestige, and admiration within the context of social recognition and respect. We use the English word 'reputation,' which includes the notions of being respected, esteemed, and admired within a social context.

the *potlatch*,[62] the ceremonial lending of valuables, and the destruction of such items, such as copper plates, woollen blankets, etc. The "passions of ostentation," which, as Rodbertus[63] believes,[64] "were stronger in antiquity than today" (He refers to examples of extravagant displays of gold and silver from antiquity and points to the 33rd book of Pliny;[65] primitive humans were also indulged in it. Hoard-money (*Hortgeld*)[66] or ornament-money (*Kleinodgeld*) plays a special role in such **displays** (*Zurschaustellung*). A beautiful wooden sculpture from the Berlin Museum of Ethnology depicts a chief of the aforementioned Kwakiutl Indians, holding a large copper plate in his arms, as they are used as money by the tribes of the Northwestern American coast.[67]) Originally, these plates had religious significance. They were displayed and revered in special houses. It is plausible that such a possession bestows 'social distinction.' However, the use of these finely crafted copper plates has not remained limited to religious purposes; they were also brought out and ostentatiously displayed on secular occasions. That is the meaning of this statuary art. A house post (totem pole) located in the Museum of Natural

---

[62] [tn] See footnote 59.

[63] [tn] Johann Karl Rodbertus (1805-1875) was a German economist and social theorist, known for his contributions to economic and social thought, particularly in the field of political economy. Rodbertus was critical of the prevailing economic conditions of his time, and his ideas were influenced by thinkers such as Karl Marx and Friedrich Engels.

[64] [tn] Rodbertus (1870:187).

[65] [tn] Gaius Plinius Secundus, commonly known as Pliny the Elder (23-79 AD) was a Roman author, naturalist, and philosopher. He is best known for his work "Natural History" ("*Naturalis Historia*" in Latin), which is one of the largest and most comprehensive encyclopaedias of the natural world from ancient times. Pliny the Elder's "Natural History" consists of 37 books, and it remains a valuable source for understanding the state of knowledge in the Roman Empire.

[66] [tn] Money that takes the form of valuable items stored as wealth.

[67] Refer to an illustration in Adam (1923).

History in New York depicts the same representation of a chief holding one of those copper plates used as money in his crossed arms.[68] Given such a money-usage, one could indeed speak of prestige-money (*Prestigegeld*), ostentatious-money (*Prunkgeld*), or swagger-money (*Protzgeld*).

The depictions on the well-known bronze plates from Benin can be similarly interpreted, depicting traders with Manilla rings,[69] [▷38] which were iron money rings weighing up to 4 and 5 kilograms and were in usage on the Upper Guinea coast.[70] The same applies to the numerous plates of the same source that have come down to us, depicting natives carrying bells. "We have to consider all these bells," says von Luschan, "primarily as ornaments or symbols of distinction."[71] The question arises whether we are not dealing here, at least in a series of cases, with bell-money (*Glockengeld*) that served as 'ceremonial money' (*Zeremonialgeld*).

As a third example of the money-expending of primitive money for ostentation, it is worth noting the practice of piling the rolls of shell-money[72] around the deceased's laid-out body during funeral ceremonies,

---

[68] An illustration in Quiggin (1948:302).

[69] [tn] The term '*manilla*' is believed to have Spanish and Portuguese origins, referring to a 'bracelet' or 'hand-ring.' They are horseshoe-shaped iron objects that were used as a form of money, as a medium of exchange and a store of value in certain regions, including parts of West Africa and other parts of the world, during the colonial era. The earliest use of *manillas* can be traced back to Calabar in West Africa, where they served as a means of exchange, with a slave costing 8–10 manillas in 1505. *Manillas* are reminiscent of torcs or torques due to their circular, open-ended, and rigid design.

[70] Cf. The work by Luschan (1919) consisting of 1 volume of text and 2 volumes of plates. Text volume: p. 41, Figures 45 and 46; p. 47, Figure 55; p. 48, Figure 56; p. 49, Figures 57 and 58; p. 55, Figure 65; p. 99, Figure 177.

[71] The text volume of Luschan (1919:369).

[72] [tn] It refers to cylindrical or elongated forms made from shells that were used as a form of money in certain cultures. These shell-money items were often strung together to create long rolls or strands, and they held value as a medium

akin to wreaths.[73]

In all these examples, the intention is to demonstrate a person's reputation or distinguished status through a particular goods-usage (*Gütergebrauch*). This goods-usage is either a factor (among others) in the emergence of money or it is (at a later stage of development) already a form of money-expending (*Geldverwendung*)[74] itself.

Once the presented connections are understood, it becomes clear that money originally often emerges as **'ceremonial money,'** as will be shown later. This means money that is used only during solemn state activities and ritualistic activities, or significant family events.[75] Such money – in New Caledonia it is stored in the "sacred basket" (*heiligen Korb*) – changes its possession only rarely, and in secular trade, it is not initially used at all.[76]

The question that arises here is: under these circumstances, how does a 'change of possession' (*Besitzwechsel*) occur, and how do these valuable items come to be used in exchange-intercourses? [p39] Certainly, it is understandable that a distinction or a socially significant possession would appear desirable in the eyes of those who lack it; after all, it is a prerequisite for certain rights. The acquisition of wives, entry into the secret union, advancement to a higher rank class, resolution of disputes, atonement for transgressions, legal validity of contracts, and many other things depend on such possession and its corresponding use. Equally understandable, however, is that those in possession of such precious-items, which

---

of trade or as a representation of wealth. These rolls of shell-money were placed around the deceased's body during funeral ceremonies, serving as a form of ostentatious display or symbolic tribute.

[73] Cf. The illustration in Gerloff (1940:64, Plate III).

[74] [tn] See footnote 2 for the meaning.

[75] Cf. Oppenheim (1941:49), and Leenhardt (1930).

[76] [tn] See Mauss (2002/1925) for similar ideas.

emphasise if not determine an individual's place within the clan (*Sippe*)[77] or society, guard these items anxiously.

Furthermore, it should be added that to the primitive human, every possession always carries more than just the 'power of disposal and control' (*Verfügungsmacht*)[78] over an object. He is emotionally attached to his possessions. Each individual item is to him both a source of magical force (*Kraft*) and a part of himself. That is why he associates his personal well-being with each of his possession-goods (*Besitzgut*), no matter how modest they may be. Naturally, this hinders or complicates the disposal of such possessions. Transferring ownership (*Eigentum*) to another person, according to the 'mental landscape' (*Vorstellungswelt*) [79] of these individuals, carries the risk of causing harm to one's own self and affecting one's well-being. The ancient customs associated with the transfer of possession or the ownership-transfer among all peoples, or those that were connected, can be explained by this emotional attachment of primitive humans to their possessions. The Germanic farmer took three grains from the bushel of grain that he lent to the needy neighbour; he took three hairs from the head of the sold livestock. Thereby he preserved the well-being of his farm. J.P. Mills reports of the Lhota Nagas [80] that when they sell something from their personal ownership, the seller retains a tiny fragment of it; otherwise, the buyer might wish to "magic him."[81] These are two examples of the aforementioned from entirely different cultural circles.

---

[77] [tn] See footnote 58.

[78] [tn] See Translation Note on p. 350.

[79] [tn] The mental or cognitive framework through which a person or a society perceives and interprets the world

[80] [tn] An indigenous community residing in the northeastern region of India, primarily in the state of Nagaland.

[81] Mills (1932:44) cites Hoyt (1926:83). For Germanic customs, see Grönbech (1937:105 ff., 1939:64 ff.).

[₰40] Ethnology and folklore studies can easily expand upon them.

Such beliefs, to which many others are added (Gerloff 1940:113, 195 f.), naturally oppose the 'change of possession of precious-items' (*Besitzwechsel der Kleinode*). And it is not just true of the Germanic people, as W. Grönbech describes them:

> The world from which the laws and the established usage (*Gebrauch*) of this people originate is one in which precious-items have their own names and personalities.[82]

The same is reported about the precious-items of certain indigenous peoples.[83] Thus, as much as the fortunate possessors of such possessions insist on holding onto them, the have-nots desire to acquire them. So, what could possibly provide the reason to divest oneself of such essential items held in distinct personal esteem (*Wertschätzung*)?

Certainly, there are various occasions for such actions. However, one of the strongest and therefore most common motivations seems to be the intention to establish those social connections that are created by the change of the possession-good by its transfer. The significance of such a bond is indeed capable of outweighing the loss that the 'alienation of possession' (*Besitzentäußerung*) entails. This has been excellently demonstrated for the ancient Germanic life-sphere by W. Grönbech.[84]

The 'change of possession' takes place among the Germanic people – and, as should be mentioned here, not only among them but also among most, perhaps even all, indigenous peoples through the avenue of gift-giving, primarily through the mechanism of gift-exchange

---

[82] [tn] Cf. See also Mauss (2002/1925: 30, 31).

[83] Cf. For example, Gerloff (1940:43, 78, 81 & 103).

[84] Cf. Grönbech (1937, 1939). Particularly see the sections on "*Kleinode*" [precious-items] (1939:7 ff.), "*Gabentausch*" [exchange of gifts] (1939: 46 ff.), and "*Kauf und Pfand*" [purchase and pledge] (1939:64 ff.).

38

(*Gabentausch*). [85] Indeed, the gift necessitates a reciprocal-gift. A gift without a reciprocal-gift is so foreign to the Germanic concept of ownership that in the Lombard Edict of Liutprand, [86] whose application is evidenced by numerous documents, they denied the legal validity (*gesetzliche Gültigkeit*) [87] of an unreciprocated gift. [88] Such a 'change of possession' is commonly referred to as a gift-exchange. [p41] However, this [concept] has nothing in common with an exchange in the economic sense; for it is repeatedly emphasised that it depends on the intention with which something is given, not on the economic value of the compensation. That a clever person can exploit this is recounted in the *Gautreksaga* [89] in

---

[85] [tn] See Translation Note on p. 353.

[86] [tn] Liutprand of Cremona, also known as Liutprand of Benevento (c. 920 – c. 972) was an important figure during the 10th century in the Lombard Kingdom and the Holy Roman Empire. He served as a diplomat, bishop, and chronicler, providing valuable historical and cultural insights through his writings. The Lombard Edict of Liutprand could be a legal decree or document that was issued during his time as ruler of the Lombard Kingdom.

[87] [tn] For example, when a gift is given, there might be certain expectations or conditions associated with it, and parties involved might want to ensure that these expectations are met. If the gift is not reciprocated, the validity of those conditions, rights or expectations may be denied. This concept might seem strange from a modern perspective, but in certain historical or cultural contexts, the act of giving and receiving gifts could be deeply intertwined with social norms, expectations, and obligations. The denial of legal validity for an unreciprocated gift reflects how legal systems can be influenced by cultural practices and social norms.

[88] *Fontes Juris Germanici Antiqui* [Sources of Ancient Germanic Law] (1869) and *Monumenta Germaniae Historica, Leges* [Monuments of German History, Laws], Volume IV.

[89] [tn] The '*Gautreksaga*' is a medieval Icelandic saga, named after its main character, King Gautrek. It is a type of narrative prose literature that was written in Old Norse during the Middle Ages, containing stories of mythical and heroic characters, often with elements of adventure, magic, and historical events.

the story of Gjafa Refr[90] (the Gift Fox (*Gabenfuchs*)[91]), who cleverly traded his only possession, a grindstone, from exchange to exchange, ultimately acquiring the king's daughter as the outcome.

Such a gift-exchange, a practice that has been reflected in the proverbial wisdom of the older Edda[92] (Gerloff 1940:46 ff.), is more than a mere transfer of ownership. It always signifies alliance, brotherhood, and the forging of friendship. Germanic culture knows no other way than that with the transfer of an object, the friendship of the previous possessor is also conveyed. That is precisely the motive behind gift-exchange. In this sense, Grönbech states:

> This dual acquisition of the physical and spiritual aspects in one is what the Germanic soul understood as purchase" (Grönbech 1939:69).

Therefore, people used to speak of gift-bond (*Gabebund*) and gift-brother (*Gabebruder*) (in Old English, "wedbroder"[93]), or even of gift-purchase (*Gabekauf*) (Grönbech 1939:76). The act of giving in all its forms, from

---

[90] [tn] Gjafa Refr is a character in the '*Gautreksaga.*' It is of Norse origin name. '*Gjafa*' is likely derived from the Old Norse word '*gjafa*,' which means 'gift' or 'to give.' 'Refr' is a common Old Norse name.

[91] [tn] The term 'Gift Fox' likely emphasises the character's cunning and skill in utilising gifts or trades to achieve his goals.

[92] [tn] '*Edda*' is a collection of ancient Norse mythological and heroic poems. There are two main collections known as the 'Poetic *Edda*' (or 'Elder *Edda*') and the 'Prose *Edda*' (or 'Younger *Edda*'). The 'Poetic *Edda*' contains a collection of poems that were composed in Old Norse and are rich in mythological and legendary content. These poems were passed down orally and were eventually written down in manuscripts.

[93] [tn] '*Wedbroder*' is an Old English term that can be translated to 'pledge-brother' or 'oath-brother' in modern English. It refers to a person with whom a formal and solemn bond of friendship or alliance is established through the exchange of pledges or oaths.

the dowry (*Brautgabe*) to the guest-present (*Gastgeschenk*),[94] always carries an obligation within it. As Grönbech states, "It binds, no matter under what circumstances it is given." Perhaps it is explained by this binding obligation inherent in the voluntary gift that in some peoples (such as the Kiziba of East Africa[95]), presents are only allowed to be exchanged among equals or from those of higher status to subordinates, but never the other way around. The obligation imposed by the presentation of the gift and undertaken with the acceptance of the gift thus opens the door to the psychological mystery of the 'change of possession.' At the same time, it explains the worldwide prevalence of this primitive goods-traffic (*Güterverkehr*). As already noted, gift-exchange is not a form of 'change of possession' unique to Germanic culture alone. [p42] The process aligns itself, rather, with the general human behaviour pattern that can be termed the principle of reciprocity and retribution, which, as anthropologists and sociologists have frequently observed, governs and regulates the life relationships of indigenous peoples.[96]

Gift-exchange is the most important and widespread form of gift-traffic (*Gabenverkehr*),[97] meaning that it is the primal method through which goods-transfers (*Güterübertragung*) resulted in earlier and earliest stages of culture. From the **gift-traffic** — to anticipate this and delve into it further later on — **money emerges**.

However, when certain goods have become money, they continue to serve gift-exchange for a long time even in their role as money. In New Caledonia, according to Leenhardt,[98] neither a message nor a contract is

---

[94] [tn] See Translation Note on p. 353.

[95] Rehse (1910: 100).

[96] Cf. Somlo (1909: 87 and 94); also refer to Thurnwald (1931-34: Vol III, 112). Numerous examples are especially found in Hoyt (1926), see footnote 81.

[97] [tn] See footnote 85 for the meaning of gift-traffic (*Gabenverkehr*).

[98] [tn] Leenhardt (1930).

considered valid unless a piece of shell-money is exchanged along with it. The same applies to insults considered serious offences in New Caledonia. Their atonements can only be initiated if the offender sends a piece of string-money (*Geldschnur*)[99] to the offended party. However, the matter is only considered settled when the offended party, in turn, sends back a piece of shell string.

Even more significant is the **'money-gift-exchange'** (*Geldgabentausch*): in family matters in New Caledonia: during the birth of a child, the maternal uncle, among others, receives a piece of shell-money string. In return, the maternal uncle also gives a piece of shell string-money as a reciprocal-gift. During the engagement, which takes place in childhood, the parents exchange equal-length shell string-money.

Not only is the ceremonial use of money clearly evident here, but also the binding force of gift-exchange.

Therefore, money in its original usage is a binding gift and as such, a symbol of established connections or relationships. Some objects, such as the ring, have the ability to preserve their symbolic meaning long beyond the era of gift-traffic.

[₱43] In this gift-exchange, as demonstrated in other contexts as well, the original focus is not on a fixed value-magnitude of the gift or even on a value equality (equivalence) between the gift and the reciprocal-gift. Tacitus[100] emphasised the contrast to Roman thinking and reported to us

---

[99] [tn] It likely refers to a specific amount or portion of money made from strings of shells, which holds cultural and symbolic significance in New Caledonian society.

[100] [tn] Publius Cornelius Tacitus (c. 56-120 AD) was a Roman historian and senator known for his writings on the early Roman Empire. He is famous for works like the 'Histories' and the 'Annals,' which provide valuable insights into Roman history, politics, and culture. One of his notable works is "*Germania*," a treatise on the customs and lifestyle of the Germanic tribes. Tacitus' writings are highly regarded for their detailed and often critical analysis of Roman society

about such practices and attitudes among the Germanic people:

> To give the departing guest what he asks for is custom; the same willingness can be demanded of him. They love to give gifts to each other. But this giving does not lead to reckoning, and this receiving does not create obligations" (Tacitus, 98:21).

It is only at a later stage of societal development that the economic, or rather the calculative valuation of things, replaces the friendly appreciation of the living personal relationships mediated by them. It is evident that with the rise of the economic perspective, the deliberative, calculative assessment of gift-traffic, the valuation, and the utilisation of the hoard-good that serves as money undergo a transformation. W. Grönbech describes this significant shift in the assessment of things in the Germanic cultural sphere with the words:

> The gold ring has found its supreme judge in the weight scale, whose [standard] weights[101] calculate in units and their fractions.

It is a long path originating from the distant prehistoric past, which, long before the Germanic peoples and the same applies to all known civilised cultures, has reached its conclusion in the full light of history. The gift, which may have been an emotional value (*Gefühlswert*) in whatever form, has become a material-value (*Sachwert*) expressed in measuring and counting, i.e., it has become money.

In this way, the history of ownership reveals two things to us : on one hand, the 'inclinations towards amassing of possession' (*Neigung zur Besitzansammlung*), specifically treasure-buildup (*Schatzbildung*)[102] or hoarding, observed among numerous peoples, and on the other hand, the beginnings of 'change of possession through giving-aways' (*Besitzwechsel*

---

and its interactions with other cultures.

[101] [tn] The small, standardised pieces of metal or other materials used for measuring weight on a scale.

[102] [tn] For the detailed meaning of *Schatz* (treasure). refer to p. 48.

durch Vergabungen). Certain things are hoarded, and these hoarded objects can serve as gifts, primarily for ceremonial gift-exchange, which means they are used as means of disbursement (*Leistungsmittel*). [▶44] Certainly, one might not readily call these hoarded goods that occasionally enter circulation 'money' as such; however, some items from among them can indeed become money. This happens when one or more, in contrast to others, are consistently used for certain giving-aways; when they also pass from one hand to the other as levies (*Abgabe*), offerings, priestly rewards (*Priesterlohn*), bride-price (*Brautpreis*), ransom-money (*Lösegeld*), contributions to allies (*Bundesgenossenbeitrag*), war tributes, or guest-presents. Many examples of this have been provided in my work (Gerloff 1940) and others will be presented here later on. However, all the mentioned gift-givings are considered as gift-exchanges.[103] Certainly, this is not of insignificant importance; in fact, this guarantees the recurrence of the process, which results in certain items from gift-exchange or other types of gift-traffics evolving into money.

Swords and shields, helmets and horns (drinking horns), cups and finger rings (or rings in general), are the recurring items in the descriptions of gift-exchange in the Germanic myths of gods and sagas of heroes. However, at most, the last two have gained monetary significance (*Geldbedeutung*); certainly and irrefutably, the rings, in any case (Gerloff 1940:42 f.). The process of becoming money can be well illustrated using the example of rings. Arm and neck rings are worn by Germanic warriors as symbols of their rank (Grönbech 1939: 38). These rings are therefore precious-items that signify distinction, and they are accordingly valued. Kings accumulate them in their treasuries to distribute lavishly on occasion. In Germanic heroic songs, the king is the ring-distributor (*Ringverteiler*); the followers are referred to as ring-takers (*Ringnehmer*). In the Bjarkalied,[104] there is

---

[103] Cf. Laum (1924:36 and 39).

[104] [tn] '*Bjarkalied*' refers to a heroic poem or lay from Germanic literature,

mention of the rings that Hrolf[105] scattered among his men. In the Beowulflied,[106] it is the queen who gave the hero arm rings and neck rings after the victorious battle. Hiltgund, as told in the "Waltharius" epic, takes two chests filled with gold from the queen's treasure as she flees from Attila's court with Walther.[107] The contents of these chests probably consisted entirely, but certainly predominantly, of rings; for first a hundred, then two hundred, Walther offered as part of this treasure to Gunther,[108] [p45] who was blocking his passage, as the Waltharius poem tells us.

The Germanic myth of Draupnir, Odin's ring, which dripped eight rings of equal value every ninth night, also teaches us the significance our

---

specifically from the Old Norse tradition. It is known for its portrayal of heroic deeds and adventures. The term 'Bjarkalied' can be roughly translated as 'Lay of the Bjarkar,' with 'Bjarkar' possibly referring to a legendary or heroic group of individuals.

[105] [tn] Hrolf, often referred to as Hrolf Kraki, is a legendary Danish king and hero from Old Norse sagas and legends, known for his legendary exploits, battles, and adventures.

[106] [tn] The *Beowulflied* refers to the epic poem *Beowulf*, which is one of the most important works of Old English literature, composed in the early medieval period, likely between the 8th and 11th centuries. Its setting is Scandinavia. It is an epic poem that tells the story of the hero Beowulf and his battles against various monsters, including the legendary creature Grendel and a dragon. This sentence refers to the passage or section in the epic poem where a queen or noblewoman bestows arm rings and neck rings (torcs) as gifts to the hero Beowulf after his successful battles.

[107] [tn] *Waltharius* is a medieval Latin epic poem that tells the story of the warrior Walthari and his adventures. Hiltgund is a queen and plays a significant role in the story's narrative. Attila (c.406 - c. 453), often referred to as Attila the Hun, was a historical figure who ruled as the leader of the Huns during the 5th century. Walther is one of the main protagonists and is portrayed as a heroic warrior who embarks on various adventures and battles.

[108] [tn] A king and warrior in Waltharius.

ancestors attached to the ornamental ring.[109]

So I give you the ring, red from the fire,

In which Odin's son turned to ashes.

From it, eight equally heavy ones drop,

Every ninth night.[110]

In the Nordic cultural sphere, it can be clearly demonstrated that rings gained monetary significance.[111] In Icelandic, a ring is called "baugr." In

---

[109] [tn] In Norse mythology, Draupnir is a magical ring associated with Odin, the chief god. Draupnir was created by the dwarven brothers Sindri (also known as Eitri) and Brokkr. Loki, the trickster god, had made a bet with two other dwarves, and he challenged the brothers to create items that would rival the treasures of the other dwarves. Loki tried to sabotage their work, but despite his efforts, the brothers managed to create remarkable items, including the ship Skidbladnir, the golden boar Gullinbursti, and the powerful hammer Mjolnir. As for Draupnir, it was a magical ring that had the ability to produce more rings. Every ninth night, eight new rings of equal quality and weight would drip from Draupnir. This ability to multiply itself made Draupnir a symbol of Odin's wealth and power. Odin often used these rings as offerings or rewards, and they were considered tokens of his favour. The story of Draupnir is found in the Prose *Edda*, a collection of Norse myths and legends written by the Icelandic scholar Snorri Sturluson in the 13th century.

[110] The Eddic ([tn] See footnote 92) tradition of Odin's Dripping Ring reappears in the folk belief of the Heckepfennig or Hecketaler*.

[tn] * '*Heckethaler*' (or '*Heckepfennig*') is a term related to a North Hessian folk belief. According to this belief, a '*Heckethaler*' is a coin that, when combined with other coins, has the power to multiply new coins for its owner, leading to increasing wealth. This belief is rooted in local legends and traditions, and it is named after the district of Holzhausen am Reinhardswald in North Hesse, Germany. The term reflects the idea that certain coins possess a magical ability to generate more coins for their possessor, contributing to the growth of their wealth.

[111] For examples, see Gerloff (1940: 43 f. and 83.) for other cultural spheres.

the Old Icelandic legal code *Grágás* (literally, Gray Goose (*Graugans*)[112]), the section about penance-money (*Bußgeld*) is referred to as "*Baugetal*," which means 'list of rings' (*Verzeichnis der Ringe*) or 'ring-table' (*Ringtafel*). Another example: In the rules for the payment of *Wergeld*,[113] as outlined in the Gulathing Law,[114] the individuals are categorised into three groups of men, each of which had to pay or receive one of the main rings. G. Vigfusson, the learned author of an Icelandic-English dictionary, rightly states that "Baugr in old times simply means money."

It [Baugr] is the treasure or hoard that the king or warlords gather, not meant to let it rust in disgrace, as Hrörek,[115] the king of greed and the hoarder of treasures did (in the Bjarkalied[116]), but rather to distribute it among the followers. The joy of possessing these precious-items, however, is shared between leaders and their followers. This sentiment resounds

---

[112] [tn] The term 'Gray Goose Laws,' used to describe the laws of the Icelandic Commonwealth in the 16th century, could refer to several possibilities: (1) The laws were written using a quill made from a goose feather. (2) The laws were bound in covers made from goose skin or (3) The laws were referred to as 'grey goose' due to the belief that geese lived longer than other birds, reflecting the age and longevity of the laws.

[113] [tn] A monetary compensation or payment made to settle legal disputes or compensate for injuries or deaths in ancient Germanic societies.

[114] [tn] The Gulathing was one of the four regional assemblies in medieval Norway. It was a legislative and judicial body where legal matters were discussed and resolved. The Gulathing Law refers to the legal code that was followed and enforced in the jurisdiction of the Gulathing assembly.

[115] [tn] Hrörek, also known as Hrœrekr Ringslinger, was a legendary Norse king known for his greed and hoarding of treasures. He is mentioned in the Bjarkalied (See the next footnote), a Norse heroic poem, where he is depicted as a king who amassed wealth but did not share it with his followers.

[116] [tn] Bjarkalied refers to the Old Norse poem "*Bjarkamál*" or "The Ballad of Bjarki." It is one of the heroic poems in the Poetic *Edda*, a collection of Old Norse poems that date back to the medieval period. The poem tells the story of the hero Bjarki and his adventures.

repeatedly in the sagas, giving the impression that those Nordic people were slaves to gold, silver, and iron. For, as Grönbech notes, they often "sing a hymn in praise of metals that goes against any feeling of decency. They create their greatest poetic works in praise of gold," and "the jubilation over gold resonates widely and powerfully throughout the entire poetry of the Germanic people" (Grönbech 1939:11f.). [₱46] The judgment of the knowledgeable expert of early Germanic culture is not quite as harsh as it may seem from this; for in another place it is said:

> These heroic inclinations to strive for gold and bronze and to accumulate them in spacious vaults and halls flood the souls of men, but without resulting in a visible dampening of all great emotions or a withering of the spirit.

The psychological interpretation of this behaviour – and hence this apparent digression – leads us back to the motive that we have already extensively discussed as the driving force behind the societal conduct-process, and thus for the entire cultural development and also for the emergence of money: the 'drive for distinction' or the 'need for recognition.'

Hoarding and wastefulness are encountered not only among the Nordic peoples. Countless examples of this can be found in various cultural circles in anthropology and cultural history. The motive underlying both generosity and greed is the satisfaction that the wastefulness of possessions, as well as their collecting (*Sammlung*) and stockpiling, can provide by creating social accentuation.

Treasure-buildup and treasure-utilisation are thus, as demonstrated here, prerequisites for the emergence of money – ring-money (*Ringgeld*) specifically – in the Nordic-Germanic cultural sphere. Similar situations can also be observed in entirely different cultural contexts, demonstrating the emergence of precious forms of money. Numerous pieces of evidence for this have been presented in my study on "The Emergence of Money" (Gerloff 1940), to which reference must be made repeatedly in this context to avoid repetition.

Language history also provides us with remarkable indications of the development shown here, from treasure or hoard to money. The word '*Schatz*' [treasure], Old High German '*scaz*,' Middle High German '*schaz*,' essentially signifies valuable property, precious possession, asset, or wealth. Early on, this word in various languages (Gothic, Old English, Old Frisian) acquired the meaning of money or tax, tribute, indicating a form of tribute or a means of disbursement. [p47] The Old Slavic word '*skotŭ*,' meaning livestock (*Vieh*), is considered to be related or of common origin with the Old High German word '*scaz*,' although disagreements exist regarding the connection. It is noted that the Old Frisian word '*sket*' not only signifies possession or asset but also livestock, especially cattle livestock (*Rindvieh*), which at that time essentially constituted possession. The original meaning of the foundational word could have been related to livestock or cattle, as described earlier in the text. The semantic change from livestock to money, or perhaps the equating of livestock with wealth = money, is indeed demonstrable in other languages and expressions as well, such as in Latin (*pecunia* from *pecus*[117]) and in English (where the Old English '*feoh*'[118] became '*fee*' meaning charge, fee, *honorarium*, and so on). Noteworthy is now what M. Heyne says about the development of the term '*Schatz*,' namely, that it has occurred in two directions: "1. Emphasising the preciousness of valuable items, notably metals and stones collected,

---

[117] [tn] *Pecus* is a Latin word that originally meant 'cattle' or 'livestock.' In the context of early Roman society, where agriculture and herding were fundamental to the economy, cattle were considered a form of wealth and value. Over time, the word '*pecus*' came to symbolise wealth more broadly, and it eventually contributed to the development of the Latin word '*pecunia*,' which means 'money.'

[118] [tn] '*Feoh*' is an Old English word that referred to cattle or livestock, and it was used as a form of wealth or value in early Germanic societies. Over time, this term evolved in meaning and came to represent a general form of wealth, which eventually transitioned into the broader concept of money.

guarded, and donated by ancient leaders of the *gens* (*Geschlecht*)."[119] The development of the emergence of money could not be better indicated. Furthermore, according to Heyne, the meaning of the word '*Schatz*' has then narrowed down in linguistic development to "minted precious metal, money piece in general, particularly frequent in the ancient language, also evolving here into the concept of coin (*Münze*) in general."[120]

As always, life's various forms and usages [*Gebrauch*] have left their mark on linguistic development here as well. Let's also add that the prehistoric treasure discoveries from the Danube[121] up to the far North confirm the picture presented by Germanic literature, both poetic and legal. In my view, this statement seems well-founded: In this cultural context, **money has originated from precious-items**, specifically through the established practice (*Brauch*) of using treasure pieces. [P48] **The origin of money can be traced back to the treasure-buildup or hoarding and treasure-distribution** (*Schatzverteilung*) **or treasure-utilisation** (*Schatzverwendung*).

However, what has been stated applies not only to the peoples belonging to the Germanic cultural sphere but also to others who have achieved a goods-usage that can be referred to as money or money-expending. In all these culturally distinct areas, often separated by time and space, it becomes apparent that the prerequisite for the emergence of money has been a certain treasure-buildup and treasure-utilisation. In this process, certain precious-items attain a preferred status. They are used as gifts to establish or fulfil various social obligations. In this context, the act

---

[119] [tn] See footnote 58 for the meaning of '*gens*.'

[120] See the entry for '*Schatz*' [treasure] in Heyne (1890-95). Similarly, Kluge (1899), Paul (1896), Weigand (1878) and Schade (1872-82) for more information on this topic.

[121] [tn] A major river in Europe that flows through several countries, including Germany, Austria, Slovakia, Hungary, Serbia, Bulgaria, and Romania, before emptying into the Black Sea.

of giving carries the significance of expressing acknowledgement, showing honour, reaffirming a promise, sealing a covenant, and more. In any case, it primarily holds a symbolic meaning, where the economic valuation takes a back seat. It is evident that such precious-items, with such a scope of use, are particularly valued and, for that reason, increasingly become both objects of hoarding and means for establishing social relationships. However, the transfer of material-value as such is not originally the essential aspect of this process.

The function of these precious-items or hoarded goods is thus twofold: they serve as social means of distinction (*Auszeichnungsmittel*) or social means of recognition (*Geltungsmittel*) and simultaneously act as tools for establishing social relationships, in short, social means of relationship (*Beziehungsmittel*). The fulfilment of these dual services turns hoarded goods or precious-items into money. Hoard-goods, which are regularly used in the sense explained to establish or fulfil social obligations, constitute money. We refer to this money as **hoard-money** (*Hortgeld*). Additionally, the term **ornament-money** (*Kleinodgeld*) may describe the realm of goods from which the money-good (*Geldgut*) originates.

§5. The Gift-Traffic

[₽49] The present-day world is inconceivable without an extensive goods-traffic. Perhaps this fact, albeit unconsciously, contributed to the occasionally widespread notion that, in contrast, the world of primitive societies was a life-sphere with little or almost no goods-traffic. Today, we know that this is not the case. One can confidently venture the assertion that human traffic, not only on a mental level through the exchange of feelings, thoughts, decisions, etc. but also on a physical level through the goods-transfer, is as old as human co-living itself. However, the earliest goods-traffic among humans was not distinctly economic, determined by economical motives. Instead, it was an expression of social life or social relationships in general. Of course, this does not mean that this early goods-traffic had no economical significance; rather, its economical aspect was largely hidden and obscured by the focus on satisfying other social needs.

Primitive goods-traffic takes on various forms, ranging from violent seizure (*Wegnahme*) to gifts, barter, purchase and all the way to different kinds of transfers. The overwhelmingly dominant form of primitive goods-traffic remains the same: the gift, which, rooted in the events of social life, goes along with the progression of the social life. It is the gifts to the deity or the hospitable friend, i.e., the gifts distributed during birth, marriage, and death, the gifts given and received during gatherings and celebrations, or upon the conclusion of agreements, and so on. **The goods-traffic in early culture is essentially a gift-traffic**.

It is reasonable to assume that this gift-traffic has not been insignificant in the emergence of money. Let's therefore examine whether and to what extent such a connection can be established. We can build on the explanations in the previous section, where, using the example of the ring, it was shown how the customary gift, the ornamental ring, acquired monetary significance. [₽50] Just as the ring was to the heroes and noble women of Germanic heroic poetry, fabrics were to the Germanic farmers.

Strangers brought them as guest-presents for hospitality, and departing guests were honoured with such gifts. Certain items of this nature are given preference, which is shown in their recurring use. They stand out from the variety of different gifts. This applies, as with rings, to specific types of fabrics as well. This naturally leads to other services being settled and fulfilled through these gift goods. This is a goods-usage that we refer to as money-usage.

Some of these gifts, especially those exchanged between guest and host, are referred to as presents in anthropological literature. However, this expression is misleading and is therefore rejected here. The word '*Geschenk*' [present] has originated from the verb '*schenken*,' which originally meant to pour a drink. In Middle High German, the concept of offering a drink as a gesture of welcome and hospitality gradually evolved into the meaning of providing something without compensation. Thus, the word '*Geschenk*' [present] is inherently linked to the notion of giving without expecting compensation. No reciprocal-gift (*Gegengabe*) is expected for the present, at least not demanded. The semantic meaning of the word '*Gabe*,' on the other hand, leaves the question of reciprocation open. Therefore, it is preferred in situations where it remains undecided whether giving and receiving occur based on the principle of compensation (*Entgelt*)[122] or non-compensation (*Unentgeltlichkeit*). Furthermore, in favour of this usage of the word '*Gabe*' [gift] is that the term '*Gabe*' is also employed in various compounds that encompass a wide range of forms of goods-transfer, all of which are summarised here under the term *Gabenverkehr* [gift-traffic], such as *Morgengabe* [morning gift to a bride],[123] *Opfergabe* [sacrificial gift to a deity], *Ehrengabe* [honorary gift],[124] and many others.

---

[122] [tn] See Translation Note on p. 350.

[123] [tn] It refers to a traditional practice in some cultures where a groom gives a gift to his bride on the morning after their wedding, often as a symbol of his love and commitment.

[124] [tn] It refers to a token of esteem or acknowledgement for one's achievements,

This already indicates that the occasions for the gift-traffic are very diverse: 'Consecration gifts' (*Weihegabe*) are given to the deity or its representatives; Pacification-gifts (*Befriedungsgabe*) mark the conclusion of disputes; [₽51] Family gifts (*Familiengabe*) and social gifts (*Sozialgabe*) accompany family and societal events such as birth, marriage, funeral, coming-of-age ceremonies, festive congregations, and so on. To thoroughly examine this multifaceted gift-traffic in detail would require extensive individual investigation. Here, only a few aspects can be highlighted.

As one of the oldest forms of gift-traffic, certain goods-distributions should be mentioned. The goods-distribution is, as shown in another context, perhaps one of the oldest forms of economic goods-traffic overall.[125] However, we are not here referring to the original distributions of hunting and gathering spoils and the like, but rather the distribution of valuable objects or hoarded goods that take place on festive occasions, during coming-of-age ceremonies, funeral rites, initiation into secret unions, concluding military campaigns, etc., carried out by the chief, the priest, or even the private host. Evidence for such distributions can be found from all parts of the world, spanning both primitive and historical societies. We encounter this practice particularly among numerous tribal communities in Oceania, as well as among the Native American populations across the vast areas of North America. Distributions were customary in the cultural communities of the ancient Sumerians, as well as at the residences of Germanic chieftains. The honorary title of the generous Germanic chieftain is, as previously mentioned, ring-distributor (*Ringverteiler*).

The objects of such distributions are (as in the last-mentioned example)

---

contributions, or position.

[125] Gerloff (1940:184, 197). Cf. Also, refer to my brief work Gerloff (1948). Also, Gerloff (1948b: 202 ff.).

golden or silver rings, while among the Native Americans, they include woollen blankets, copper plates, or wampum [126] beads. On the Banks Islands, during initiation ceremonies into the secret union (*Suque*[127]), long threads of shell-money are distributed. The distribution of mats is customary in Samoa. Such gift-distributions are particularly common during funeral ceremonies (Petri 1936: 207, 209).

The widespread custom of gift-distributions, as expected, naturally becomes an incentive for the gift-amassing, the treasure-buildup; indeed, it almost compels it. [P52] Most often, this task falls to the head of the family; however, the purpose is to have the means available for respectful distribution on the occasion or to be able to contribute accordingly to public distributions. The distribution-good is often already money, but just as frequently, they acquire money characteristics through their use in public distributions. Its use as a distribution-good makes it capable of circulation, granting it a circulatory function. Several ethnographic examples show how the customary-practice (*Brauchtum*) of such distributions tends to evolve into a regulated circulation of goods, which can be considered, in some aspects, as a form of money-usage.

It is evident that the significance of such gift-traffic, meaning in this case the amassing of specific goods, the treasure-buildup, and their distribution, must not be underestimated for the development of economic intercourses and especially for the emergence of money. Unfortunately, in this case, it must also be noted that the entire scope of the issue, from the perspective outlined here, has not yet received any attention, let alone a

---

[126] [tn] Traditional cylindrical beads made from shells are particularly used by certain native American tribes, especially those from the northeastern parts of North America. These beads were often strung together and used as a form of money, as well as for ceremonial and decorative purposes.

[127] [tn] The term '*Suque*' refers to the secret union that exists within the communities of Vanuatu, a country located in the South Pacific Ocean.

satisfactory scholarly treatment.

Next to distributions, we should also mention the ritualistic gift-traffic. Its significance for the emergence of money has been demonstrated by Bernhard Laum for a limited area, namely the cultural sphere of Homeric Greece (see Gerloff 1940:21).[128] Various facts from the realm of ethnology also suggest that among certain indigenous peoples, a gift-traffic has evolved within their rituals that have influenced the emergence of money, or at the very least, have contributed to transforming items from gift-traffic into forms of money-good.

The oldest congregations serve the purpose of worship. However, there is no worship without consecration gifts. It can be observed that some of the goods used as consecration gifts become money. The use of an item as a consecration gift makes it generally desirable, leading it to be used for other purposes as 'voluntary gifts' (*Dargabe*) [129] and contributions (*Hergabe*), [130] thus turning it into money. Therefore, among the consecration gifts, we often find goods that we encounter as money in [economic] intercourses. [᛭53] They are not consecration gifts because they are money; that may only be the case at a much later stage. Instead, they are consecration gifts, and it is because they are consecration gifts that they have become money or, at the very least, this characteristic of theirs has facilitated the process of becoming money.

Furthermore, friendship-gifts (*Freundschaftsgabe*) should be mentioned. Friendship relationships primarily exist among related persons at lower or the lowest cultural levels. Furthermore, we frequently encounter instances of friendship relations that extend to non-relatives and are not limited to members of one's own tribe. Hospitality is such a relationship, which, however, seems to be indeed widespread at the stage

---

[128] [tn] See Laum (2023).

[129] [tn] See Translation Note on p. 356.

[130] Refer to the literature mentioned in footnote 125 for further comparison.

of primitive culture due to the mistrust of the primitive, who is inclined to perceive hostility in everything foreign. To overcome such mistrust and to express goodwill, gifts and reciprocal-gifts are used. Likewise, the value, longevity, and strength of other friendly relationships are demonstrated and ensured through a gift-traffic. Even among primitive culture societies, such a gift-traffic seems to have already developed. As A. R. Brown, the foremost expert on the Andamanese,[131] states about them: "Almost every object they possess constantly changes its possessor" (Schmidt 1937:81).

More or less distinctly, two types of gifts can be distinguished: namely, those that require a reciprocal-gift, and those that do not necessitate an immediate return. Among the Andamanese, reciprocal-gifts are only expected and accepted from peers, not from older individuals (ibid.: 41). Among the Kyrgyz[132] people, it is reported that presents are not only customary but obligatory in the event of the death of the father, father-in-law, or influential individuals. They typically consist of silver or livestock. It is not customary to reciprocate these gifts with reciprocal-gifts. [p54] In addition to these presents mentioned, there are others referred to as 'tamur-bulmak,'[133] which are reciprocal gifts. Apparently, disputes and judicial decisions often arise when these gifts do not correspond in value to each other. If the person receiving the gift does not have anything to offer as an equivalent reciprocal-present (*Gegengeschenk*), they will not accept the gift. The habit of demanding a reciprocal-gift for a given gift is so widely customary among North American Indians that the term "Indian gift" signifies a gift that requires a reciprocal-gift in return (Hoyt

---

[131] [tn] The indigenous people inhabiting the Andaman Islands, a group of islands in the Bay of Bengal, primarily belonging to India.

[132] [tn] An ethnic group primarily living in Central Asia, particularly in Kyrgyzstan.

[133] [tn] A term used to describe mutual gifts or reciprocal giving practices among the Kirgiz people. These gifts are exchanged between individuals and are often given without the expectation of immediate reciprocation.

1926: 99). This leads to a gift-traffic that rightfully deserves the name 'gift-exchange.'

Similarly, the gift-traffic appears to occur among many peoples. The joyful or sorrowful events of daily life give rise to 'present-distributions' (*Geschenkverteilung*), while gifts given on other occasions always result in an immediate reciprocal-gift. But even those gift-distributions, as observed for example (according to Malinowski) during ancestral festivals on the Trobriand Islands[134] and (according to Wheeler) during initiations into manhood among the Australians is customary and have frequently evolved into proper 'traffic of gift-exchange' (*Gabentauschverkehr*) (Malinowski 1922: 184; Wheeler 1910:72 ff.). The Samoyed[135] gives presents to their guest, but they expect a reciprocal-present in return. The same applies to the Tungus,[136] Yakuts, Lapps,[137] and others. The reciprocal-gift has thus become a mandatory obligation. That is one aspect; the other is the belief and practice that has developed, indicating that the reciprocal-gifts must be equivalent (*gleichwertig*). Disagreements regarding the equivalence of exchanged gifts often lead to bitter disputes among these people. It is not uncommon for the tribal judge (*Stammesrichter*) to be called upon for a decision, either sentencing the return of the gift or imposing penances on the guilty party.[138] The Germanic customary laws state something similar.

---

[134] [tn] The Trobriand Islands are located in the southwestern Pacific Ocean, part of Papua New Guinea.

[135] [tn] The Samoyed refers to the Samoyedic people, an indigenous ethnic group from Siberia.

[136] [tn] The Tungus people are indigenous to Siberia, particularly in areas of Russia, China, and Mongolia.

[137] [tn] The Yakuts are a Turkic ethnic group native to the Sakha Republic (Yakutia) in Russia. Lapps (Sámi) people are indigenous to northern Europe, primarily inhabiting parts of Norway, Sweden, Finland, and Russia.

[138] References from various sources in Schmidt (1937: Vol II, 27, 56, 135, 235 ff.).

In the 'Gray Goose' (*Graugans*),[139] it is stated:

> A giver cannot take back their gift, but if they gave in the hope of compensation, or if the recipient has promised an equivalent in return, then the giver has a claim to as much as was promised.

[♭55] The Ostrogothic Law (*Ostgötagesetz*)[140] states that one can assert ownership by saying: "He gave, and I repaid." – Such provisions trace back to the idea that the exchange of presents is the proper procedure when items pass from one hand to another (Grönbech 1939:71). In general, it can be said that gift-traffic has led to the development of certain legal forms. This is evident in the fact that, as mentioned, it is subject to judicial assessment, particularly when one party believes to have received less than expected. However, where such value-assessments (*Wertabschätzung*) and value-determinations (*Wertfestsetzung*), even penances, are involved, it is likely that money and monetary value also play a role. And indeed, that is

---

[139] [tn] '*Graugans*' is the term used to refer to an Icelandic law book dating back to the early Middle Ages. This term is also the German translation for 'Gray Goose,' which corresponds to the Old Norse term '*Grágás*' (see footnote 112). '*Grágás*' is connected to the wider context of Germanic customary laws known as "*Germanische Volksrechte*." While these "*Germanic Volksrechte*" were generally written in vulgar Latin with the inclusion of Germanic terms, '*Grágás*' stands out as an example from the North Germanic region, specifically Iceland. This legal text, written in Icelandic, offers insights into legal practices and norms during the Early Middle Ages in Iceland. It serves as a testament to the preservation of legal traditions within the broader scope of Germanic legal history. "*Graugans*" is among the oldest and most original sources of Germanic law, written in a Germanic language and reflecting the unique conditions of Iceland as an island republic.

[140] [tn] The Ostrogothic Law, also known as the "*Lex Visigothorum*" or the "*Visigothic* Code," was a collection of laws used by the *Visigothic* kingdom in Spain during the early Middle Ages. It was one of the first attempts to codify Germanic customary law and Roman law, reflecting the legal system of the *Visigothic* people. The law code covers a wide range of legal topics and provides insights into the legal norms and practices of the time.

the case.

The subject of unilateral gift-traffic includes the rings and fabrics known from the Germanic cultural sphere, which are precious-items and other hoarded goods. In other cultural spheres, these can be shell arm rings, mats, precious old plates, wild boar tusks, as well as livestock pieces, and so on. As certain services with these goods become customary for other purposes, such as bride-purchase (*Braukauf*) or penance-payment (*Bußzahlung*), they evolve into forms of money.

Certainly, the gift-traffic is not limited to the usage of hoarded goods. With the progressing development of economic life, the gift-traffic also extends to more or less vital means of existence. Certain natural products like red earth, white clay, shells, skins, salt, copper, etc., or products of tribe-specific craftsmanship such as blacksmithing, mat weaving, ornament-making (e.g., ornamented bamboo combs among the Semang [141]), give rise to occasional but easily becoming regular gift-exchange. This is especially the case when peoples of lower development come into contact with those of higher technological advancement. At times, the gift-exchange can also transform into a levy-relation (*Abgabenverhältnis*) or 'disguised tribute obligation' (*verschleierte Tributpflicht*),[142] where the weaker party delivers products of its economy and, in return, receives unilaterally determined compensations.

[P56] From this list of examples related to gift-exchange, it becomes apparent that some of these items attain monetary significance, such as salt, copper, processed shells, mats, and so on.

By transforming friendly gift-traffic into a gift-exchange, a significant

---

[141] [tn] A Negrito ethnic group of people living in Peninsular Malaysia.

[142] [tn] 'Disguised tribute obligation' describes a scenario where the requirement to pay tribute is not immediately evident or transparent. It suggests an obligation to pay that might not be openly acknowledged or apparent due to various reasons, despite its actual existence.

step towards the economic development of goods-exchange has been taken, even if economical purpose-settings were not originally the intention behind the gift-reciprocation (*Gabenwechsel*). Then, regular visits for gift-exchange, known as gift-exchange journeys (*Gabentauschfahrten*), often occur. In this context, the Pangwe[143] peoples of West Africa organise regular friendship visits among families of the same clan, as well as between different clans, with the apparent purpose being an extensive gift-exchange (Tessmann 1913: 209 ff.). Most commonly, such gift-exchange journeys take place between tribes whose products can complement each other's provisions, especially between inland and coastal inhabitants. This occurs, for instance, between reindeer herders and sea-dwelling Korjaks.[144] From the Melanesian islands,[145] such journeys are often reported, such as from the Motu,[146] Siassi,[147] and Tami[148] islands, and so on.[149] The objects and means of this gift-traffic are, of course, not to be considered as money at first and without further ado, but some of them can become money. The Tubetube and the Teste, two seafaring coastal tribes of New Guinea, typically import the majority of their subsistence demand. On the other hand, they export shell ornament piece that has become valuable in the areas they visit and is used as money. Money can thus emerge in two ways during these gift-exchange journeys. One way is that a tribe, reliant on

---

[143] [tn] An ethnic group from West Africa, specifically from regions such as Cameroon, Equatorial Guinea, and Gabon.

[144] [tn] An indigenous people living in the northeastern part of Siberia, mainly in the Kamchatka Peninsula and adjacent areas in Russia.

[145] [tn] A subregion in the southwestern Pacific Ocean and includes the islands and nations to the northeast of Australia.

[146] [tn] An indigenous group living in Papua New Guinea.

[147] [tn] A group of islands located in the Bismarck Sea, part of Papua New Guinea.

[148] [tn] A small group of islands located in the Bismarck Sea, near the northern coast of Papua New Guinea.

[149] Evidence from various sources in Thurnwald (1931-34: Vol III, 119 f.).

goods-procurement (*Güterbeschaffung*) from outside sources, introduces certain items into circulation, such as arm rings, shell strings, mats, etc., which serve as a form of money for them. On the other hand, these items can also acquire monetary significance for the acquirers. For them, these items become precious-items or hoard pieces, signifying possession and thereby conferring reputation. [p57] Indeed, this seems to have often been the case in the Melanesian islands in the past. The ornamental pieces acquired through gift-exchange initially serve as adorning-money (*Prunkgeld*) and showcasing-money (*Schaugeld*), and they are only used as circulating-money (*Umlaufsgeld*) on specific occasions, such as when acquiring wives.

The gift-traffic is always an expression of social relationships. In fact, one could say that there are hardly any significant social relationships that do not find their expression in gift-traffic or are even established through it.

The strongest and most important social relationships are based on gender-related contact, that is, sexual relationships. Even these are often linked to a gift-traffic that has not infrequently appeared to have influenced the emergence of money and the development of money-usage. In some farming tribes at a subsistence level with a matrilineal inclination, it is customary for a man to reciprocate each act of love from a woman with presents in "traditional valuables."[150] Among the Papuans, a man must pay for each sexual relation with the customary shell-money used there.[151] Frank Wedekind,[152] who once sought to solve the entire social question at

---

[150] Thurnwald (1931-34: Vol II, 132).

[151] Ploss & Bartels (1927: 11, II, 206).

[152] [tn] Frank Wedekind (full name: Benjamin Franklin Wedekind, 1864-1918) was a German playwright, poet, and actor. He is best known for his ground-breaking and controversial plays, which often explored themes of sexuality, societal norms, and the human psyche. Wedekind is considered a key figure in German Expressionist theatre and had a significant influence on the

once with a proposal of this kind and simultaneously put an end to public financial distress, probably remained unaware of the inspirations behind his proposal.[153]

The widespread, friendly exchange of women, which, as has often been observed, we find both among the lower hunter-gatherer peoples in various parts of the world and also among higher primitive peoples, is also connected with a gift-exchange, whereby certain regularly customary gifts can acquire the character of money. For wherever gifts become traditional carriers of value, they must be regarded as money. [58] Here, it appears that the exchange of women transforms from a customary exchange of gifts into a form of wife-purchase (*Frauenkauf*). We will come back to this shortly.

Even the extramarital and parallel romantic lives of indigenous peoples are associated with a gift-traffic. Frequently, one encounters phenomena here that one is inclined to regard as prostitution, although this term is certainly often unjustly used for the free sexual contacts of indigenous peoples. However, this is not to be pursued here. What matters is that compensations in gifts are customary in such cases, which, through their regular use, can become a form of money or whose transformation into money is supported, among other factors, by this usage. These are processes of very different kinds, ranging from premarital free love, which, as J. J. Bachofen (1861: Preface) suggests, is a "guarantee of marital chastity,[154] the sanctity of which requires a prior fulfilment of the

---

development of modern drama.

[153] Holm (1932: 114).

[154] [tn] This means that experiencing relationships before marriage can inform and mature individuals, potentially reducing curiosity or the need to explore outside the marriage. The idea is that having already explored such feelings or connections before marriage may contribute to a more committed and stable relationship thereafter.

woman's natural duty," to hetairism [155] and commercial prostitution (temple prostitution[156]), as well as certain sacred orgies and erotic festivals associated with gift-giving, which may have significance in their own right for our subject of investigation. To demonstrate this would require an in-depth specialised investigation because, unfortunately, this aspect of these processes has not yet received the attention of ethnologists or cultural historians.

Amidst the wealth of material, reference should be made to the girls of Palau,[157] Yap,[158] and Ponape,[159] who, known as *'armegól'* (hetairai), for a period of time provide love services in the assembly houses of the young men. Certain gifts, as noted repeatedly by explorers (such as Kubary, Müller-Wismar, A. Hahl, etc.), play an important role here as compensation. "Similar extramarital relationships resembling prostitution

---

[155] [tn] *Hetaira* (ἑταίρα. pl. *hetairai*) is a term used in ancient Greece to describe a specific category of female companions, that extended beyond mere sexual transactions and included elements of intellectual and emotional connection. They were often courtesans or mistresses, who were typically educated, cultured, and provided companionship to men. These women were known for their wit, charm, and artistic talents and were often associated with intellectual and artistic circles.

[156] [tn] Temple prostitution, also known as sacred prostitution, is a historical practice in which sexual activity or rituals of a sexual nature were conducted within the precincts of a religious temple or shrine. This practice was found in various ancient cultures and religions, including those of Mesopotamia, Egypt, Greece, and India.

[157] [tn] An island country located in the Micronesia region of the western Pacific Ocean.

[158] [tn] An island located in the western Pacific Ocean and is part of the Federated States of Micronesia.

[159] [tn] Palau is an island country located in the western Pacific Ocean. Yap is one of the four states of the Federated States of Micronesia. Ponape (now known as Pohnpei) is another state of the Federated States of Micronesia.

are also known from the Sunda Islands[160]" (Thurnwald). Similarly, it appears that such intercourses are customary on the Gilbert Islands.[161]

The practice of lending women for the earning-purpose is also worth mentioning in this context. For business reasons, it is common to keep several women for this purpose.[162] [p59] A counterpart to this can be found among the Mansela-Alfuren[163] on the island of Seram. When a man enters into a marriage with a second wife, he must provide a gift to the first wife, specifically an old plate if the marriage is childless, and for each child, an additional such plate.[164] These old plates or bowls, as we know, are money, and they have indeed become money because they serve as a means of payment in these and other processes (Cf. Gerloff 1940:32, 33, 38).

The interaction between the sexes finds its most significant relationship-form (*Beziehungsgestaltung*) in marriage or the marital bond. Marriage, as far as we can see, is an event of significant social and legal importance among all people. Its significance is typically manifested through solemn activities, and its legal validity is often linked to the fulfilment of certain services. It is known that even in this context, gift-traffic plays an important role — a role that varies not only among different peoples but has also undergone significant changes over time. For the Germanic cultural sphere, W. Grönbech succinctly expressed it with the words: "In ancient times, marriage was built on presents" (Grönbech 1939: 283). That money was not an uninvolved bystander in these processes is to be assumed, or better yet, we know this. This is not meant

---

[160] [tn] The Sunda Islands, part of the Malay Archipelago, are a group of islands located in Southeast Asia, predominantly in Indonesia

[161] [tn] A group of coral atolls and islands in the central Pacific Ocean. They are part of the island nation of Kiribati, which is located in the Micronesia region.

[162] Ploss & Bartels (1927: II, 96 ff.).

[163] [tn] An indigenous group living on the island of Seram in Indonesia.

[164] Schadee (1915: 129, 135).

in the ordinary sense of a dowry marriage (*Geldheirat*) but in the sense that the gift-traffic accompanying, and often even initiating the marriage has also influenced the emergence of money.

The significance of the bride-price, along with the *Wergeld*, in the emergence of money has recently been emphasised by H. Quiggin as well. She writes:

> It would be extravagant to claim that, bride-price and *Wergeld* brought currency into existence, but they certainly established standards of value and regularised certain media of exchange.

[P60] And elsewhere, regarding the role she attributes to the bride-price in the emergence of money, she suggests that if money, as some believe, is the root of all evil, then "Eve once more marked out for blame" (Quiggin 1949: 7 and 291). Mrs. Quiggin evidently was not aware of my theory that women invented ornament and men turned it into money[165]; otherwise, she would not have blamed her gender [for the vicious role of money in society].

Regarding the extent of gift-traffic during marriage in ancient Germanic times, Grönbech says:

> Of greatest importance were the presents from the groom, or more accurately, from his clan, to the bride's family. But these main presents were complemented by numerous smaller presents. The groom gave ornament pieces to the bride and later to his wife, and the father did the same for his daughter at her wedding. Further presents were probably presented by the bride's family to the groom's relatives and by the bride to the wedding guests, and perhaps the groom made a present to each of his brothers-in-law" (Grönbech 1939: 283).

The Old English vernacular laws refer to the payments made for the bride as '*scaet*.' The connection with 'treasure' (*Schatz*) and 'money' is clear. "In

---

[165] Gerloff (1940: 143 ff. and 151).

the morning gift,[166] it is not the woman who offers to the man, but the man who offers to the woman," as stated by Tacitus (98 AD:18).

> The parents and relatives gather to approve these gifts, which are not chosen for female vanity or to adorn the bride, but cattle, a bridled horse, a shield, a spear, and a sword. Such presents constitute the dowry. On the other hand, the woman also brings something related to armour to the man.

From this enumeration, it is not clear whether, among these wedding gifts, there are any that can be considered as money or that may evolve into money over time. Both possibilities cannot be ruled out. However, it is also entirely possible that over time, other items may replace these gifts, which may be considered as money.

Among indigenous peoples, courtship and marriage are often associated with a diverse gift-traffic. [p61] As already shown in another context (Gerloff 1940:140), the gifts or gift-servings (*Gabenleistung*) made upon entering marriage, sometimes before or after, are not a purchase-price (*Kaufpreis*) but rather a giving and receiving as a symbolic activity, an expression of the established friendship, and acceptance into the clan-association (*Sippenverband*). Similarly, the Zulu term '*Lolola*,' which has become established in African studies for the suitor's gifts (*Freiersgabe*) or dowry, does not denote a purchase-price. The same applies to the Indonesian marriage-money (*Heiratsgeld*) called '*Harta*' and the '*Kalym*' (bridal-money (*Brautgeld*) or bride-price (*Brautpreis*)) found among all Asian breeders of horse, camel, and sheep.

The value of dowries varies significantly. In general, one can say that the transition from symbolically intended minor gifts to the transfer of larger values, such as greater livestock, is linked to the economic development that leads from matrilineal to patrilineal systems. [In patrilineal conditions], dowries tend to be relatively high because women, as

---

[166] See footnote 123.

labourers, have significant value, and the children belong to the father and his clan.

All of this need not be pursued further here, as the purpose is only to use the interpretation of such gift-traffic and the demonstration of its prevalence to indicate the possibility of the emergence of money and money-usage. *Harta* payments have already been discussed elsewhere (Gerloff 1940: 30). The *Kalym*, which consists of livestock, can also be paid in instalments, especially when the girl is promised in marriage while still a child.[167] The nature of dowries primarily depends on the way of life of the particular peoples involved. Among all livestock herders, these gifts consist of livestock, whether horses, cattle, or reindeer, which holds monetary significance. Additionally, among Nordic peoples, furs and skins are also common as bridal gifts. Among subsistence farmers, iron tools like hoes play a role, and small livestock may also be included. The Basumbwa[168] people, at the beginning of this century, paid dowries consisting of 150 to 1000 hoes. [P62] For the same purpose, the Basumbwa also used rolls of copper wire. However, the Wakara[169] paid only two hoes for the bride during the same period, along with at most one goat. Among the Wabende,[170] payment items included hoes, goats, and fabrics. In other African tribes, cowrie shells or ornament strings made from ostrich eggshells served the same purpose. For example, the bride-

---

[167] More details about the *Kalym* can be found in Gruenwaldt (1937:220) and from various authors in Schmidt (1937: II, 231).

[168] [tn] An ethnic group from East Africa, primarily found in the region of Tanzania and Uganda.

[169] [tn] A place in the Southern Kordofan region of Sudan.

[170] [tn] A region in East Africa.

68

price among the Basiba[171] used to be 12,000 cowrie shells.[172]

A fine example of the significance that gifts for "bride-purchase" can have in the emergence of money can be found in the customary-practices of the Kongoneger people from the Ababua[173] tribe. J. Halkin, to whom we owe a monograph on this ethnic group, says, based on Calonne,[174] regarding the payments made during the acquisition of wives: "These are knives specifically forged to pay the marital composition, and which," he remarkably adds, "have become a true currency (*monnaie*) in exchanges."[175]

The scope and extent of this dowry-traffic (*Brautgabenverkehr*) or suitor's gift-traffic (*Freiersgabenverkehr*) should not be underestimated, as it is one of the most significant and regular events in social life. It is a gift-traffic that is older, more widespread, and more general than exchange (*Tausch*); perhaps courtship and marriage are the societal processes with which the oldest gift-traffic of all is associated.

Early on and apparently in distant times that we cannot overlook, another form emerged alongside that familial gift-traffic: it was gift-exchange in the resolution of disputes and gift-servings (*Gabenleistungen*) as *Wergeld* or penance-money. The monk Gregor of Tours[176] tells of the

---

[171] [tn] The Basiba, also known as the Vasekele, are an ethnic group living in the Kasai region of the Democratic Republic of the Congo.

[172] Schultz-Ewerth & Adam (1929: I. Ostafrika, 113 ff. and 251).

[173] [tn] It refers to the Baboa people (singular Boa, also Ababwa, Babua, Babwa, Bwa) in the Democratic Republic of the Congo.

[174] [tn] The source of reference is not identified. Calonne refer to Charles-Alexandre de Calonne (1734 -1802), a Controller General of Finance to Louis XVI in 1783.

[175] [tn] Halkin (1910: 513). Our translation from French.

[176] [tn] Monk Gregor of Tours (Gregory of Tours, 358-594 AD) was a Frankish historian and bishop known for his "*Historia Francorum*," a significant historical work about the Merovingian kings and the early history of the Franks.

resolution of disputes between Leuvigild, the King of the Goths, and Theodomer, the King of the Suevi,[177] and he concludes with the words: "They exchanged gifts and both of them went to his home" (Grönbech, 1939: 48). [P63] In this passage, the monk describes a practice and process that seems to be very ancient. Disputes between leaders, kings, tribal chiefs, and so on — public feuds, one might say — are concluded with a gift-exchange. Just as old as these mutual payments, if one could call such a gift-exchange, are the unilateral payments used to atone for and settle the conflicts and wrongdoings of the people: *Wergeld* or penances. It is evident from this that there could be a connection with the emergence of money, as in the language of the Palau[178] Islanders, any form of payment is simply called "penalty-money" (*Strafgeld*).[179]

Above all, *Wergeld*, the atonement-payment for manslaughter, appears to be almost customary among all peoples. Provisions concerning it, such as its collection, determination, payment method, and distribution, are among the oldest legal statutes in existence. Instead of using terms like 'penances' or '*Wergeld*,' the old Nordic laws often referred to them simply as "rings." The Gray Goose (*Graugans*), as mentioned in the ring-table (*Baugatal*[180]), sets the penance for manslaughter in rings and regulates,

---

[177] [tn] A group of Germanic peoples who lived in central and northern Europe during antiquity. They are known for their migrations and were prominent in the early history of the Iberian Peninsula (modern-day Spain and Portugal) during the late Roman Empire and the early Middle Ages.

[178] [tn] An island country located in the Micronesia region of the western Pacific Ocean.

[179] Kubary (1895:9).

[180] [tn] 'Baugatal' is a specific reference to a section of Old Norse poetry known as the '*Baugatal*' or 'the Catalogue of Rings.' It is a poetic catalogue found within the Poetic *Edda*, a collection of Old Norse poems (This poetic catalogue was likely used as a mnemonic device to help people remember the various amounts and items that were appropriate for different situations and degrees of kinship). The '*Baugatal*' provides details about the amounts of gold rings and

similar to other Germanic customary laws, precisely what amount of rings and ring fragments each clan member is entitled to as *Wergeld* based on their degree of kinship proximity. Other legal offences are assessed in terms of penance-payments. According to the Gray Goose (*Graugans*), the standard is the three-mark penance. This is the recurring monetary penalty equivalent to 144 ells[181] of legal woollen fabric or one and a half cow's worth.

Among other peoples, we also find, as is natural, a certain similarity in the goods that serve as dowries and those determined by the legal-order as a means of penance-payment (*Bußzahlungsmittel*). Among the Basumbwa, the manslaughter penance for a chief's son is 1000 hoes, for a wealthy person 500, and an ordinary man 200. Among other African tribes, livestock, slaves, textiles, copper wire rolls, and ivory are used as *Wergeld* or penance-money. In Samoa, mats are commonly used for this purpose. [P64] Among the Kirgiz people, atonement-money (*Sühnegeld*) is determined in horses, while among the Samoyed people,[182] it is specified in reindeer. The usage that turns a good into money is expressed just as much in the determination of *Wergeld* or penance-rates (*Bußsatz*)[183] as this determination turns those goods used for 'damage compensation'

---

other treasures that should be paid as *Wergeld*' in cases of manslaughter or injury, based on the status and kinship of the individuals involved. This catalogue is used as a source of legal and cultural information about the Viking Age and early medieval Scandinavia.

[181] [tn] An old unit of measurement for length or distance, often used as a cloth measurement and was approximately 45 inches or 1.143 meters in length.

[182] [tn] An indigenous Finno-Ugric people who inhabit the northern regions of Scandinavia, which includes parts of Norway, Sweden, Finland, and the Kola Peninsula of Russia.

[183] [tn] The term '*Bußsatz*' refers to the determined amount of money or value that must be paid as a penance for an offence or misconduct. This amount is often set by laws or traditions and is meant to compensate for the harm caused or the wrongdoing committed.

(*Schadensvergütung*) into money.

Among the oldest societal relationship-orders associated with gift-trafficare the secret unions (*Geheimbund*) and secret societies found throughout the world. The anthropological and sociological studies that focus on these [secret] unions and related practices like men's houses, clubs, and similar institutions have given very little attention to the gift-traffic and payment systems within these [secret] unions. Therefore, our knowledge about the role that these [secret] unions and their customs may have played in the emergence and development of money is quite limited. This knowledge is primarily based on occasional and somewhat random remarks and reports found in the scattered literature that addresses these institutions.[184]

Such [secret] unions, whether were formed as 'age-group associations' (*Altersklassenzusammenschlüsse*) for asserting status in the generational order or simply as men's unions for purposes other than supporting law enforcement, as cult societies, as means of political associating (*Zusammenschluss*) and party formation, etc., often use the payment as a way to strengthen their power, whether entrance fees are collected for granting membership, especially for different levels, or whether levies are extracted from outsiders, a practice that has occasionally developed into systematic tax collection and tribute extraction. [⁋65] The items paid in such payments are either already money or their use for the mentioned purposes gradually turns them into money, at the very least solidifying their monetary character.

H. Schurtz aptly characterises the nature of these institutions:

> The character of secret unions is the same everywhere: the majority of the male population, possibly excepting only the youngest age

---

[184] The most famous work is Schurtz (1902). Additionally, you can refer to the articles by Höltker (1931) and Nevermann (1933), along with the literature cited in these two publications.

groups, tends to belong to them, and only the very poor devils who cannot afford the entrance fee remain excluded; they are usually also doomed to perpetual bachelorhood since they cannot afford a bride-price either" (Schurtz 1902:380).

The extent of these payments is illustrated by the recurring reports that candidates often spend years trying to gather the necessary funds for entry into the union, sometimes receiving loans from their friends for support. The cost is usually higher for advancing from one grade to another because increasingly higher payments are required for each higher grade. So what happens to the funds acquired by these unions? The answer: they are hoarded. Just as individual families or chiefs hoard shell-money rings, porcelain bowls, mats, ivory, etc., some of these secret unions turn their clubhouses into treasure houses through this practice. These funds are also used for various contributions, covering the costs of communal festivities, and serving gift-exchange with other unions and various other purposes.

As an example, the Kakihan union, a secret union in West Seram,[185] was mentioned earlier (Gerloff 1940:30 f.). Money-hoarding (*Geldhortung*) takes a central stage in the life of the secret union in Oceania, the *Dukduk*,[186] which is most well-known at least nominally. Membership in the union is, of course, contingent upon substantial payments, which often lead to significant debts for the initiates. In return, members become participants in the shell-money treasure, and enlarging this treasure appears to be their primary task. In small groups, accompanied by the wearer of their masks, they traverse the entire area to collect shell-money payments. [p66] The shell-money is also significant in various rituals and

---

[185] [tn] A region located in Indonesia, specifically on Seram Island in the Maluku Islands, which is part of the eastern archipelago of Indonesia.

[186] [tn] *Dukduk* is a traditional secret union or men's initiation society found in various parts of the Pacific Islands, particularly in Papua New Guinea, the Solomon Islands, and other neighbouring regions.

customs of the *Ingiet*[187] society, which is nearly as renowned as the *Dukduk*.

What shell-money is for these unions, that is mat-money (*Mattengeld*) for the natives of the New Hebrides.[188] Their cult group *Suque* society[189] appears to have developed a sophisticated payment system.

Prinz Maximilian zu Wied[190] reported about the Mandan, a Native American tribe from the upper Missouri region, that each age class has its own badges, songs, and dances, for which aspiring members must pay to obtain and learn. Dances and songs seem to be something that is frequently bought and sold, both among members of their own tribe and with other tribes.

Indeed, these unions or associations, regardless of the basis on which they are founded, often serve as carriers of a certain money-usage. Their structures and ways of life have contributed to the emergence and development of money. This is particularly true where a "change of motives" has transformed these organisations into societally structured ones, as is often the case. The transformation often relates to possession-related facts, focusing on 'acquisition of possession' (*Besitzerwerb*), 'expansion of possession' (*Besitzvergrößerung*), and, not least, 'preservation of possession' (*Besitzbewahrung*). Thus, these societal institutions, such as the Melanesian societies, have acquired a strong

---

[187] [tn] A secret men's society among the Tolai of East New Britain, commonly associated with sorcery and black magic.

[188] [tn] A former name for the island nation of Vanuatu in the South Pacific Ocean.

[189] [tn] See footnote 127 on *Suque*.

[190] [tn] Prince Alexander Philipp Maximilian zu Wied-Neuwied (1782 –1867) was a German explorer, naturalist, and ethnologist who conducted extensive research and exploration in North America during the early 19th century. He is known for his detailed observations and writings about the indigenous peoples and wildlife of the region.

plutocratic character. In fact, from mystery societies, they may have even become pure extortion societies (*Erpresserbund*). It is evident that money, and particularly money-hoarding, plays a significant and rapidly growing significance.

The societal life of ancient and early cultures includes many other forms of gift-traffic in addition to the ones mentioned. For example, the widespread practice of adoption (*Ankindung*) [of a child] is often associated with such gift-traffic. Adoptions occur among primitive societies for various reasons. These details are not of particular interest here, except insofar as they result in a gift-traffic. [P67] Compensations paid to the natural parents are customary, for example, among the Copper Eskimos[191] and among the Tami and Jabi[192] in New Guinea. Such one-time services may have little significance for the emergence of money and monetary intercourses. However, it is different when adoption establishes a continuous gift-traffic, as is the case in Samoa, where finely woven mats (*tonga*) play a significant role (Lehmann 1936:113 ff.).

Marriage, atonement-order (*Sühneordnung*) and federation (*Bündewesen*), as well as many other societal practices in the earliest cultures, are indeed linked to gift-traffic. Among the items involved in this gift-traffic, there are often goods that fulfil the essential services of money and can be considered money. The question regarding the emergence of money in this context can be framed as follows: Are these goods used as gifts because they are money or have they become money because they are regularly used as gifts to establish societal relationships within those specific social circles, and therefore also prove to be useful in forming other

---

[191] [tn] The Copper Eskimos, also known as the Copper Inuit, are indigenous people living in the Arctic regions of Canada, particularly in the area around the Coppermine River in what is now the Nunavut territory. Their name derives from their use of copper, which they obtained from trade and hunting implements.

[192] [tn] Both are islands in Papua New Guinea.

social relationships? Clearly, in the history of these relationship-orders, there are examples of both scenarios. However, there is a lack of comprehensive ethnographic and cultural-historical collection of material as well as scholarly analysis to provide specific evidence for each case. More important than the direct proof of the connection between such and many other processes and the emergence of money, which may be challenging to establish, is the recognition that this gift-traffic, older than the exchange-intercourse, must be considered as the social life-sphere in which the earliest monetary phenomena occur.

§6. The Hoard-money

Is it just an arbitrary whim of linguistic spirit (*Sprachgeist*)[193] that 'money' means "having recognition (*Geltung*)"? Or do Schiller's words hold true here: "What appears to us as blind chance often rises from the deepest sources!"[194] [P68] The answers to this question must be provided by the explanations present in this work regarding the emergence of money. However, the process described still requires supplementation in various directions.

The prerequisite for good to become money is, as has been shown, that it appears generally desirable for some reason and is therefore also generally, i.e., within a certain circle, desired. Such highly desirable goods are initially and primarily goods that satisfy the social need (*soziales Bedürfnis*) for an acknowledgement (*Anerkennung*) or distinction (*Anerkennung*), i.e., that powerful need which characterises **homo ambitiosus** and which is the true foundation of human society, as Pareto once expressed it.[195]

---

[193] [tn] It refers to the collective linguistic consciousness, conventions, and cultural understanding of language within a particular community or society.

[194] [tn] Schiller, Friedrich (1793), *Über Anmut und Würde* (On Grace and Dignity), Act 2, Scene 3 '*Wallensteins Tod*' [Wallenstein's Death], p. 3 of 3.

[195] [tn] This phrase is likely referencing the term '*homo politicus*' found in Vilfredo Pareto's sociological and political theory, as presented in his book "*The Mind and Society*" (Pareto, 1935/1916-7). '*Homo politicus*' encompasses the notion that individuals are primarily motivated by their political and social interests. Pareto contended that people are driven by a complex interplay of social and political factors, often pursuing their interests within the broader context of society and politics. He argued that individuals make decisions based on their own assessment of what serves their best interests while navigating the constraints and opportunities presented by the political and social systems they inhabit. The concept of '*homo politicus*' is intimately connected to Pareto's overarching theories concerning the distribution of power and the dynamics of elite classes in society. Pareto's work delved into the ascent of elites to power, their maintenance of control, and their influence on political and social systems,

On the other hand, the naïve idea is erroneous that certain goods are therefore preferentially sought after and become money precisely because they have proved to be particularly easy to sell or particularly marketable in exchange-intercourse. These goods are *not* necessarily money *because* they are used as intermediate exchange goods (*Tauschgut*) everywhere, given or taken, when the supply of goods from those involved in the exchange does not match both parties' desires, and as a result, direct exchange cannot successfully achieve its goal.[196] This explanation of the emergence of money "as a natural fruit of exchange-intercourse" (K.

---

with individual behaviour being a vital component of these processes.

[196] [tn] It was mentioned by Carl Menger. To quote,

> With the growing understanding of the above economic interest, especially due to inherited insights and the habit of economic action, the most marketable goods in accordance with local and temporal conditions have become those which everyone not only has an economic interest in accepting in exchange for their own less marketable exchange goods but is actually willing to accept. The most marketable goods are those because only they, in relation to all other goods, are the ones with higher marketability, and thus, only they become generally used. The history of exchange media in all times and among all peoples, as well as the traffic phenomena still observed today in countries with primitive cultures, confirm the above development based on the economic nature of humans and the situation in which they find themselves. We can see everywhere that the most marketable goods, tailored to local and temporal conditions, also serve the function of generally used exchange media, alongside their use for practical purposes. The significance of 'habit' in the emergence of generally accepted means of exchange is evident. The exchange of less marketable goods for those with higher marketability is certainly in the economic interest of each individual economic agent in the cases under consideration here. However, the general and willing acceptance of the medium of exchange not only requires an understanding of this interest but also the 'habituation' of economic subjects to a procedure in which they exchange goods for items that may be entirely useless to them in themselves (Menger 1909:559-560, our translation).

Knies)[197] not only contradicts historical facts but is, as easy to understand, nothing more than a circular argument; it assumes what is then derived as a conclusion from the facts.

All primitive money-goods are, therefore, 'precious-items' *(Kleinode)*, although this phrase must, of course, be understood correctly. That is, they are goods that must be regarded as precious-items according to the 'mental landscape' (*Vorstellungswelt*)[198] and possession-relations (*Besitzverhältnis*) of primitives or early humans. Hoard-money is predominantly ornament-money. Only much later do we encounter among the goods that have become money also items related to physiological needs, such as salt, tobacco, etc. The disposal and control (*Verfügung*) over these goods, especially their consumption, often occur in a way that can be described as displaying oneself, essentially being just one of the countless manifestation-forms of the 'need for recognition' (*Geltungsbedürfnis*). [p69] Money is formed from a large number of all these goods – among which the precious-items certainly take the lead – although it always becomes only one or the other.[199] This suggests that merely having the essential service of being a means of distinction or a means of recognition alone is apparently not sufficient to turn good into money. However, the other aptitudes the good must be equipped with to become money are not easily determined, or to be more precise: there are various qualifications depending on the fundamental services that money is supposed to fulfil under specific conditions. Why do such diverse objects as sound instruments (bells, *mokkos* [metal drum], gongs), porcelain plates

---

[197] [tn] The source of this quotation is not identified.

[198] [tn] See footnote 79 for the meaning.

[199] [tn] In other words, when a society adopts a form of money, it tends to select one specific type of good or item to function as money, rather than using all of them simultaneously.

and jugs (*tempayans*[200]), ivory, bronze cannons, large stone discs (*fä*[201]), fine weaving, copper plates, cups, and building materials, among many other things, become money? **As mentioned, their possession or their usage grants 'social recognition'** (*soziale Geltung*) **or expresses social differentiations. That is one aspect; the other is their aptitude to establish or express social relationships through their use as gifts**.

Mythical beliefs and 'magical ties' (*magische Verknüpfung*) often play a role in the selection. The origin of money-good is sometimes unknown or linked to legendary stories, and the consecration of old age almost always characterises such money. This applies, for example, to the pearl-money of the Palau Islanders and also to most forms of money in Indonesia. In 1880, the Antwerp naturalist Colfs wrote in his diary about the bronze drums of Alor,[202] which were undoubtedly a form of money:

> I have seen these famous Moko.[203] They are preserved like ancient relics, and their value can go up to a thousand florins. When the indigenous people hold festivals, they display them and use them as tambourines to accompany their dance.[204]

This is an excellent description of this hoard-money. It is treasured like old relics. [Þ70] The value of individual pieces varies, but in some cases, it is very high. During the major tribal festivals, it is brought out and displayed, and ultimately, it also serves as a musical instrument, making it a genuine instrument-money (*Gerätegeld*).[205]

Similar accounts are also reported about other early money (*Frühgeld*). Regarding Caledonian money, which is pearl-money (*Perlengeld*), it is

---

[200] [tn] A large earthenware jar for storing water.

[201] [tn] A large circular stone with round holes hewed out in the centre.

[202] [tn] An island in Indonesia, part of the Lesser Sunda Islands.

[203] [tn] Bronze kettledrums from Alor Island, Indonesia.

[204] Vordermann (1888:225).

[205] [tn] It refers to money originally used as an instrument.

described in the guide to the Basel Museum of Ethnography:

> The finer varieties are kept at family shrines, attached to elegantly woven so-called coin heads, often adorned with sculpted human faces.[206]

The objection that these and similar hoarded objects used in payment-traffic (*Zahlungsverkehr*) are not money is easily refuted, as colonial administrations have often recognised these items as money in their decrees and provisions (*Verfügung*), using them in their dealings with the indigenous people. Money-penances are set and collected in such means of payment, service-performances (*Dienstleistung*) are paid for with them, and taxes are collected in them.[207]

Another excellent ethnographic example of hoard-money is Samoan mat-money, known as "*il tonga*." The mats are highly valued and in high demand among the indigenous people (Gerloff 1940:40). While they have also been used as a means of exchange and payment in more recent times, they still primarily serve as family precious-items. As such, each precious piece has its own name and is associated with a story that has mythological content. On significant occasions, mat distributions take place. Events in family life are occasions to present mats to the chief. The same happens when he grants titles. On other occasions, it is not the chief but his speaker (a kind of minister) who receives such mats. All of these are processes that can be described as money-usage, especially since, as mentioned earlier, these same mats are occasionally used as a means of exchange and a means of payment.

Even from the last days of German dominion, it was reported from the Palau Islands: [ᵽ71]

> The local money is the general means of intercourse and means of exchange; it is either glass-money (*Glasgeld*) or a kind of porcelain-

---

[206] Oppenheim (1941: Bd. LII, 49 ff.).

[207] Cf. Examples from Gerloff (1940: 37 and 91).

money (*Porzellangeld*) or a red, yellow, or green clay substance ranging in size from a pea to finger length.

Each money piece has its specific name and value. The monetary unit is the price of ten baskets of taro. The largest money pieces, equivalent to 100 to 500 marks in the German coin, do not circulate but are kept as family treasures. Our informant casually speaks here of money pieces that have a disproportionately high value, do not circulate, and are kept as family treasures. It is, therefore, a form of money that deserves the name 'hoard-money' (*Hortgeld*). A characteristic of this money is that it only occasionally comes into deployment and typically has a limited scope of circulation.[208]

This money has two distinctive characteristics: it does not represent a specific monetary value-magnitude, and it often lacks convenience or practicality. But these two requirements are not necessary for this money; because the traffic processes in which it is used are not commercial transactions, and they are also so rare that it does not matter whether the transfer of money is more or less easy and convenient.

In all of these cases, it is a goods-utilisation that I believe can rightly be described as money-usage (*Geldgebrauch*). On the other hand, when, based on older, widespread, and still widely held opinions, the question is raised whether a hoard-good can be rightfully called money at all, or whether hoarding is contrary to the very essence of money, the response is: so many pieces of evidence have already been provided here and elsewhere (Gerloff 1940: 26 f. and 31 ff.), which support the view presented here, that the overwhelming abundance of facts should be enough proof. Nevertheless, let's briefly address such objections. This is a matter of terminology, which means finding an appropriate name for a specific set of things or processes. [P72] Choosing accurate designations is a means of

---

[208] The references for these statements are found in Schultz-Ewerth & Adam (1929: II, 676, 524, and 625).

scientific understanding. A correctly chosen designation that sensibly categorises an object within a series of phenomena can significantly enhance its scientific comprehension. Language usage will always need to serve as a guide in this regard but cannot be the final arbiter of the decision. In the present case, we can indeed rely on language usage. In numerous ethnographic reports, hoarded objects are referred to as money. As evident from the many cited references, researchers have no reservations about referring to hoarded family precious-items as money. So, according to their conviction, these items are apparently used as money. The same is evident from government decrees of some colonial administrations. Examples of this were also provided. Hoarded goods of the natives are referred to as money in such provisions and decrees and are accepted as money in interactions with the administration!

It remains to be discussed whether such terminology is appropriate or should be rejected for reasons of scientific insight. Apart from the fact that it would not be advisable in scientific teaching to oppose a widespread language usage that corresponds to the facts of life, I also believe that the concept of hoard-money is beneficial for understanding the becoming (*Werden*) and the entire nature of money. It precisely fulfils what we must demand from a scientific concept. It connects the characteristics of the generic concept with those of the specific concept, thereby placing it in the system of related phenomena in such a way that it significantly serves classification, comparison, and the scientific understanding of the totality of phenomena as a whole. Indeed, in matters of this kind, it is ultimately the purposefulness of the chosen boundaries and differentiations that matters. They must prove their usability (*Brauchbarkeit*) in the research work itself. If you apply this benchmark, it can hardly be denied that the classification of monetary phenomena into hoard-money, exchange-money, etc., highlights characteristic stages of the evolution of money.

[73] To understand the emergence and nature of hoard-money, one must realise that the goods- stockpiling or hoarding seemingly held social significance even at one of the earliest stages of human existence. As an

outgrowth of primal drives, – as social psychologists often speak of, such as the 'drive for possession,' 'drive for amassing,' 'drive for appropriation,' and the like – it is one of the fundamental elements of social development. "The 'drive for the treasure-buildup' (*Trieb der Schatzbildung*)," says Karl Marx," is unlimited by nature."[209]

Hoarding is one of the causes that give rise to the first social tensions. An example from the history of language can shed light on its prevalence and significance as well as the existing connections with our subject of investigation. The Greek term *keimēlion* (κειμλιον) originally means the lying property, kept as a treasure in the house. Then, it refers to any valuable or rare possession that is hoard-good or kept as a keepsake (*Andenken*). Furthermore, it can also refer to such precious-items intended to be a lasting, valuable possession as a gift or present. The dichotomy between gift and lasting keepsake demonstrates the purpose-change in the determination and use of these goods, i.e., how hoarded goods can become money. The term *keimēlion* thus encompasses hoarded goods of all kinds that, when hoarded, represent wealth and are also used as gifts (honorary presents, prizes of victory) and therefore eventually become a form of money. Ancient Greek instrument-money (*Gerätegeld*) (such as tripod vessels, axes, etc.) provides several examples of this phenomenon.[210]

From the many examples,[211] let's cite just one from the *Iliad*, where Adrastos speaks to Menelaos[212]: "Many *keimēlia* are laid up in my rich father's house, brass, and gold, and woven iron." And then he adds, "From

---

[209] Marx (1962/1890:147).

[210] [tn] Refer to Laum (1924/2023).

[211] Boisacq (1923:427).

[212] [tn] Adrastos (or Adrestus) is a leader of the Trojan allies, hailing from a city in Anatolia. Menelaos (or Menelaus) is a Greek king and the husband of Helen, whose abduction by Paris of Troy serves as one of the central causes of the Trojan War.

this, my father is willing to offer you an immeasurable ransom" (Book II, Line 47). The lodging-money (*Liegegeld*) [213] becomes ransom-money (*Lösegeld*) here. Consequently, hoarded goods can also be seen as items within an old, possibly ancient, system of gift-traffic.

[¶74] They are used as peace-gifts (*Friedensgabe*) after the resolution of disputes, as a welcoming gift from the host, as a token of gratitude from the departing guest, as a dowry from the suitor, and in various other contexts. However, hoarding had a different significance in older cultural stages than it does today. The possession gives a social reputation to the possessor (*Besitzer*), but it is hardly a means to a lofty way of life or even an appreciative (*genießerisch*) existence. The hoard-good is coveted because it serves as a means of social classification and rank-differentiation (*Rangunterscheidung*) or because it may even bestow magical force upon the possessor. In short, it serves human endeavours to gain recognition. When some items from the hoarded goods category are selectively singled out as more or less regular or commonly used objects in the gift-traffic, they become money. Through the earning (*Erwerb*) [214] of this money, 'social distinction' (*soziale Auszeichnung*) is gained, its transfer to others conveys 'social recognition,' and at the same time, social relationships can be established.

---

[213] [tn] A fee paid for a bed or lodging, often during travel or while staying at an inn or accommodation. The sentence mentions a transformation or shift in the concept of '*Liegegeld*' (lodging-money) into '*Lösegeld*' (ransom).

[214] [tn] The German word '*Erwerb*,' typically translated as 'acquisition,' is rendered as 'earning' when it refers to the act of gaining or acquiring something, often in the context of earning money or obtaining assets.

§7. Money and Ownership

The prerequisite for the emergence of money is the existence of individual ownership, either private or personal ownership (*persönliches Eigentum*).[215] We now know that even at the earliest stage of human development accessible to our knowledge, there was already personal ownership. Therefore, the prerequisite for the emergence of money was already present at this stage.

The earliest forms of personal ownership encompassed: 1. 'Disposal and control' (*Verfügung*) over food. 2. Items related to personal attire (ornament and clothing). 3. Equipment and tools, including items used for various tasks, like ships and utensils. 4. Ground and soil, including all immovable assets associated with the soil, such as ownership of huts or individual trees. This indicates the extent of the range of goods from which money-goods can be separated. Ownership, as the exclusive 'authority of disposal and control' (*Verfügungsbefugnis*) over certain objects, is a legal-relation (*Rechtsverhältnis*). [⁊75] It has emerged from possession, which originally is nothing more than a fact. However, in society, it becomes a legal-relation, namely a rulership-relation (*Herrschaftsverhältnis*) over things[216] that are recognised by the legal-order and endowed with legal consequences.[217] To genetically consider ownership, one must begin with

---

[215] [tn] See Translation Note on p. 353.

[216] [tn] The Latin word '*dominium*' (meaning 'rulership' or 'domination') originally denoted a master or slave owner, with its root stemming from '*domus*' (an adjective meaning 'of the family'), which was also used to describe servants within the household. A similar relationship can be observed between '*familia*' (family) and '*famulus*' (slave). However, it is important to note that the term '*dominium*' was initially employed exclusively within the context of human relationships. Over time, as slaves came to be regarded as possessions rather than human beings, the concept of '*dominium*,' originally associated with humans, began to be applied to inanimate objects (Graeber, 2011: 201).

[217] [tn] This statement is a subject of controversy. If 'personal ownership' refers

possession. The concept of ownership evolves from possession as a fact. From the fact of possession to the awareness of ownership is a significant leap. It is the transition from the animal to the human. There is no known stage of humanity in which the members are entirely devoid of this awareness, even if actual goods-possession is very modest. However, the fact of this ownership-consciousness (*Eigentumsbewußtsein*) becomes most striking to us when we learn that even among preliterate societies, there exists an 'intellectual ownership' (*geistiges Eigentum*), namely ownership of songs and chants, of magical incantations, and the like.[218]

Possession and ownership signify an elevation of personality. Therefore, the earliest possession-goods are expressly personal items: initially,

---

to mere primitive possessory rights, the statement may remain innocuous. However, if it also alludes to the protection of 'personal ownership' that is 'perfected' by the legal-order as mentioned here, it implies the concept of 'property rights' in the modern sense, which are safeguarded by the law and used as collateral to create debt, akin to the property theory of money (Heinsohn and Steiger 2000). In the latter case, the creation of personal ownership 'already' presupposes money of account, as Smithin points out (2018:47),

> (T)he very concept of property, at least the one interesting to economists, must always have some definite monetary value. This monetary quantification of property is the reason why it can be used as collateral. As in the example of the house, the underlying concept of 'property' itself, unlike the more primitive concept of 'possessiveness,' already presupposes a money of account.

Cf. Also refer to Max Weber, when he said,

> From an evolutionary perspective, money is the creator (*Schöpfer*) of 'individual ownership' (*Individualeigentum*); it possesses this characteristic from the very beginning, and conversely, there is no object with the character of money that has not had the individual 'character of possession' (*Besitzcharakter*) (Weber, 1923:208;1927:236).

[218] Lowie (1928:551 ff.). See also the statement by Maass (1949: 12, Note 1), which reads "'Intellectual ownership' rights existed before property rights in material objects," along with the ethnological references provided in this context.

intellectual ones like proverbs, stories (which are told), incantations, or even dances, and then material ones like weapons, ornament and clothing. This extends to the point where these latter possessions are taken into the grave upon death.

The primordial possession (*ursprünglicher Besitz*) is considered inalienable.[219] This is related to the emergence of claims (*Anspruch*) of possession and ownership on one hand and the development of possession and ownership on the other. However, the old debate about the emergence of ownership shall not be raised here. In contrast to the various theories regarding the emergence of ownership, which are often just attempts at justification, the opinion supported by ethnological and socio-psychological observations is that primitive ownership is not based, as frequently claimed, on the labour or effort expended in the creation or 'acquisition of possession-goods.' Originally, labour did not enjoy such esteem. [P76] Instead, it is founded on the notion of 'magical ties' between things and the person who possesses them. The blessing or force (*Kraft*) inherent in things is only present in them when held by the rightful possessor. For this individual, possession represents an extension of his self. It is therefore understandable why such possession is considered inalienable, and it marks a significant stage in cultural development when things become transferable.

If the 'acquisition of possession,' i.e., the emergence of personal possessions, is the first step in the development of ownership, then the 'disposal of possession' (*Besitzveräußerung*) is the second. The psychological inhibitions that exist between the first and the second steps, and the overcoming of these inhibitions, have already been alluded to. In the same vein, the widespread 'alienation of possession' (*Besitzentäußerung*), as manifested through lavish consumption, wastefulness, and the 'distribution of possession,' may also play a role. As

---

[219] [tn] See Weiner (1992) regarding inalienable possession.

the practice of 'disposal of possession' becomes established, the path is taken in which the transitions of possession-relation from a personal relation to a technical one. This lays an important foundation for the emergence of money.

Another significant development of ownership, which unfolds in a different direction, is important for the emergence and development of money. This is the possession-aggregation (*Besitzanhäufung*). The stockpiling (*Aufspeicherung*), stacking (*Aufstapelung*) or hoarding of possession-goods initially appears entirely foreign to the mindset of primitive humans. This is because, in accordance with their way of life, such possessions are seen as cumbersome baggage that hinders their mobility. Certainly, the idea of precautionary-measure (*Vorsorge*) does exist in ancient cultures, even more so in primitive cultures, especially among those known as harvest peoples living in temperate or cold regions. This leads to the layout of stockpiles, which means amassing and stockpiling of certain goods for later immediate usage or consumption, rather than for the purpose of treasure-buildup. Nevertheless, this marks an important step in cultural development.

[77] Another significant advancement occurs when amassing and stockpiling are not for the purpose of later consumption but for the creation of assets that primarily serve the purpose of bestowing social reputation (*Ansehen*). It does not necessarily have to be fundamentally different goods that serve the two mentioned purposes. Therefore, the intentions pursued can indeed overlap. However, typically, the chosen goods are different because surpluses of the economy serve one purpose, while rare items serve the other. To the extent that possession of such goods acquires the significance of a social accentuation of the possessor and, not infrequently, serves as a means both of setting and breaking social barriers, amassing and stockpiling, often to a considerable extent, take place.

We find, among various peoples and cultures, that stockpiling and hoarding, along with the usage of storages filled with various hoarded goods, serve as means to acquire societal power. The usage of these goods initially manifests simply in the display of possession-goods, in creating an impression of abundance, and in the exhibition of splendour. Social reputation, or put differently, an outstanding societal status, is less achieved and maintained through mere ostentation, meaning simply displaying and showing off possessions, than through their generous, extravagant usage and consumption, which is aimed at public recognition and often extends to ostentatious extravagance. As demonstrated in a different context (as shown here on p. 79 and in Gerloff 1940:35 ff., 61-62), the "inalienable" family possessions circulate. They become part of a gift-traffic and, furthermore, based on this usage, they also become a means of disbursement (*Leistungsmittel*) in general. In other words, they become a means of payment or money.

Ownership is the prerequisite for buying and selling. However, initially, every 'change of possession,' regardless of the reasons and methods, is subject to significant hindrances [ᵖ78] because the owner (*Eigentümer*), as previously explained in a different context, believes that their well-being is linked to the 'command of disposal and control' (*Verfügungsgewalt*) over their possession. Ownership of a house, farm, livestock, weapons, the harvest, and so on, implies dependence on these things and responsibility towards these things.

It is a long journey during which the hoard-good loses the character of being a possession intimately linked to the person of the owner, until it ultimately becomes nothing more than a technical object whose sole purpose is to provide specific services, namely, monetary services (*Gelddienst*). This not only involves a transformation in the social significance of these goods themselves, which have become money but also from these goods, i.e., money, emanates a social re-evaluation of all forms of goods-possession, of all ownership. It is the social transformation of all measurable value (*Größenwert*) into value-magnitudes (*Wertgröße*).

The explained societal conduct-process delineates two important stages of social development: the formation of wealth through possession-aggregation or goods-accumulation, and the mobilisation of this wealth through money and by means of money. From the 'drive for appropriation' and the 'drive for amassing,' or whatever one may wish to name this primal force, emerges a need that becomes a dominating desire governing all human emotional life and activities throughout this course. The goods-acquisition (*Gütererwerb*) becomes a passion that seizes and dominates the contemplations and aspirations, first of individuals, then of more and more people, and ultimately of the entire society. Society, to use an expression by R. H. Tawney, becomes an "acquisitive society" (Tawney 1920), meaning a society driven by the quest for acquisition. However, we are already going beyond what should be outlined in this section. Just one more thing should be added: the earning-pursuit (*Erwerbssuch*) that arises from deep-rooted primal forces is not, as one might assume, a trait unique to or particularly characteristic of the economic person. It is the same passion to which the primitive human already indulges and to which they are obedient, accumulating items like taro or mats, shell rings (*Diwara*[220]) or ivory, iron tools or *Manillas*,[221] copper plates or woollen blankets, and so on. [79] In ownership and money, which socialises ownership, the human 'need for recognition' finds its significant means of satisfaction, constantly reigniting the craving. Human *doxomania*[222] has found its narcotic.

---

[220] [tn] A type of traditional ornament or jewellery, especially in Indian or South Asian contexts.

[221] [tn] See footnote 69.

[222] [tn] *Doxomania* (δοξομανία) combines '*doxa*' (δόξα), meaning 'opinion' or 'glory,' and '*mania*' (μανία), which refers to a strong enthusiasm or obsession. '*Doxomania*' generally refers to an excessive or obsessive 'need for recognition,' approval, or glory. It describes an intense craving for a good reputation, honour, or acknowledgement by others, often to an unhealthy or irrational degree.

§8. Exchange-Money and Purchase-Money

As we have seen, gift-traffic does not just lead to the emergence or use of hoard-money; that is only the case in very specific types of gift-traffic. Instead, it is entirely possible for regular usage of a good to become established within such gift-traffic, the good which is not hoarded but introduced into circulation as a means of acquiring gifts and then continues to be used by the recipient for monetary service. Such money, based on its original but by no means based on exclusive usage, is referred to as exchange-money (*Tauschgeld*).

A good becomes exchange-money by being used as a mediating good in exchange-intercourses. However, it does not happen as one might commonly imagine, that certain goods are permanently and exclusively chosen for this role. Instead, typically, goodwill only occasionally serves this purpose. Indeed, initially, there are only a few exchange-intercourses, and they often occur at significant intervals. However, during the interim periods, the mediating good is by no means idle, waiting to be used as money. Instead, it serves other purposes, such as satisfying the need for adornment. If it has not been consumed in the meantime, it can be reused as an exchange-good when needed.

Whether one should already consider such a good as money for the purpose of such use is a matter of debate, as is well known. However, this debate does not affect the situation of the emergence of money. A. H. Quiggin has an opinion on this matter:

> It must frankly be admitted that many objects are called 'Currency' which are never current. [▶80] They may serve as standards of value or as symbols of wealth, two of the functions of money, but they are never used in ordinary trading. They pass from hand to hand, or from group to group, in important transactions, and play a large part in gift-exchange and in 'bride-price' but they cannot be termed currency, still less, money, in their proper senses" (Quiggin 1949:4).

I cannot subscribe to the view that the means of exchange function is essential to the money-concept (*Geldbegriff*). One will neither do justice to the essence of money nor come closer to its understanding if one does not distinguish between money with different functions. We will need to delve further into this matter.

In anthropological reports, it is not uncommon to find information that indigenous tribes may be aware of the concept of money without actually using it in 'commerce and trade' (*Handel und Wandel*). This is simply because there is little to no trade in their communities. However, as soon as a certain level of market-intercourse (*Marktverkehr*) develops, the groundwork for the spread of exchange-money is laid. Exchange-money is **market-money** (*Marktgeld*). The earlier mentioned gift-exchange journeys often evolve into regular market-encounters (*Marktbegegnungen*), where one or another of the market goods may indeed become money. In such cases, it can very well happen that one tribe regularly produces a sought-after good for their exchange journeys, which they use for purchases during the trade-encounter (*Tauschbegegnung*). Subsequently, the other tribe may use it as a means of payment. However, this is not because it serves as or could serve as exchange-money, which is typically not the case, but because it is a means of recognition that is universally desired. "What was initially used as an exchange-tool (*Tauschwerkzeug*)," as von Wieser once said, "was not yet money in our sense,"[223] but he seems to have admitted that it was already money. In short, the difference is that those older exchange-tools tend to temporarily assume the role of money. These are goods that repeatedly find their way to a final purchaser, a final consumer. However, one can doubt whether this happens because it is the actual purpose-designation (*Zweckbestimmung*) of these goods, or what seems to be more accurate in many cases, because there is not so much for money to do at this stage of societal development [p81] as to be constantly employed in circulation.

---

[223] [tn] Wieser (1926:44).

However, as exchange-economic intercourse grows, there are more opportunities for the 'exchange mediating good,' i.e., for money. As a result, this good no longer finds a final consumer who would consume it but is continuously passed on in exchange for goods or services or to settle various obligations.

The 'exchange mediating good' has become the "eternal commodity" (*ewige Ware*); it is the "*marchandise tierce*," i.e., the third commodity, as French authors (such as Wolowski and others) have called it. This term appears to refer to the threefold classification of economic goods introduced by K. Knies: means of consumption (*Genußmittel*), means of production (*Produktionsmittel*), and means of exchange (*Tauschmittel*).[224] The classification of goods into one category or another is not an inherent characteristic of the goods but rather a matter of their usage. For example, wine and tobacco can serve as means of consumption, means of production (e.g., for medicines), or means of exchange, just like gold and silver. But evidently, the aptitude for one purpose or other often outweighs that for the third. In theory, any good can serve as a means of exchange or money; however, in practice, only a limited number, despite the wide variety of goods that may have temporarily played the role of money, have done so historically. Decisive for the money-usage of goods is whether and to what extent they can fulfil the essential functions of money more or less effectively. This naturally leads to a process of purposeful selection (*Auslese*), which results in a restriction of the goods used as money until finally only a few, or even just a single good, serves as an exchange-medium (*Tauschvermittlung*). It is the good through which the exchange of all other commodities and service-performances are facilitated most effectively. However, this also means that the value of all other goods is typically expressed in terms of quantities of this one good.

Initially, the emergence of exchange-money occurs in a very limited

---

[224] [tn] Knies (1885: I. Bd. 20ff.).

sphere of social intercourses because primitive economies satisfy only modest needs through exchange, specifically the so-called "fine demand" (*Feinbedarf*) (Thurnwald 1922), while "basic demand" (*Grobbedarf*) is covered through self-provision. [82] However, it is precisely the 'fine demand,' the 'luxury demand' that is not foreign to any ethnic group or time period, and that consistently exhibits strong expansion, that drives the development of exchange-money and monetary economic exchange-intercourses.

At this point, it is worth noting another fact, as mentioned earlier, that "intellectual ownership" (*geistiges Eigentum*) is often the first subject of buying and selling among many societies. R. H. Lowie reports on various Eskimo tribes that personal ownership of material-goods, even equipment for fishing and hunting, is foreign to them. It is quite different from the magical formulae that ensure hunting success. They can only be acquired through specific exchange-goods, which mean money. The institution of payment is a prerequisite for the effectiveness of the formulae. [225] A number of other examples can be found in the reports of the Hamburg South Sea Expedition. For instance, Müller-Wismar mentions from the island of Yap that dances are bought and sold. Texts and dance figures are the inviolable personal ownership of the creator, who alone can dispose of them. In the case of a disposal, the performance-right (*Aufführungsrecht*) passes into the sole possession of the buyer. [226] As our field researcher adds to his report, the prices paid demonstrate that people know how to appreciate the services of their spiritual heroes on Yap. On Yap, medical prescriptions are also considered as 'intellectual ownership,' and one can only use them if they have been acquired through purchase.

Similar reports come from the inhabitants of the island of Dobu (South

---

[225] Lowie (1928: 551 ff.). See also the previously cited statement by Prince Maximilian of Wied on p. 73.

[226] Müller-Wismar (1917: 263).

Melanesia). Incantations play a significant role in their daily lives, whether it is related to the growth of fruits, protecting trees from theft, awakening love, or cursing a neighbour with illness and death; [▶83] all of these can only be achieved through magic. However, the magic spells for these purposes must be purchased at a high cost.[227]

Kaj Birket-Smith reports:

> In New Guinea, not only masks and other dance equipment but also the right to perform the associated sacred ceremonies are subject to purchase and sale.[228]

The name 'exchange-money' is based on the emergence of this money, its original purpose-designation of being a mediating good for exchange-intercourse. However, the expression does not quite accurately reflect the underlying situation. Exchange is the surrendering of one good for a contribution of another good, with the implicit assumption that neither of these two goods is money. A change of goods-possession that occurs through the mediation of money is commonly referred to as a purchase or sale. Therefore, money only facilitates the exchange, but it does not swap (*tauscht*) [between two non-money-goods]; instead, it 'purchases.' Exchange-money is, therefore, purchase-money (*Kaufgeld*).

This is certainly not its only function. Rather, once introduced into circulation in this capacity, it quickly expands beyond this scope by being used for various other purposes. Above all, one thing should not be overlooked: Exchange-money or purchase-money has emerged and, from its very beginnings, has increasingly served the facilitation of the goods-traffic because it has always been a good that simultaneously satisfied other strong needs, especially directly or indirectly fulfilling the 'need for recognition.' This is the cause of the general aspiration for these goods and thus their so-called "marketability" (*Marktgängigkeit*). The strong demand   arising   from   the   social   'need   for   distinction'

---

[227] Benedict (1949: 131 ff.).

[228] Birket-Smith (1948: 191).

(*Auszeichnungsbedürfnis*) makes them become the commonly used means of exchange. Thus, one can probably say that the psychological roots from which hoard-money and exchange-money emerge are the same. [‡84] Therefore, we also see that hoard-money and exchange-money originally coincide in many societies, meaning that they cannot be initially distinguished by the nature of the goods, nor by their aptitude and service.

The term exchange-money is therefore not an invention of purposefulness; it has not been introduced from economic prudence, but it has emerged from a social gift-traffic that corresponds or is capable of corresponding as much to *doxomaniacal* [229] as to 'economical needs' (*ökonomisches Bedürfnis*). It is only with the development of this gift-circulation into a proper exchange-intercourse that money becomes a necessity for executing exchanges; it becomes a means of economical intercourse (*Mittel des ökonomischen Verkehrs*), more precisely, a compensated goods-traffic and service-traffic (*Leistungsverkehr*) that serve the sustenance. Money is no longer just a means of satisfying '*doxomaniacal* drives,' inclinations, and strivings, although these still retain their significant force and remain effective in the background. Instead, it has become a means of satisfying 'economical needs.' This expansion of its scope marks a new phase in the development of money, one that opens up possibilities of the utmost social and cultural significance.

It is self-evident that the new role of money leads to an adaptation (*Anpassung*) in terms of its purpose-designation towards material and form, not only externally marking this new chapter in the history of money but also influencing retroactively the essence of money itself. The transition from the impressive corporeality (*Körperhaftigkeit*) of the money piece to the material-less money symbol and ultimately to the 'measurement-unit money' (*Maßeinheit Geld*), not bound to any material sign, is revealed.

---

[229] [tn] See footnote 222 for its meaning.

§9. The Money-Usage

The history of the emergence of money demonstrates that depending on the location, time, and other circumstances, different goods have become money at different times. Some of these goods tend to maintain this role for an extended period, while others have taken on the role of serving as money or being money only temporarily. [▶85] The reasons for this changing role-playing, however enlightening they may be, will not be pursued at this point. But we should consider the question of what role a good must actually assume to become money or the role it takes on when it becomes money. This question has already been addressed in the discussions about hoard-money and exchange-money. Let's continue from there. It has been demonstrated that the goods originally performed monetary services are items that signify distinction in possession and confer reputation or otherwise grant recognition (*Geltung*) to the possessor. Such goods used as means of recognition are naturally widely desired. Consequently, they become carriers of a certain social intercourse: social means of relationship. Various examples of this have already been provided. To clarify what is meant and further substantiate the points made, here are some additional examples:

In Melanesia, certain shells are desired and hoarded by everyone. As we are informed in the compilation on indigenous law in the (formerly) German protectorates, it is the desired goal of every family head to acquire as many of these shells as possible. And why? Because it "confers reputation and enables the purchase of supplies for war." However, as the reporter adds:

> The main function of this money (he calls the shells money!) is to lend it to others for wife-purchase and thus bring younger men into [economic] dependence [on older individuals who controlled or provided these shells].[230]

---

[230] Schultz-Ewerth & Adam (1929: II, 625).

The Ababua and Buschongo, African tribes in the Congo region, hoard ornamental knives called '*lipombo*,' which symbolise wealth and bestow reputation upon their possessors. These knives are called '*lipombo*,' which roughly translates to 'women's ornament' (*Frauenschmuck*).

Most peoples have known money as a means of recognition for a long time and used to make use of it before the exchange of goods or the payment of labour services became common. The first step in this process is the hoarding of certain goods: the treasure-buildup. Sometimes, this hoarding is a tribal matter. The chief has a treasure house constructed where the shell rings or money mats are stored. These treasures are only brought into the daylight on certain particularly solemn occasions to be splendidly displayed. [▶86] "On one of the most important of these events," writes Finsch, "the possessor is especially festively adorned and, among all his wealth, is even paraded, albeit only as a corpse [in a funeral]."[231] During these funeral ceremonies, money-distributions are customary. Such distributions also occur on other occasions because, precisely by lavishly sharing the accumulated treasures, they serve their purpose of bestowing reputation upon the original possessor.

The pursuit of distinction, the quest for reputation within one's comrades, often finds expression in the most peculiar forms of human behaviour. It is also the motive behind seemingly senseless acts of money-destructions (*Geldvernichtung*) that occur in various cultural contexts. Such treasure-destruction (*Schatzzerstörung*) (blankets, copper plates) is well-known, especially among certain Native American tribes in North America. However, it can also be found among other cultures, often in connection with funeral ceremonies. Various motivations may underlie these practices. One motive is the reverential thought of leaving the deceased person with their possessions, often accompanied by the fear that the spirit of the deceased will seek revenge for taking possession of their

---

[231] Finsch (1914:16).

inherited assets by inflicting various misfortunes. Another motivation is the sacrificial mindset (*Opfergedanke*),[232] which can lead to excesses that might even result in the economic ruin of the surviving family members. Through sacrifices, the reputation of the deceased in the spirit world, as well as their status and power there, is intended to be favourably influenced. Sacrifices are also meant to ensure that the deceased does not harm the living. Above all, the consideration that the accumulated treasures, such as shell-money rings among certain South Sea peoples, quantities of fabric (pangue, makute.[233] Cf. Gerloff 1940:118) in some parts of West Africa, and pearls in Indonesia, are seen as provisions for the journey to the afterlife and one's stay there, also plays a role.[234] [ß87] This entire customary-practice reveals to us a money-usage that is older and more widely spread than any other.

Money, as a means of recognition, serves the "drive for self-assertion" (Gerloff 1940: 28), i.e., ambition; its usage aims to satisfy the love of ostentation (*Prunkliebe*), which can manifest itself in both treasure-amassing and treasure-distribution, as well as treasure-destruction. The treasure-buildup, the treasure-display (*Schatzzurschaustellung*), the treasure-distribution, and ultimately, the treasure-destruction are indeed the initial forms of money-usage. The money of ancient or early cultures is a hoard-money. It serves as showcasing-money and ostentatious-money, as prestige-money or swagger-money. The fact that at this stage of monetary

---

[232] [tn] It refers to the concept or mindset of making sacrifices, often in a ritualistic or religious context, with the belief that these sacrifices will have a positive or purifying effect, or as a way to honour deities or the deceased.

[233] [tn] Both are types of fabric used in various cultural practices, likely for crafting or ceremonial purposes.

[234] Also, Refer to the illustration in Gerloff (1940:64-5). Cf. Gerloff (1940:113 and 195), as well as Thurnwald (1929: II, 624). In another context, Bernhard Laum has demonstrated the significance of the sacrificial cult for the emergence of money in Homeric Greece: See Laum (2023/1924).

development, such usage represents a proper form of money-usage is also evident from the fact that it is the same goods that initially perform monetary services as a means of payment from person to person, such as bridal-money, penance-money, feud-money (*Fehdegeld*),[235] and so on. What J. Halkin reports about the Ababua,[236] that the hoarded ornamental knives became real money (ibid: 62), can also be said of certain other hoarded goods in different cultural areas that serve or served as means of representation and ostentation.

A peculiarity of early money-usage is that different money types regularly coexist, with each type being usable only for very specific services or purchases. This is particularly evident in some South Pacific islands and island groups where relatively complex and strictly observed monetary orders exist.

A prime example is the monetary system described by Armstrong[237] on Rossel Island in the Louisiade Archipelago.[238] There, two money-types (*Geldart*) coexist. The '*Dap*' is made from Spondylus shells[239] and the '*Kö*'

---

[235] [tn] This term is primarily associated with Germanic legal traditions and refers to the compensation paid to a victim or their family as a form of restitution for a crime, particularly homicide or injury. The payment was meant to provide compensation to the victim or their family and prevent feuds or further conflicts. '*Fehde*' can be translated as 'feud,' so '*Fehdegeld*' relates to settling disputes and preventing blood feuds. This term is similar to '*Wergeld*,' which is more commonly associated with Anglo-Saxon and medieval English legal traditions.

[236] [tn] An ethnic group living in the Congo region of Central Africa. They are part of the diverse cultural and ethnic landscape of the Democratic Republic of the Congo.

[237] [tn] Armstrong (1928).

[238] [tn] Rossel Island, also known as Yela, is an island located in the Louisiade Archipelago, which is part of Papua New Guinea in the southwestern Pacific Ocean.

[239] [tn] A genus of colourful sea mollusks, often referred to as 'thorny oysters' or 'spiny oysters.' These mollusks are known for their striking and vibrant shells,

is made from small shell discs, each strung in sets of 10. There are 22 different values of *Dap* and 16 different values of *Kö*. The former are the higher denominations. The possession of the highest valued ones is a chief's privilege. However, what is crucial is that each monetary unit, whether *Dap* or *Kö*, can only be used for very specific things or purposes.

[▮88] From this arises another characteristic of early money-usage, which is found in many peoples: a system of lending (*Darlehnssystem*). The multitude of money types with a relatively small money supply and a strictly limited scope of use for each type forces, wherever payments are to be made, the acquisition of the only qualified money types. This is most commonly observed in the context of the bride-price. On Rossel Island, it is the fifth-highest value *Dap* that is required for wife-purchase, and as a result, there is a high demand for it.[240] It is not uncommon for a young native to remain unmarried simply because he lacks a specific money type.[241] A black man returning to his home village from the mining districts of Transvaal, even if he has plenty of pounds sterling, may still not be able to acquire a wife. Sterling and indigenous money are often not convertible to each other.

Another peculiarity of early money-usage is that it is regularly associated with magical and mythical elements. Money-expending does not take place for purely economic or rational purposes; instead, it is originally a by-product of ritual activities or a socially significant occurrence emerging from everyday life, such as coming-of-age ceremonies, marriages, funerals, and so on. It is always an act intertwined with supernatural ties. This often extends to the selection of money types used for various occasions. For

---

which are sometimes used as decorative elements, money, or ornaments in various cultures.

[240] Cf. Einzig (1949: 42ff.); Quiggin (1949:183). Similar examples can be found in the monetary system of the Palau Islands. You can refer to Gerloff (1940: 98) and Finsch (1914: 105 and 154) for more details.

[241] Quiggin (1949:117) and Einzig (1949: 187).

example, among the various types of mother-of-pearl-money on Palau, there is one known as "mourning-money" (*Klagegeld*) because it is used at funerals.

Even in cases where people already pursue well-considered economic purposes with money, the practice often persists such that respective transactions can only be carried out on special occasions. For example, they may only occur during festival events held at specific times. It is therefore not so "unfathomable reasons" as Paul Einzig thinks that in the Admiralty Islands[242] exchange-activity (*Tauschhandlung*) regularly takes place in connection with marriages, [ʔ89] so that marriages are allegedly often only arranged in order to have a pretext for trade and to bring money to the groom.[243]

Primitive humans early on required money primarily for two purposes: for the authority figures (chief or priest) and for acquiring a wife. Furthermore, money was needed for club expenses, festival costs, ornament, and various trinkets. So, it is not entirely far-fetched when Kant, in his otherwise less successful discussions about money, suggests that "what initially was a commodity eventually became money" through "being demanded as a levy (*Abgabe*) from subjects."[244]

Experience has shown that primitive peoples are often inclined to adopt foreign objects of usage, which they use as toys and ornaments. However, they are reluctant to adopt devices and tools that are means of production, as their use would require a change in their economic way of life.

The desire to acquire new pleasure and useful goods compels one to obtain means, to earn through work, and to sell one's own products. The means, in this case, is money. In this way, even tribes that have had little

---

[242] [tn] A group of islands located in the southwestern Pacific Ocean. They are part of Papua New Guinea and are situated northeast of the country's mainland.

[243] Einzig (1949:77).

[244] Kant (1797: 122 ff. and 126).

contact with trade are drawn into the commodity-trade and gradually introduced to money-usage. Contact with money gradually leads to an economic transformation that starts from the consumption side and brings about profound social changes as a result. However, as long as only occasional individual products are sold, there is no transformation of the economy; such a transformation only occurs when production aligns with sales or when indigenous peoples venture outside their village community or tribal community for money earning.

So, originally, money-usage was not directed toward an economic purpose. Just as experience taught the economic usefulness of certain social activities, experience also taught the advantages of a certain form of money-usage. Through slow and prolonged experience, these advantages are recognised and simultaneously become motives for action. [p90] This process serves as an example not only of the 'law of continuity in cultural change' (*Gesetz der Stetigkeit im Kulturwandel*)[245] and the 'law of the plurality of motives' (*Gesetz der Vielheit der Beweggründe*)[246] but also the law of the frequent purpose-change in cultural-goods (*Kulturgut*)[247] often associated with a change in motivating reason (*Beweggrund*).

Another law of social development that confirms the emergence of money is as follows: all social actions related to material-goods begin in the realm of consumption and not in that of production. The consciousness of 'common belongingness' (*Zusammengehörigkeit*) among humans, which leads to association, social organisation, social creations, and human

---

[245] [tn] It suggests that cultural shifts and transformations tend to occur gradually and continuously over time rather than abruptly or in sudden leaps.

[246] [tn] It implies that cultural changes and developments are influenced by multiple factors, motives, or forces rather than being driven by a single cause or motivation.

[247] [tn] Objects, artefacts, practices, knowledge, cultural heritage or other elements that are considered valuable and significant within a particular culture or society.

achievements, first finds its field of influence in the world of material-goods through the shaping and the order of consumption. This also applies to the first money-usage, which primarily belongs to consumption. The display, distribution, or even destruction of money are acts of consumption. It is a lengthy process that leads from this initial money-usage to the one we are familiar with today, which transforms money from an immediate means of recognition into an economic means (*Wirtschaftsmittel*) that is unparalleled in significance and scope compared to any other. Money as a means of recognition, however, is the 'primordial appearance of money' (*Urerscheinung des Geldes*).

The further history of the development of money-usage is the history of the monetary framework itself. It led to the development of various forms of money and the expansion of its purchasing power (*Kaufmacht*)[248] into the modern monetary system. Both of these aspects will need to be addressed separately in different contexts.

---

[248] [tn] See Translation Note on p. 354.

§10. Class-money

Just as all cultural possessions (*Kulturbesitz*), i.e., the ownership of
material as well as intellectual cultural-goods (*Kulturgut*), originated as
class-possessions (*Klassenbesitz*), so did money. Its original usage, as
demonstrated and shared with other cultural-goods, serves the satisfaction
of the 'need for recognition.' This means that at its inception, it was a
cultural-good or cultural instrument (*Kulturmittel*) of the privileged or
upper stratum (*Schicht*) of society.

[**91**] In societies at a lower stage of development, social differentiations
find their expression primarily in goods-possession (*Güterbesitz*) and
goods-usage, rather than in the way and means of satisfying daily life needs.
Regarding the Paressi-Kabisi, an Arawakan tribe in Central Brazil, M.
Schmidt states:

> The stockpiles of material-goods exceeding the measure of
> immediate individual demand, be it for their exchange against other
> material-goods or for the acquisition of service-performances, is
> solely the prerogative of the ruling class. Only they have the right to
> accumulate assets.

He adds that among other indigenous societies at a similar stage of
development, a comparable pattern of behaviour likely occurs.[249] If this is
the case, and it is likely to be agreed upon, then it is understandable that
money possession (*Geldbesitz*) and money-usage in their beginnings are a
characteristic of the status and lifestyle of aristocratic strata. It is only over
the course of a long period that an expansion of the usage-range of money
occurs beyond the circle of the initial users. This happens according to the
well-known process of the appropriation of a cultural-good by the lower
strata through imitation of the behavioural pattern of the upper classes.
The cultural-good is adopted by a broader segment of society. Such a
transition of cultural-goods from an aristocratic sphere of use into the

---

[249] Schmidt (1920:196, 1917: 52 ff.).

usage domain of another, typically larger group, often involves a purpose-change of the object and, consequently, its usage-range, thereby frequently granting it a new and unforeseen significance and impact. This also applies to money. With the dissolution of the aristocratic stratification (*Schichtung*) of society and its replacement by a society primarily based on the economic power-possession (*Machtbesitz*), money not only gains entry to a larger user base but also assumes a new role within it.

[⬤92] The primitive money thus appears as a goods-possession and goods-usage,[250] which for its owner becomes a symbol of belonging to a particular class, indeed making it virtually a class-symbol (*Klassensymbol*). This is connected with the original function of money, which is to be a means of recognition. This original service of money is not only characteristic of ancient and primitive money-form but also of a developed money-form like the coin. Berhard Laum pointed out in another context that in ancient times, the right to mint money often belonged to different authorities depending on the type of metal. In Persia, for example, the minting of gold coins was a royal prerogative, while the issuance of silver coins was left to satraps,[251] dynasties, and cities. The Roman emperors reserved the minting right of gold and silver coins for themselves while granting the minting of bronze coins to the Senate. This division of minting rights can only, as Bernhard Laum suggests, "be an expression and means of societal hierarchy (*Rangordnung*)."[252] The same applies, even more so, to the use of coins. The more valuable coins are used in transactions with the nobility or between the nobility themselves. The coin was, like the money ring that was its precursor, originally primarily a

---

[250] [tn] It means that, money, in its earliest form or conception, was closely linked to tangible possessions and the utilisation of those possessions and not just an abstract unit of exchange. It was also a representation of one's ownership of tangible assets.

[251] [tn] Provincial governors or administrators in the ancient Persian Empire.

[252] Laum (1929:48)

symbol of honour and esteem (*Würde*), rather than a profane exchange value. If Roman gold coins of the same imprint have different weights, it is, as explained by numismatists, because these coins were intended to be distributed at imperial festivities to participants of different ranges of people according to their esteems.[253] From anthropology, we also know of examples that show the money signs (*Geldzeichen*) in use are class signs. This applies, for example, to the money that has already been mentioned several times, i.e., the money which was used on the Palau Islands.

Just as co-living (*connubium*[254] and *convivium*[255]) externally signifies belonging to a class, so does money-usage. Primitive money is a class-money, meaning it is money that is exclusively used by a specific social class and typically can only be used by members of that class.

[♭93] When the terms 'class' and class-money are used here, it is meant to express that it concerns the money-usage of a group positioned at a specific social level, without delving into whether the societal gradation (*Abstufung*) is regarded as tiering (*Staffelung*), stratification, or genuine class formation.[256]

Money always originates within a particular class of society, a higher or upper class, and initially, money-usage is exclusively reserved for them. Money-usage then spreads within broader circles from this domain.

---

[253] Cf. Examples at Laum (ibid.: 49 f.).

[254] [tn] It referred to the legal right or concept of marriage and who one could marry within Roman society. *Connubium* determined the eligibility for marriage between different individuals, particularly in terms of their social or legal status. It played a crucial role in regulating and defining the boundaries of marriage within the Roman legal framework.

[255] [tn] Communal dining or feasting associated with ancient Roman society, often with a specific group of people. It can indicate social gatherings and events where people from a particular class or social group come together to share meals or festivities.

[256] [tn] See Translation Note on p. 355.

However, this does not mean that these circles readily adopt the money of the upper class. While it can certainly happen, it is also not uncommon for different classes within a society to use different forms of money. This is related to the original significance of money, which is to serve as a means of recognition. For the nobility, means of recognition are something different than for the peasants. For example, among the ancient Germanic peoples, rings served as the money of the nobility and their retinue. Rings were the money used in aristocratic transactions. However, for the peasants, their money consisted of fabric or livestock. Besides the fact that ornament-money of the upper strata is not suitable for the lower strata, the diversity of money-types arises from the consciously maintained segregation of societal strata, which does not allow the lower strata to use the same money-goods as the upper strata. Just as on the Trobriand Islands, located east of New Guinea, the ceremonial trade game known as *Kula* involves the exchange of goods, some of which can be considered money-goods, only among the members of certain distinguished clans, mainly the chief's families. Similarly, money-usage and monetary intercourses were originally limited to those at the upper rungs of the social ladder.

Certain goods acquire their monetary function by being used in social ceremonies. These are goods with a representative character, such as ceremonial weapons, ornaments, and musical instruments like bells and gongs. They become **'ceremonial money.'** It is evident that the usage of these ceremonial goods is usually a matter of social status. [94] The 'ceremonial money' also appears to be a class-money, meaning it is always in the possession of the upper-class members and can only be used by them.

Anthropology has hardly delved into the question of the class-bound origin of money. The information available from ethnologists' fieldwork consists mainly of incidental hints that a good serving as money can only perform this monetary service in the hands of certain individuals. For instance, in his travel report "The Palau Islands in the Pacific Ocean" (1873), K. Semper mentions "three types of money used by the nobility"

(Gerloff 1940:98). Senfft,[257] the former district officer of Yap, refers to the well-known stone money of these islands, known as '*Fä*,' saying:

> Although thousands of these money pieces are in the possession of Yap as communal and private property, there are villages and individuals who do not claim ownership of any *Fä*. The villages of the 6th and 7th ranks, as well as their inhabitants, are prohibited from possessing or acquiring stones that are over four spans in size.[258]

The chiefs, in contrast, retain all the large pieces of stones that are mined in the quarries of the Palau Islands and are often difficult to transport by sea from the moment they arrive on land. Additionally, the lower-status individuals on Yap are not allowed to possess stone money with a diameter exceeding four spans.

The mentioned district officer Senfft, like other researchers, refers to '*Fä*' as men's money and '*Jar*,' which are mother-of-pearl shells, as women's money (*Frauengeld*). He states:

> The *Jar* is more in the ownership of women. Therefore, everything obtained from them is paid for with *Jar*, but never with *Fä*.

According to J. Kubary, mother-of-pearl shells on Yap and turmeric balls[259] on Truk[260] are considered women's money. Thurnwald, who relies

---

[257] [tn] Paul Albrecht Senfft (1865-1931), a German colonial administrator and ethnologist who served as the district officer (Bezirksamtmann) of Yap in the German colonial administration during the late 19th and early 20th centuries.

[258] Deutsches Kolonialblatt (190: 871).

[259] [tn] Small spheres or pellets made from turmeric, which is a yellow spice derived from the rhizomes of the turmeric plant. Turmeric is commonly used in cooking, especially in Asian cuisine, and it has a distinct bright yellow colour and a warm, earthy flavour. In some cultures or historical contexts, items like turmeric balls may have been used for various purposes, including medicinal, culinary, or even as a form of trade or money.

[260] [tn] An older name for the Chuuk Atoll, which is part of the Federated States

110

on Müller-Wismar, provides slightly different information, but he also confirms the situation that matters here: he says:

> Not only do the chiefs usually distinguish themselves through special ornaments, but special forms of value are also in circulation among them or the nobility, for example, on Yap, money made from the cowrie shell, [❧95] while the well-known millstone-money (*Mühlsteingeld*)[261] made from aragonite[262] has gained recognition (*Geltung*) indiscriminately.[263]

We also hear numerous reports of a money-usage among the pearl-money forms used in the South Seas, which serves as evidence for what is referred to here as class-money.[264]

Finally, certain forms of Samoan mat-money may also have the character of class-money. These are the clothing mats known as '*ie toga.*' Their production requires not only great skill but also a significant amount of time, with higher-quality mats taking several months or even years to create. The mats represent the wealth, power, and influence of the Samoan family (Finsch). There are about ten different types of mats distinguished based on the occasions for which they are used. A special group is formed by the state-mats known as '*ie o le mala,*' which are in the possession of the oldest and most noble families. These mats are considered sacred and often have individual names. They are only brought out and used on very significant state occasions, such as when forming alliances. The other mats are used more frequently as a means of payment, but according to their value, they are also only used as money in large denominations. They are used as payment for house and canoe builders, for tattoo artists, as dowries

---

of Micronesia in the western Pacific Ocean.

[261] [tn] A type of stone used for grinding or milling grain or other materials.

[262] [tn] A mineral composed of calcium carbonate ($CaCO_3$).

[263] Thurnwald (1931-34:IV, 258)

[264] Petri (1936:209).

for chief's daughters, and for distribution during family events, especially for acquiring titles and esteems.[265] The various types of Samoan mat-money appear to be, in part, remnants and, in part, descendants of an originally purely aristocratic class-money.

A mention by Merensky[266] also seems to indicate the existence of a class-money, as cited by H. Schurtz (1898:104): Merensky reports:

> When we first visited the Basuto of North Transvaal[267] in the year 1860, the natives soon drew our attention to a special type of pearls or corals, which were of high value and were almost exclusively worn by reigning chiefs and their wives. [⟡96] In particular, a yellow and a black variety had a high reputation and were often used as atonement-money (*Sühnegeld*) or tribute, through which sub-chiefs gained the favour or protection of the superior chief."

In this context, it should also be pointed out that often, goods that are worn as signs of acknowledgement and distinction have the tendency to become money, just as conversely, money signs are worn as badges. The most well-known example is rings, especially neck and arm rings, which, as mentioned earlier, are awarded as a form of distinction and at the same time are money or become money over time. Among the Massai,[268] in addition to rings, bells (bell-money) also serve this purpose. Wherever ornamental pieces are money, and as shown, this was originally not uncommon, perhaps even the rule, this money also serves as a symbol of

---

[265] Finsch (1914:407) and Helmreich (1914-1915:124) and the literature cited there.

[266] [tn] Hans Merensky (1871-1952) was a renowned South African geologist and entrepreneur known for his discoveries in mineral resources, particularly platinum, and his contributions to the mining industry.

[267] North Transvaal refers to a region in South Africa that was historically part of the former Transvaal province.

[268] [tn] A Nilotic ethnic group primarily located in East Africa, specifically in Kenya and Tanzania.

112

rank or status. Max Weber goes so far as to claim that "the possession of certain means of payment was a primary characteristic of social status."[269]

Very often, cowrie shells also serve as symbols of bravery, and it remains to be seen whether they were originally money or became money through their usage in various ways. When a Dahomey[270] warrior has killed an enemy, the gunstock[271] is decorated with cowrie shells.[272] In the Angami Naga,[273] cowrie shell ornament is also a symbol of martial achievements.[274] Among the Alfuren on Ceram,[275] shell adornments on the war shield are the badges of warrior performances. The same applies to the native Americans in North America and on some islands in the South Pacific.[276] In these and other cases, we repeatedly encounter the fact that the goods that serve as symbols of rank and dignity also have a usage that we can describe as money-usage.

[P97] In summary, it can be observed that all money begins as class-money, meaning it is a form of money whose usage is specific to a particular class or even reserved for them. The primitive money-good often comes from the realm of luxury goods. Its usage represents a form of

---

[269] Weber (1925: 40. 77).

[270] [tn] A historical kingdom and later a French colony located in West Africa, in the region that is now part of the modern-day country of Benin.

[271] [tn] The part of a firearm where the shooter holds and stabilises the weapon. It is the wooden or synthetic portion at the rear of a firearm, often called the buttstock or simply the stock.

[272] Duncan (1848: I, 261. 78).

[273] [tn] One of the major Naga tribes in Northeast India, primarily found in the state of Nagaland.

[274] Butler (1855: 148).

[275] [tn] Ceram, also known as Seram, is an island located in Indonesia, specifically in the eastern part of the country. It is part of the Maluku Islands, which are sometimes referred to as the Moluccas.

[276] Cf. Landtman (1909:50).

expenditure through which membership in a class or a particularly distinguished status within the class is expressed. The typical class-money is 'hoard-money.' It is 'elite-money' (*Herrengeld*) or the money of the elite class. The expansion of money-usage occurs in such a way that this class-money is either adopted by a socially lower class, or the subordinate class develops its own money that corresponds to its needs and expenditures. In this case, members of different classes use different forms of money. The purpose-change, which money typically undergoes when expanding its usage, results in a selection among various money-goods. In most cases, the money-good used by the larger group proves to be superior and displaces other money-goods. The money of the upper class almost always loses its character as money in this process. Along this developmental path, money transforms from a means of recognition into an economic means. Money as an economic means is democratic money, meaning it is not bound by class in its usage and is not determined by class in its possession. Destroying handed-down classes can indeed create new ones or even strengthen the old ones, further separating them based on possession and non-possession.

III. The Essence of Money

§11. The Concept of Money

[**98**] A material, for example, a plant extract, which is medicinal, cannot yet be considered as medicine, nor is a material with a certain nutritional value necessarily a food; instead, those substances are only referred to as medicine (*Arzneimittel* = means of medication) or food (*Nahrungsmittel* = means of nutrition) when they are *customarily* used as such. So, it is the *usage* (*Gebrauch*) or the *use* (*Verwendung*) that allows us to designate such goods as medicine in one case and as food in the other case. The same applies to the goods we call money. It is a certain usage or a specific manner of usage through which such goods become money. However, the question of what kind of use must be present to justify the designation of money is not as easy to decide, as in the two chosen examples above.

The concept of money can only be understood within the 'context of meaning' (*Sinnzusammenhang*) in social events, which demonstrate a certain goods-usage that is referred to as 'money-like' (*geldmäßig*). The money-like goods-usage is based on *psychological* facts that lead to consistent behaviour, aligned judgment, and action of socially connected individuals in the evaluation and utilisation of such goods, specifically money-goods. Here is the answer to the question of what conditions must be met for a good to be used as money: It is not only the aptitude of the good or certain properties that determine its aptitude but also a certain *mindset* (*Gesinnung*) of the people using the good, i.e., a mindset of the monetary society [or money-use society] (*Geldgesellschaft*). This mindset is a bond (*Band*) that envelops the participants and becomes a binding [agent] (*Bindung*) for them, which is far from benevolence or arbitrary discretion and is felt as 'order and law *without* external pressure and coercion.'

[**99**] From this, a *consistent behaviour* emerges, which is the

prerequisite for a good to be used as money. The frequently posed question about the correct money-concept is posed incorrectly. It can only be a matter of forming a concept that corresponds to the respective facts of money-usage. Money-usage itself, however, like all social life, is subject to continuous change, transformation, and development. It can indeed be said that a significant portion of the disagreements regarding the concept of money stems from the object (*Gegenstand*) itself,[277] which is the result of historical development. The money-concept that emerges from the observations we gather from ethnographic and early historical accounts of a certain money-usage corresponds *only* to the facts of these early stages of the historical development of money. When Adolf Wagner once said, "A concise, **unified** money-concept derived from a single (main) function cannot be properly formed,"[278] it essentially conveys the same idea, because the historical development of money shows us a transformation in the functions of money, or at the very least, a shift in the meaning and ranking of these functions, or, as I prefer to say, in these fundamental and essential services, namely the monetary services, which the conceptualisation must naturally take into account. Therefore, I also believe it is right to differentiate between various money-concepts corresponding to different stages in the historical development of money.

For someone approaching the concept of money as it is understood today, the emergence of money and thus essential aspects of the historical development of money must remain concealed. Primitive societies are not acquainted with money in our sense, nor do they possess a modern

---

[277] [tn] It means money.

[278] [tn] Adolf Wagner (1835- 1917) was a prominent German economist associated with the Historical School of Economics, known for his contributions to economic history, public finance, and the formulation of 'Wagner's Law,' which posits that government spending tends to increase with a nation's income growth. The source of the current quotation has not been identified.

monetary mindset, whether it be that of liberal *oikonomia* (*Ökonomie*)[279] or any form of managed economy (*Wirtschaft*). However, they do have a notion of money, are familiar with a certain form of money-usage, and often exhibit a prominently discernible monetary mindset. The Germanic culture knew nothing else but that possession was acquired through an offering of friendship. [❡100] "However," as Grönbech adds, "neither inclinations nor greed were diminished by it." This is also the case with other peoples. The differences between selfless yearning (*Gebedrang*) [for gestures of friendship] and selfish greed for possession disappear. "For a Germanic, love and advantage could no more be separated than the soul and body of the ring or the axe" (Grönbech 1939:72). It is certainly no coincidence that here the ring and axe are mentioned when discussing yearning and greed for possession.

If we adhere to the history of the emergence of money, without claiming that it can provide us with something definitive or even something binding regarding the concept of money, we can still observe the following: ethnographic and cultural-historical literature teaches us that among all peoples and in all times, certain goods have had the significance of social means of recognition, meaning that the possession and use of these goods confer reputation within the circle of fellows and thus power. They are social means of power. Such possessions are linked to social differentiations and social privileges. As a result, these goods are particularly suitable for use as a means of distinction, for social classification, for the formation of social bonds, and so on. It is precisely because of the aptitude attributed to these things by the opinions and behaviours of the socially connected people, and these goods are generally desired and therefore hoarded not because of their technical characteristic. Everyone seeks to acquire and possess them, and at the same time, their use expands rapidly and easily beyond the initial purposes. To the extent that

---

[279] [tn] See Translate Note at p. 351.

this is the case, i.e., to the extent that goods are both collected and hoarded as bearers of social esteem (*Wertschätzung*) on the one hand, and on the other hand, in a certain sense, regularly used in exchange for the formation of social relationships or fulfilling social obligations, and especially transferred, these goods are called money. This is the money-concept that corresponds to the beginnings of the development of money.

The concept of money developed above is based on notions that correspond to a money-usage as encountered in the early stages of the development of money. [p101] What von Zwiedineck once conjectured, in fact, holds true – as long as one avoids the rationalistic connotations associated with the term "purposive institution" (*Zweckeinrichtung*). He states:

> Not only the society of a division of labour but also the preceding political human communities, it seems, have developed money as a purposive institution.

However, with the development, expansion, and growth of the economic society, the money-usage takes on a different character. Money becomes a means of exchange. As is well known, in the second chapter of the first book of his famous work "The Wealth of Nations," Adam Smith spoke of the inclination of human nature to trade – to truck, to barter, and exchange one thing for another. However, he leaves open whether this inclination belongs to the original drives of human nature, which cannot be accounted for, or, which is more likely, is the necessary consequence of reason and language capability. Based on this assumption, it appears to the founder of classical national economic theory and all his followers that the emergence of money as a general means of exchange is not a problem at all but sheer self-evidence. However, this assumption is just as mistaken as the innate desire for exchange in humans and the resulting obviousness of the idea of exchange.[280] Ethnology teaches us that among primitive societies,

---

[280] It is entirely mistaken, therefore, when O. Schrader says, "The idea of

there is no trace of such a "natural" inclination, and there can be no talk of an obvious understanding of the purposefulness of using a means of exchange. Many societies are reported to have had no knowledge of the exchange of economical goods at all before coming into contact with the Europeans. While they may have had a form of gift-traffic, they did not engage in barter trade (*Tauschhandel*). The step from gift-traffic to barter trade is no less significant than the one from in-kind exchange (*Naturaltausch*) to exchange using money. [᭄102] Certainly, many societies, even at relatively early stages of culture, have a goods-usage that could be described as a money-usage, but this money does not serve as an exchange-medium. Buying and selling for money continue to be rejected even in more developed economic conditions for a long time. This is connected to those notions of 'magical ties' through which the primitive person feels linked to the things in their environment. The sale of livestock, according to the early tribal cultures' pastoralists, takes away the luck of the herd. Therefore, reindeer are never sold but only exchanged for other animals. It is also evident that money is not intended to facilitate goods-exchange in the eyes of primitives because, as mentioned in another context, the first exchange-activities are not directed towards the acquisition of material-goods at all.[281]

It is not our task to attempt to delve into the psychological foundations of these notions and activities. Their presentation should only teach us that among all peoples, it has been a long journey of psychological development until means of exchange-intercourse (*Tauschverkehrmittel*) through money became established, until exchange-money emerged. Exchange-money, like hoard-money, originates from gift-traffic. This has already been demonstrated. Exchange is originally a manifestation-form of

---

exchanging a foreign good for a part of one's own possessions is so obvious that we may presuppose it at every cultural level" (1907:290).

[281] Cf. Lowie (1928: 551 ff.) and the explanations above on p. 94.

social relationships and as such an expression of social connectivity. Originally, it did not or only to a very limited extent played an essentially economic role. Instead, it gradually grows into this role, although to such an extent that it becomes the primary carrier of economic life. However, it is not direct exchange, in-kind exchange, that assumes this role because this form of exchange is too cumbersome. Instead, it is an indirect exchange, which involves the exchange that utilises a general means of exchange.

With the usage of a means of exchange to facilitate exchange-intercourses, another aspect is connected, which becomes established as a consequence of this usage and at the same time paves the way for the general economic expansion of exchange-intercourses. [P103] That is the utilisation of the common exchange-good as a means to express economic valuations in numerical terms, i.e., in prices. The general means of exchange thus becomes the general means of price-expression (*Preisausdrucksmittel*). At the same time, another general mode of use is linked to it: the usage as a means of payment, which is already familiar in the hoard-money stage.

Economic evaluations and the price-calculations based on them are indeed not necessarily tied to a general means of exchange but often precede the usage of such a means for a significant amount of time. However, the goods in which such evaluations are typically made (e.g., livestock; see Gerloff 1940: 135 ff.) are not yet called money. It is only when the good serving as a price-measure also regularly serves as a means of exchange or as a means of payment that it becomes money. However, historical development typically does not follow the path from the unit of account to the general means of exchange, but rather the reverse; the good that becomes a general means of exchange tends to also become the unit of account and the means of price-expression. At the same time, older units of account that coexist are gradually abandoned. Only the name of the older unit of value is often retained and may even be transferred to the general means of exchange and means of payment.

The money of this stage of development is thus a general means of exchange, a means of payment, and a means of price-expression. These are its essential services. Goods are then commonly called money when they are regularly used as a general means of exchange and, consequently, also as a means of payment and a means of price-expression.

The conspicuous essential service of money, being a general means of exchange, has led to the misconception of viewing this aptitude as the sole money-purpose. However, this view is erroneous. Exchange-money is only one stage in the development of money, and facilitating exchange is just one essential service of money at this stage of development. Therefore, not every form of money inherently possesses the 'service of facilitating exchange' (*Tauschdienstleistung*), and it is not contradictory for believers of a new economic order that bypasses exchange through money to believe that money (namely as a value-measure and unit of account) should and can be retained, [p104] even if it is no longer a means of exchange. However, one can indeed describe the 'service of facilitating exchange' as the great catalyst in the development of money. It leads to the valuation of goods and services in terms of money, even if they are not actually exchanged. Through the path of the exchange service, money acquires a general 'economic value-generating function' (*wirtschaftliche Wertfunktion*). It becomes an expression of economical evaluation and a means of practical economic reasoning (*Mittel der praktischen wirtschaftlichen Vernunft*). All economical values and value-relationships (*Wertbeziehung*) are expressed in terms of money. This is a situation aptly captured by H. Sauermann in the words: "The economy extends as far as money reaches."[282] However, at this stage of its development, money is not only an organising factor (*Ordnungsfaktor*) in the economy but also, by being so, it becomes an economic means, whose services in their significance and impact extend far beyond the organising function (*Ordnungsfunktion*). Exchange (*Tausch*) and economy (*Wirtschaft*)

---

[282] Sauermann (1931:425).

[individually] are possible without money, but an exchange-economy (*Tauschwirtschaft*) cannot exist without money. Money creates the exchange-society (*Tauschgesellschaft*). This society becomes an "evaluation society" (*Bewertungsgesellschaft*) (K. Soda) that uses money not only for exchange but also as a general economic means of intercourse (*Verkehrsmittel*), through which the conversion of proceeds into income, the distribution of the social-product (*Sozialprodukt*), and the realisation of all economic claims take place. This money is, therefore, a '**general commercial-money**' (*allgemeines Verkehrsgeld*).[283] At this stage, money is the good that serves as a universally accepted means for conducting exchange-intercourses and transferring asset claims in a specific economic domain.

The difference from the previous stage is only gradual. It simply consists of the fact that money which has its life-sphere essentially in the turnover of goods (*Güterumsatz*) or in the market has become money that is the universally used, recognised, and valid good wherever economic value-transfers (*Wertübertragung*) take place. Thus, money has gained socially effective force and significance infinitely. [P105] Naturally, even for money in earlier stages, the beginnings of an expansion of its social domain of influence can be identified. The determining factor for the fact that we can observe a stage of the development of money here is solely the fact that everything found as beginnings in the direction of developing a 'general commercial-money' in earlier stages has found its final development here. In [economic] traffic, there is nothing else for the exchange-medium and value-transfer but one and the same money. Externally, this development is characterised by the fact that the money signs are given a specific form.

However, even here, the development does not come to a halt, and as before, the further development of money, which leads to a

---

[283] [tn] See Translate Notes on p. 352 for the meaning of commercial-money (*Verkehrsgeld*).

transformation, builds upon beginnings that go far back in time. It is the usage of certain value-magnitudes in societal-economic intercourses, such as a piece of livestock or a quantity of grain or oil, a unit of weight in metal (indicated by names like Libra, Mark, etc.), as a measurement-unit for the evaluation of goods-possession and services, for the assessment of obligations and compensations. It is evident that once an exchange-money or commercial-money has been established, it can be used in the same way as a measure (*Maß*) and benchmark (*Maßstab*), and indeed this is the case. For the settlement of not only exchange-economic intercourses but any service-traffic (*Leistungsverkehr*), it is not the physical money-good, i.e., the material-money (*Sachgeld*), that is used, but the monetary unit (*Geldeinheit*) as a unit of measure (*Maß*) for [such] service. But even this is not absolutely necessary. The balance can be debited or credited and can be offset in the next service-traffic when the opportunity arises. Services and counter-services are now measured only with the monetary unit (*Geldelle*), as they say. The money has become a **money of account** (*Rechengeld*). However, up to this point in the development of money, everything has remained the same, except that the increasing trade relies more and more on the measure rather than the measure-good (*Maßgut*) itself. The significant step in the further development of the monetary framework, which is now being taken almost unnoticed and unconsciously at this point, is that the measurement-unit (*Maßeinheit*) no longer remains a mere form but acquires a specific content. [P106] From an abstract measure of magnitude, it becomes a positive magnitude that includes income portions (*Einkommensteil*) that represent purchasing force (*Kaufkraft*). [284] From a common denominator for value-comparisons and value-clearing (*Wertverrechnung*), it has become a meter (*Zähler*) for magnitudes of purchasing force.

---

[284] [tn] See Translation Note (p.354) for the difference between 'purchasing power' (*Kaufmacht*) and 'purchasing force' (*Kaufkraft*).

The course of development is as follows: The usage of some form of money thing leads to using the 'unit of material-money' (*Sachgeldeinheit*) or a certain quantity of material-money (*Sachgeldmenge*) as a unit of account, for example, in setting penances, compensations, levies, etc. This unit of account becomes a measure of purchasing force. By expressing income portions within this measure of magnitude, these income portions themselves become a measured value (*Maßgröße*) that is regularly used for payments. It becomes the proper (*eigentlich*) money.

Money is a measure of magnitude and a measured value of purchasing force, which the socio-economic service-traffic uses as a value-standard, a means of price-expression, a means of payment, and a means of clearing (*Verrechnungsmittel*).

This money can appear in the handed-down form of money signs, whether they have material value or not, and can be transferred from hand to hand. However, much more frequent and much larger are the payments that occur without the use of money signs through somehow documented transfers (clearings) of income or asset portions, which, when expressed in the 'measurement-unit money,' themselves represent a specific measured value of money.[285] Whether in income or assets that enter the market, in the 'measurement-unit money,' the magnitude of purchasing force expressed in money is the actual, the real money. This is the definition of money in the current economic stage.

One can raise the question of whether the conceptual delimitation presented here correctly captures the monetary phenomenon, especially whether the magnitudes of purchasing force expressed in 'measurement-unit money' can be reasonably referred to as money, or whether it would

---

[285] J. Dobretsberger says the following:

> It is therefore expedient to use the term money both for the concrete purchasing force document and for the abstract purchasing force unit; language usage does this, and monetary policy refers to both (1946: 37).

be preferable to restrict the money-concept to money signs or 'measurement-unit money.' [⍴107] Answer: This would mean completely excluding oneself from understanding the manifestations of money and, in turn, the understanding of essential processes in social and economic life. It is not the money embodied in money signs, and even less so the 'measurement-unit money' used as a means of account (*Rechnungsmittel*), that are essential forces of social order and economic fabric [underlying structure], but rather the *magnitudes of purchasing force* expressed in the 'measurement-unit money' are the carriers and coiners (*Präger*) [i.e., shapers] of social and, above all, economic relationships. Essential ties in social life, especially the entire world of economic activity, the entire service-traffic with its price mechanism, are based on this money. Certainly, money signs and monetary accounting (*Geldrechnung*) play a certain role in social conduct-process, in their order and formation (*Gestaltung*). However, this role is insignificant compared to the far-reaching power that money, as a magnitude of purchasing force, exerts in society. Money as a magnitude of purchasing force is the driving force behind socio-economic movements and, at the same time, it determines their goals and pace.

Thus, it can be said with some reservation that money has evolved from being a physical object into a representation (*Vorstellung*), a process that has been a prerequisite for the development of abstract thinking and the building up of language, marking the transition from animality to humanity. With this change, the significance of the money-good or money-goods has diminished, while the realm of monetary representations (*Geldvorstellung*), and consequently their meaning, has undergone massive growth. This development carries the risk that money, to use an expression employed by K. Lamprecht in a different context, becomes a "psychic dominating agent (*psychische Dominante*)" of society, significantly and diversely influencing group conduct (*Gruppengehabe*). However, it encounters a certain counterbalance in the fact that as money, as a measure of purchasing force, gains significance in the societal environment of the individual, the influence of money embodied in material-goods or symbols (signs and emblems) is gradually diminished as an inherited social means of power (*Machtmittel*) and thus as a dominant component of societal existence.

[p108] The described developmental path is the process of the abdication of gold as a money-good and its replacement by a magnitude of purchasing force expressed in a handed-down measurement-unit, which serves as societal 'compensation for services' (*Leistungsentgelt*).

126

§12. Societality²⁸⁶ of Money

Money is a societal good. A table, a pair of shoes, etc., are personal goods. They serve an individual's demand-satisfaction (*Bedarfsbefriedigung*) independently of others. Money is not such a good; it is a societal good that only gains validity (*Geltung*) within society and through society.

That money is a societal phenomenon is by no means a new insight, but it is rather a neglected one and, in its significance, not sufficiently appreciated, as I believe. When, for example, Adam Müller says, "The societalisation of people finds its expression in money," he does not characterise the essential social relevance of money. In fact, one could say that cause and effect are being confused. For money is primarily not an expression but a means of societalisation.

Just like Adam Müller, H. C. Carey also failed to correctly recognise the societality of money, despite referring to money as "An Instrument of Association" and discussing the doctrine of money under the heading "The Instrument of Association" (*Das Werkzeug der Association*) in his textbook on economics and social science. When he refers to money as "the great instrument provided by Providence to facilitate association and combination," his subsequent explanations indicate nothing more than that money is an "exchange-tool," (*Tauschwerkzeug*) a means for the labour-saving execution of exchange-intercourses.²⁸⁷

[p109] Or when Michel Chevalier says, "*La monnaie est indispensable à l'homme, du moment qu'il vit en société*" (Money is indispensable to man as soon as he lives in society),²⁸⁸ he, like all those who follow in the footsteps of Adam Smith, is solely considering the necessity or

---

²⁸⁶ [tn] See Translation Note on p. 350.

²⁸⁷ Refer to Carey (1870: 319 ff.). For further reference, see J. W. Jenks (1885: 57 ff.).

²⁸⁸ Chevalier (1851: Tome III, 1).

purposefulness of money as an exchange-medium arising from the division of labour.

Although von Wieser admits that money is a societal phenomenon, i.e., one that "cannot come to life without societal powers," he only means to express, as he himself realised, that money does not entirely stand on an individualistic basis.[289]

The societality of money is not something incidental to money, but it is its essence (*Wesenheit*). Money is therefore more than just a social means of relationship, as there are numerous others. It is, in fact, an element of the realisation (*Verwirklichung*) of society itself. It possesses the force (*Kraft*) to establish society. It is one of the means that create the connection between individuals that we call society, a connection that is established through social action. This is the uniqueness of money: it is a product of society that, in turn, generates society. While it is not a prerequisite for society, it is the most potent means of the development of society. However, this is – and this is a further characteristic of the peculiar social power of money – by no means at the expense of the individual personality, but quite the opposite: just as money makes the social existence of the individual possible, it means assurance (*Gewährleistung*) of personal existence in its unity to a significant degree if not entirely at the same time.

The societality of those processes that lead to a goods-utilisation, commonly referred to as money-usage, is evident, based on what was discussed in the first part of this study. As shown, these processes by no means exclusively involve *economic* relationships; [p110] in fact, initially, they do not extend to such relationships at all. It is from the general 'social habit of use' (*soziale Verwendungsgewohnheit*) of money that the more specific economic or exchange-economic aspect emerges.

When we explore the causes of the 'social habit of use' that allows

---

[289] Wieser (1929:242).

certain goods to become money, we are attempting to make visible and conscious the starting point and beginning of a cultural phenomenon of immeasurable significance. Money, as society employs it as a technical means, becomes a dynamic element in societal development and thus a force that shapes society itself.

Like all social facts, money also exhibits a series of stages in its development, ranging from those facts that already acquired a solid form down to those yet-to-be formed phenomena, from which social life is shaped and unfolds. The question of at which point in this progression one can already speak of money is futile, as its answer is tied to more or less arbitrary assumptions and contributes nothing to the elucidation of those social facts themselves.

When money is referred to as a social fact here, it is actually *a quid pro quo*,[290] or more precisely, it is not about money itself but about money-usage. Money-usage is the social fact. The social fact consists, as one can say in reference to Durkheim's studies on the sociological object, of a particular kind of action, thinking, and feeling that exists outside the individual and is endowed with compelling coercive power (*Gewalt*), by virtue of which the social fact imposes itself over the individual.[291] The social fact we refer to as money-usage is thus a customary way of doing and behaviour with regard to the usage of certain goods within a given society. As a result, these goods acquire a specific meaning or function that we call their 'social value-generating function' (*soziale Wertfunktion*). It is worth emphasising once again that this function precedes the purely economical function.

[𝄢111] In this passage, 'social value-generating function' refers to the

---

[290] [tn] A Latin phrase that means 'something for something' or 'this for that.' It refers to the exchange of goods, services, or favours where one party provides something in return for something else.

[291] [tn] Durkheim (1982/1895:52).

service (*Leistung*) of money within society, which consists of continually creating new societal formations (*Gestaltung*), specifically connections of interests within groups in action. Money, in this sense, constitutes society. Behind this concept lies a specific direction of feelings and desires, needs and satisfactions, domination and submission, and giving and receiving. However, money, unlike any other, serves as the means of effect (*Bewirkungsmittel*) and the means of expression (*Ausdrucksmittel*) for all these strivings and aspirings. It acts as the motor (*Motor*) and the bond for these formations of connections while also serving as the outward visible sign that signifies our encounter with a societal phenomenon, the presence of society itself. Therefore, money is not merely an expression of societal relationships; it is also a means of human group formation (*Gruppengestaltung*). It not only expresses social connectivity but also creates such connections. From the moment it comes into existence, it becomes an incessantly active cause of societalisation. It transforms individuals into links in the chain of a greater whole, signifying society itself.

One could raise the question of whether these connections already exist beforehand and only find a particular form of expression in money. The question must be answered in the negative. While there are certainly social connectivities for which money is nothing more than a coincidental form of expression, much more frequently, it is money itself that creates the social connectivities that would not be conceivable at all without money or that are significantly shaped in terms of their nature, duration, and strength by money.

The societalisation of people was originally limited to small groups. With the development of their intellectual capabilities, there was a gradual adaptation to an extended societality through the formation of ever larger groups. Money is a means of this adaptation. It is certainly not an absolutely necessary societal means of existence (*gesellschaftliches Daseinsmittel*). However, once introduced, it contributes to the increase in societalisation to a degree matched by only a few other cultural-goods, primarily because it strongly influences the construction of society. [₱112] In step with the expansion and densification of society, which it itself brings about, money undergoes its ongoing development (*Fortbildung*) and transformation (*Umbildung*), adapting to the needs of societal life. The continuation of this adaptation holds the seed for the change in the essence of money. Just as society itself is subject to constant change, so is money. Therefore, there will never be money that perfectly corresponds to the needs of society because these needs themselves are constantly evolving.

In the usage of money, society experiences itself. As Simmel once said:

> Giving is one of the strongest sociological functions. Without continuous giving and taking within society, even outside of exchanges, no society would come into being at all.[292]

If this is true, and who could doubt it, then the role of money in societalisation is also defined. Then, money is the element that increases acts of giving and taking to an infinite extent (excluding the intellectual exchange, which Simmel primarily seems to refer to). Therefore, money can be seen as a societal ideogram (*gesellschaftliches Sinnbild*), containing a meaningful statement about society itself. It is one of those forms of connection through which social life is expressed. This form of connection differs from others in that it has taken visible form in money signs.

In the usage of money, society establishes a regulation of life (*Lebensregelung*). Simultaneously, it encroaches upon the handed-down social life-order (*Lebensordnung*) and establishes a legitimacy (*Gesetzmäßigkeit*) of social action. Such a regulation of life can be of various kinds, as we know, and the battle (*Kampf*) over the money-design (*Gestaltung des Geldes*) is a battle over this regulation of life, where opposing demands can be made based on [respective] legal convictions and cultural attitudes: for example, such as a battle over stable versus rusting-money, or limited versus unlimited purchasing power of money. [₱113]

---

[292] [tn] Simmel (1908: 444n1).

Money is thus more than a mere fact; it is the expression of social connectivities in which it actively participates and continuously alters.

All social changes are reflected in money and find their expression in the monetary framework (*Geldwesen*). Thus, money proves to be a means of differentiation and integration of society, following Spencer's law of development from the coexistence of similar, unconnected parts to the coexistence and interdependence of dissimilar, connected parts.

When discussing the societality of money, one must also acknowledge the contributions of Aristotle. While Aristotle may have misunderstood the societal source of money, he certainly recognised its societal significance. He can be regarded as the first great Western thinker who, although influenced by his aristocratic beliefs and the belief in the natural legality of slavery, clearly understood the societal role of money. In Book 1 of "Politics," at the end of Chapter 9 and the beginning of Chapter 10, Aristotle explains the consequences of the introduction of money-usage. [293] The introduction of money, roughly speaking, displaces household-management (*Haushaltskunst*) or *oikonomia* (*Ökonomie*),[294] which is in accordance with nature, and replaces it with the art of earning (*Erwerbskunst*),[295] which knows only one means of acquisition, namely, profitable commodity-sales. The art of earning is concerned only with making money because the beginning and end of its exchange-intercourses always and exclusively involve money. The wealth generated by this art of money earning knows no bounds! Similarly, the art of earning or the

---

[293] [tn] It seems that Gerloff is referring to Aristotle (1872), which has a different chapter structure compared to Aristotle (1932). For our reference, we will use Aristotle (1932) since it adheres to the standard chapter divisions in Aristotle's Politics. Chapter 9 and the start of Chapter 10 in Aristotle (1872) approximately align with 1257a - 1258a in Aristotle (1932): Book I, Chapter III, lines 11-22, (pp. 41 -51).

[294] [tn] Refer to Translate Note at p.351.

[295] [tn] See footnote 214.

monetary economy has no limits, for it seeks nothing but wealth and money in general. However, household-management, which is not limited to merely making money, has a defined purpose, even though it may not always be conscious of it. Acquisition (*Erwerb*) is thus of two kinds: one is commercial, and the other is related to household-managing. The latter is necessary and is highly respected, while the former, which is solely concerned with trade, is rightly criticised. Accordingly, *oikonomia* (*Ökonomik*) is praised, while profit-seeking money-making (*chrematistic*) [296] is severely condemned. [p114] Aristotle does not recognise the economic contribution made by trade and merchants but only sees the outward aspect: the pursuit of money-earning (*Gelderwerb*), "which knows no bounds." The mercantile art of earning, which views its purpose as the ever-increasing multiplication of money possession, has, as the wise philosopher vehemently observes, infected even household art of acquisition, as well as the entire political, economic, and artistic life, so that "all their energies are occupied in the business of getting wealth."[297] Thus, money-making (*chrematistic*) spreads and undermines political virtues such as the will to fight (*Wehrwillen*) [for the state] and civic spirit, posing a danger to both the people and the state.

One must read the accusations raised in Chapter 9 of "Politics"[298] literally to understand Aristotle's critique of society but also to recognise its one-sidedness. This one-sided perspective has often provoked

---

[296] [tn] See footnote 40 for its meaning.

[297] [tn] Full quotes:

> (A)s therefore the desire for life is unlimited, they also desire without limit the means productive of life. And even those who fix their aim on the good life seek the good life as measured by bodily enjoyments, so that inasmuch as this also seems to be found in the possession of property, all their energies are occupied in the business of getting wealth (Aristotle 1932:47; 1258a; 1872:35).

[298] [tn] See footnote 293 to refer to Aristotle (1932).

contradictions among interpreters of "Politics." Aristotle does not see – and perhaps could not or did not want to see – what the introduction of money meant for the liberation of human society, and how the spread of the monetary economy initiated a democratic revolution. J.G. Schlosser, in his translation of "Politics,"[299] astutely notes regarding Aristotle's arguments:

> As correct as it is that the art of finance (*Finanzierkunst*), which deals only with money as a symbol of things, knows no bounds, it is incorrect in many respects to suggest that household management has inherent bounds. Household management, as Aristotle himself sees it, is supposed to provide for all of a person's needs. If humanity had remained faithful to nature, this art would indeed have found its bounds in the nature of human beings and the environment surrounding them. However, human imagination has led people elsewhere and awakened needs within them that have no bounds; thus, household management has also lost its bounds.
>
> It may be that the invention of money, by facilitating trade, has allowed human imagination to roam freely. However, money itself is not solely to blame. I rather believe that in the face of many great evils brought into the world by money, we do not owe this invention alone the fact that now nine-tenths of the people have to serve the fortunate one-tenth in the possession of the properties (*Liegenschaft*)."[300] [301]

[115] Aristotle's criticism is not actually directed against money itself,

---

[299] [tn] Schlosser (1798).

[300] Schlosser (1789: Part 1, 57).

[301] [tn] It means that the unequal distribution of property and wealth existed before the invention of money. Money itself alone is not to blame for this inequality, but it has been used to perpetuate and exacerbate these disparities. The author is pointing out that the root causes of social and economic inequality go beyond the existence of money and are related to property ownership and distribution.

whose importance as a means of exchange the philosopher fully acknowledges. Instead, it is aimed at the emergence of a money-centric mindset that threatens to disrupt the societal structure of the Aristotelian world. In a society characterised by a feudal or military nature, money may indeed play a less significant role as a means, especially when compared to a society whose order and institutions are primarily based on purely economic foundations. However, precisely for this reason, it is often perceived as an alien element in such societies. The societal force of money is not only society-building but also society-destroying. By facilitating the emergence of new societal forms, it simultaneously often leads to the downfall of others.

Indeed, money has not played a role in the emergence of fundamental forms of society. However, in the course of social development, it exerts a profound influence on the formation of numerous societal forms and leads to the creation of new societal structures. It facilitates organisational collaboration within society, not only in the economic realm but also in the political and cultural domains. Money is the bond that not only enables the formation of numerous societal structures but also holds them together over time. It not only strengthens existing social relationships but continually establishes new ones and ultimately, through these, brings about a transformation in the very nature of human beings.

Thus, in the habitual arrangement of human group conduct, money plays a role of the utmost significance. As an expression of human relationships or of new forms and modes of co-living, it acquires a social significance that few other institutions and means of communal life have. [P116] Although it is only a means of expressing social existence and not an efficient cause (*causa efficiens*),[302] it brings about reinforcement and

---

[302] [tn] In Aristotle's philosophy, '*causa efficiens*' refers to the efficient cause, which is one of the four causes he identified to explain the existence and characteristics of things. The four causes are (1) *Causa Materialis* (material cause), which pertains to the physical substance or matter from which

intensification of societalisation in all its forms of development. Furthermore, the primary significance of its social impact lies in the fact that the means of expression continuously and retroactively transform the forms of expression and their psychological content. In other words, the technical means of expression not only alter the forms of expression but also the content of the social fact itself, of which it is a reflection. Thus, societal existence is changed and reshaped through the means of its forms of expression. This will be further elaborated upon in the subsequent part of this exposition.

---

something is made; (2) *Causa Formalis* (formal cause), which deals with the essential form or blueprint that defines an object's nature and characteristics; (3) *Causa Finalis* (final cause), which relates to the purpose or end for which something exists or is create; and (4) *Causa Efficiens* (efficient cause), which concerns the agent or force responsible for bringing something into existence or causing an event to occur. In the context of '*causa efficiens*,' it refers to the active cause or the agent that brings about a particular effect or result. In particular, it focuses on the processes and agents that initiate change or creation in the world.

§13. The Essential Services of Money

Every theoretical perspective has a dual purpose: it aims to describe the generality or types of state of affairs (*Sachverhalt*) or phenomena in which the state of affairs presents itself to observation, and then to explain the connections expressed in this state of affairs. The result is an understanding of the connections and processes involved, which may, under certain circumstances, be referred to as laws.

The phenomena that the societal theory of money considers are the services of money as expressed in money-usage. These services of money are diverse in nature. When we speak here of the essential services of money, we mean those services that transform goods into money in the first place, that establish the moneyness (*Geldsein*) of a good.

This is not to say that a good must fulfil all the monetary services recognised as essential services of money to be considered money. Instead, as previously explained, depending on the changes that money undergoes during its development and continues to undergo, various services should be considered essential for moneyness at different times. Some misconceptions in fundamental questions of monetary theory stem from a misunderstanding or a narrow conception of the essential services of money, or as one can also say, the monetary service (*Gelddienst*). [p117] It is too narrow if, for example, not only in terms of the emergence of money but also regarding its monetary service in the societal economy, fulfilling the role of money is primarily or solely seen as facilitating sales.

Society is a 'communal life' (*Lebensgemeinschaft*) characterised in some way. Consequently, for a societal theory of money, the question naturally arises: what are the services of money within this communal life? The intention behind this question is not to break down the monetary phenomenon into its components, but to recognise its meaning and understand it as a 'carrier of meaning' (*Sinnträger*). The preliminary answer to our question is: money is a 'carrier of services' (*Leistungsträger*) in various societal domains. As a result, its essential services are also of various kinds. The original 'social habit of use' of money, as shown, is that of a means of recognition (*Geltungsmittel*). The essential service through which money comes into life should not be understood to mean that this single essential service immediately turns goods into money. Nor should it be implied that any means of recognition is automatically considered money. Certainly, numerous goods have proven particularly suitable throughout history for obtaining recognition (*Geltung*)[303] or being an 'expression of recognition' (*Geltungsausdruck*), without these goods ever becoming or having become money. The intention is only that the good or goods that originally became money were all 'recognition-goods' (*Geltungsgut*) (usually precious-items).

A means that confers societal recognition is not only a means of expressing social rank-status and power-status (*Ausdrucksmittel sozialer Rang- und Machtstellung*) but is therefore also a means of societal power-exercise (*Mittel gesellschaftlicher Machtausübung*).

The essential service of primitive money, being a means of recognition, is therefore inseparably linked to the other services, being a social means of power (*Machtmittel*). As a social means of recognition and a social means of power, money becomes a means of accentuation within society, leading to differentiation, and thereby also segregation (*Absonderung*) and dissociation (*Trennung*). [118] However, therein lies the germ for a reversal of this service into its opposite: from a good that serves as a means of recognition for accentuation or segregation against others, it becomes a social means of binding (*Bindemittel*) that creates social relationships within the group as well as among different groups. Women, allies, protection from the powerful, and so on can be acquired with those goods that serve as means of recognition, precisely because they are such means. When these goods are used as bride-prices, tributes, offerings, gifts, etc., they create social relationships and simultaneously become a social means

---

[303] See Translation Notes on p. 352.

of binding. This situation seems to be the idea that the American sociologist Albion W. Small has in mind when, without pursuing this thought any further, he calls money 'a medium of social contact.'

As such a social relationship-bearer (*Beziehungsträger*), money appears to us already in its embryonic form, namely where certain goods serve treasure-buildup, which, however, are community assets (*Gemeinschaftssach*). The treasure-display and treasure-distribution, and finally the treasure-destruction driven by the 'drive for recognition' (*Geltungsdrang*) as shown, are indeed the **initial stages of money-usage**.

Money is thus a social means of relationship, namely the one that, through the more or less regular transfer of certain goods, establishes an intercourse between individual people or groups and thus creates a kind of those mutual relationship-engagements that signify society *par excellence* (*schlechthin*). **In the context of the social habit of using a good as a means of recognition, when others join in transferring such goods to establish social relationships, it is only then that this good truly becomes money or is the process of monetary formation considered complete.**

All of this has already been explained in the discussions regarding the concept of money, but in this context, as with many other points in this paragraph, which may be seen as repetition, it naturally needs to be mentioned once again. The new 'habit of use of recognition-goods' extends to various social relations. However, in all cases, these are value-transfers. [p119] Initially, these transfers do not occur for immediate economic reasons but with the intention of establishing social relationships. When the good is exchanged and received, as explained in another context, a bond is formed, signifying or resulting in friendship, marriage, reconciliation, and so on. Only gradually does this process also acquire economic significance. The economic evaluation of the goods-transfer gradually takes precedence and becomes more or less determining for this activity. A significant expansion of the service range of money is the consequence. **Money becomes an economic means.**

Money undergoes a semantic change, which has a great impact on its ongoing development and further development. This process is an example of the 'the law of purpose-change' (*Gesetz des Zweckwandels*) or 'the law of semantic change' (*Gesetz des Bedeutungswandels*),[304] which states that usages, such as activities and symbols, change their fundamental purpose over time and thus undergo reinterpretation and a new understanding accordingly. By having the original purpose recede into the background or become entirely lost, the custom or activity is imbued with a new purpose ('the law of purpose-change' or 'the law of semantic change'). Such a semantic change is often accompanied by the tendency to elevate the means to the end (the 'law of the means becoming the end' (*Gesetz der Zweckwerdung des Mittels*) or the 'law of autonomy of the means' (*Gesetz der Verselbständigung des Mittels*). If the 'law of semantic change' implies a purpose-change, then the 'law of the means becoming the end' is the elevation of the means to an end. Money is one of the most impressive examples of the reinterpretation of means as goals and their elevation to a purpose.

When it is said that money is an economic means, it means that it is a work tool (*Werkmittel*) in the purposeful means-deployment (*Mitteleinsatz*) for the best satisfaction of human purposes (which is what we mean by economics), the use [quantity] of which proves to be the smaller, i.e., economically more advantageous means compared to others. This is the case in several respects as below:

1. Money enables the valorisation of goods and services independently of the vagaries of the supply of natural counterpart goods (*naturale*

---

[304] [tn] The semantic change specifically addresses the phenomenon of words or symbols changing their meanings over time. It is also sometimes referred to as a 'semantic shift.' On the other hand, the 'purpose change' signifies changes in how language is used for different purposes over time.

140

Gegenleistung).[305]

2. Conversely, money enables the acquisition of any desired counterpart, regardless of the nature of one's own inventory of goods or the type of one's own services that can be offered.

[P120] 3. Money enables the purposeful means-deployment in the economy. It serves as the benchmark against which all economic actions are oriented, and their success is measured.

4. Money is a means of dividing and distributing economic returns, a means of income-allocation (*Einkommenszuteilung*) and income-distribution (*Einkommensverteilung*).

These aptitudes of money correspond to the services attributed as essential to money in the economic society, which establish the moneyness of economical (*ökonomisch*) money. First and foremost, **the essential service of money is to be a means of exchange.** This refers to the use of money as a "means of indirect exchange" (*Mittel des indirekten Tausches*). This means that, especially with the advancing division of labour, the direct exchange of available goods and services for any needed or desired others is usually not possible. Therefore, those willing to exchange rely on temporarily accepting goods as compensation for their offerings, which they anticipate can be exchanged for the desired goods and services in the future. These goods regularly used as means of exchange may, under certain circumstances, become money. Money, as a means of exchange, is a good that is accepted by everyone in transactions as compensation for goods and services, and for this very reason, it provides the assurance that goods and services of other kinds can be acquired with it at any time.

To the extent, as money becomes the foundation of the exchange-economy and is increasingly drawn into broader segments of the

---

[305] [tn] It means that money allows for the exchange of goods and services without relying on specific natural products or barter-like transactions as counterparts. Instead, it provides a universal medium of exchange.

population, which occurs with the transition from household-economy (*Hauswirtschaft*) to artisan economy (*Kundenwirtschaft*) and further to market-economy, money acquires a significance that goes far beyond its role as a means of exchange. On one hand, it becomes a **means of earning** (*Erwerbsmittel*), and on the other, it becomes a **means of account** (*Rechnungsmittel*).

The use of money as a means of exchange leads to the association of certain 'value-magnitude representations' (*Wertgrößenvorstellung*) with money. Money becomes a representation of the value-magnitude of goods and services. The means of expression is the number, with reference to the monetary unit. [₽121] In this case, it becomes the unit of account. Money serves as a unit of account corresponding to a 'value-magnitude representation,' acting as a **value-measure** (*Wertmesser*) or, as it is better expressed, as **a means of price-expression** (*Preisausdrucksmittel*). Based on these services, the other function is established: serving as the means of account and, consequently, the means of expression for economical judgment, a means for organising the deployment of goods in production and consumption, in short, serving as the benchmark for economic management (*Wirtschaftsführung*). As a 'value-magnitude representation' and means of account, money serves as a benchmark by which the economic value of goods and services is measured and expressed. Consequently, it is also used for quantifying compensations for goods and services, as well as for converting economic returns into income and distributing it. Money is, as this service has been called, a **participation-measure in the social-product** (*Beteiligungsmaß am Sozialprodukt*). However, as demonstrated in another context, money is more than just a measure of magnitude for evaluation of goods and services or for determining a share of the social-product; it represents participation or the potential (*Möglichkeit*) for participation in the social-product itself. Simultaneously, through payment, it serves as a means of transfer of social participations (*Mittel der Übertragung sozialer Beteiligungen*).[306]

The service of money as a possibility of participation and a participation-measure in the social-product is closely linked to the usage of money as a means of payment. This has led to the opinion that the aptitude as a means of payment does not constitute an independent monetary service but is merely the consequence or the other side of these or of other fundamental services of money. This question will need to be addressed later. Here, the aim was simply to list those services of money that are considered essential for its moneyness under various circumstances. The next task is to dissect the individual services of money themselves and present them in terms of their significance and impact. In this regard, the observation already implied in what has been said here will become even clearer: **the essential services of money evolve and change with the needs of the society that uses money**.

---

[306] Cf. Elster (1920: especially. §§ 3, 4 & 7).

§14. Money as a Social Means of Relationship

[𝔭122] As demonstrated in the discussions on the societality of money, money is one of the significant forces through which social relationships are formed and existing ones are strengthened. It is one of the forces that generate societal relations and merge separate groups into a society. Certainly, "the social" is the substance, and money or the money-usage is just one form of the social. In other words, social relationships are the original foundation, which finds its expression in money or through money. However, new social ties emerge in money-usage, alongside the deepening, strengthening, or transformation of existing ones. The usage of money not only expresses social connectivities but also creates them. Under the condition of a specific organisation of societal intercourses, money-usage itself leads to particularly shaped social relationship processes and formations, the significance of which extends to various realms of human purpose-settings. The social impact of money is not limited solely to the domain of economy or *oikonomia* but extends far beyond it. Therefore, the subject of the societal theory of money is not on money-usage as an economic event but as a social phenomenon. This is not to suggest that the economic aspect of money-usage is disregarded, but rather that it represents just one, albeit the most significant, specific case of the social relationship-environment (*Beziehungsverhältnis*) created by money.

The society-forming and society-binding force of money is inexhaustible, as it continually creates new societal ties. It brings about a certain alignment of interests, primarily in economic matters, but also in intellectual and political realms. Money-usage presupposes a socially connected relation just as it establishes one. Money acts as a bond that continually gives rise to ever new ties between the relationship-bearers. [𝔭123] Such a social relationship system created by money can be referred to as a "**monetary community**" (*Geldgemeinschaft*). It is more than just a payment-community (*Zahlungsgemeinschaft*), meaning it is not merely a connection of economies through a common means of payment. The monetary community arises through money-usage, but at the same time, it affects its expansion, strength, and effectiveness through its inner and outer development, thereby achieving its own perfection. It creates a unity of evaluation, not only of economic goods but also of social recognition-goods, thereby imparting to societal existence not only a specific imprint but also a distinct psychological attitude. It is one of the most potent means for shaping society and intensifying societalisation (*Vergesellschaftung*).

Money is the social means of relationship that creates certain societal formations or structures, or at the very least significantly contributes to their emergence and operation, if not enabling them altogether. The versatility of the societal services of money becomes particularly evident here. The range of relationship-communities (*Beziehungsgemeinschaft*) formed by money encompasses structures of such diverse types as social classes on the one hand and the national economy on the other. At a certain stage of its development, society itself becomes unequivocally a monetary society (*Geldgesellschaft*), meaning a society in which relationships not only appear to be oriented through money but also exist in their cohesion and in essential aspects of their exertion through money and money-usage.

When it has been said that money is not an absolutely necessary societal means of existence, this applies to the general concept of society. However, certain societal formations, especially those that are among the most advanced, are inconceivable in terms of their structure and functioning without money or would, at the very least, be very incomplete without money. This applies not only to socialisations (*Vergesellung*) within the realm of economics but also to many other structures that extend far beyond economic matters, encompassing power-relations and dependency relations among people as their content. [P124] Levies of all kinds, sacrificial offerings, tributes, contributions, various services to authority, as well as gift-distributions among equals and subordinates, originally mostly occurred in the form of material-goods, i.e., in kind.

However, what is peculiar is that they gradually almost entirely adopt the money-form, in the development of which those goods often play a determining role. They retain this form permanently and find their continuity and growth in it. It is precisely through the money-form that these services become a social means of binding, connecting individuals and groups into relationship-communities in a way that no other material means can equally achieve. Certain societal forms of life which give the character of the conduct of an era, even often an entire age, such as capitalism, are hardly conceivable without money or would, in any case, present a completely different face without this means of existence.

As a social means of relationship, money embodies a certain life-order that undoubtedly does not derive its original meaning from money but, in its usage, increasingly acquires a characteristic imprint, a style and rhythm determined by money. When one perceives the substance of the social within social relationships, as a widely held sociological belief, then it is difficult to place any other equally important means of existence alongside the significance of money for society.

§15. Money as a Social Means of Recognition

In a cultural-historical study, "Hunters, Farmers, Traders" (1939), L. Franz states: "The goal of human life-struggle (*Lebenskampf*) is threefold: recognition (*Geltung*),[307] knowledge, preservation (*Erhaltung*)."[308] It is quite indicative that in this enumeration, not the drive for preservation (*Erhaltungsdrang*) or the drive for knowledge (*Wissensdrang*) but the 'claim for recognition' (*Geltungsanspruch*) is mentioned in the first place as a desire and striving that already dominate prehistoric and early historical man. Indeed, gaining recognition is the goal of the life-struggle; that is what the history of all peoples teaches us. [p125] It also teaches us about the behaviour of individuals within a group. As shown, money has emerged as a means to satisfy the 'need for recognition' of *homo ambitiosus*.

The respected English economist A. Marshall referred to money as a benchmark (*Maßstab*) of motives for human action, i.e., a measure of motive.[309] As he explains, once one can gauge the intensity of personal needs by the amount of money a person is willing to expend to attain a desired satisfaction, or by the sum required to prompt them to exert a certain effort, the foundation for a scientific consideration is established. Therefore, an examination of this benchmark is the starting point (and nothing more!) of economics. He then continues (with a slight

---

[307] [tn] See footnote 29.

[308] [tn] It refers to the preservation or maintenance of one's existence, well-being, or way of life.

[309] [tn] Marshall (1920:782). The whole text is

> For instance, the statement that the dominant position which money holds in economics, results rather from its being a measure of motive than an aim of endeavour, may be illustrated by the reflection that the almost exclusive use of money as a measure of motive is, so to speak, an accident, and perhaps an accident that is not found in other worlds than ours, When we want to induce a man to do anything for us we generally offer him money.

contradiction to what was just mentioned): Money is the focal point of economics not because it is considered the primary goal of human endeavours, nor because material wealth is the main subject of study for economists. Instead, money holds this central position "because in this world of ours it is the one convenient means of measuring motives of human activities on a large scale."[310] Therefore, he also suggests that the fact that money plays such a significant role in economics primarily stems from its role as a benchmark for motives in human action, rather than its role as the ultimate goal of human endeavour.[311]

Apart from the fact that all of this applies only to a very specific form of money, namely, the money of the liberal economy in its era, something entirely different is of interest in this context, and hence Marshall's remarks that the almost exclusive use of money as such a benchmark is, so to speak, a coincidence, "an accident that is not found in other worlds than ours."[312] He says:

> It is quite possible that there may be worlds in which no one ever heard of private property in material things, or wealth as it is generally understood; but public honours are meted out by graduated tables[313] as rewards for every activity that is done for others' good. [P126] If these honours can be transferred from one to another without the intervention of any external authority, they

---

[310] [tn] Marshal (1920:22).

[311] Cf. A. Marshall, *Principles of Economics*, H. Ephraim (tr.), Book I, Chapter V. Salzburg 1905, pp. 62, 64, 69 footnote 2.
[tn] This reference appears to be from the German edition based on the 4th edition of the English original, translated by H. Ephraim and others, published in Salzburg in 1905, We have not verified the Marshall's 4th edition. The content is shown in the 8th edition of Marshall (1920:782). See footnote 309 above.

[312] [tn] See footnote 309.

[313] [tn] Graduate tables refer to tables or scales with a structured and systematic division or marking of values.

148

may serve as a convenient and exact benchmark of motives just as money does with us. In such a world there may be a treatise on economic theory very similar to the present, even though there be little mention in it of material things, and no mention at all of money.[314]

Marshall is mistaken if he believes he can identify a difference here. He overlooks the emergence of money and misunderstands its role in our society. His mistake lies in the fact that what, according to his assumption, would be transferred as a reward, etc., from person to person in that other world, would be nothing other than the 'money' of that world, a money that fundamentally would not differ from ours at all; because it would also be a means of recognition.

Jhering has once explained that money and honour serve the same function in the human conduct-process: When the Roman citizen did not demand payment for his services to the state, i.e., without tangible coin, it was because he was compensated in another way, "which, for the man of higher social classes, had exactly the same allure (*Anziehungskraft*) (and one may perhaps add, exactly the same significance) as money did for the lower class: namely, in honour, reputation, popularity, influence and power."[315] It can hardly be described better than with this enumeration of how the service of money as a means of recognition is characterised.

The aptitude of a good to serve as a means of recognition, a means of social differentiation and a means of social accentuation, is the first prerequisite necessary for becoming money. If this aptitude is granted to a good by the behaviour of a group, then the possession instinct, "the sense of property" – the leitmotif of the Forsyte Saga[316] – is awakened. In the

---

[314] [tn] Quoted directly from Marshall (ibid.:782), without translating German.

[315] Jhering (1877:116).

[316] [tn] The central and recurring theme or idea throughout the Forsyte Saga is the concept of possession and the strong desire for ownership or property. The "Forsyte Saga" is a series of novels written by British author John Galsworthy. It

'acquisition of possession' and its multiplication, and in the lavish way of life made possible by possession, in ostentatious display (*Prunkentfaltung*) and extravagance (*Verschwendung*), the 'striving for recognition' (*Geltungsstrebe*) seeks to find satisfaction. Thorstein Veblen has shown how the mere preservation of the caste requires voluntary and ostentatious waste of ownership and [▶127] how such possession-squandering (*Besitzvergeudung*) is further increased by the competition in the display of wealth by members of the leisure classes.[317] Waste naturally precedes the acquisition of wasteful goods. It typically leads to hoarding or treasure-buildup. This is, of course, also just a means to an end, namely the deployment (*Bereitstellung*) for recognition-activities (*Geltungshandlung*), such as public treasure-displays, public treasure-distributions, and public treasure-destructions. The regular usage of certain goods such as mats, rings, woollen blankets, copper plates, etc., for such purposes, especially, of course, for distribution, allows us to see here, as emphasised several times before, the embryonic form of money. For it is these goods that subsequently also serve the familiar uses of money today, namely, as a means of compensation. Thus, wasteful goods become money due to their regular usage in distributions, etc. Likewise, money, as a recognition-good (*Geltungsgut*), is the ultimate wasteful good. Everything that possession signifies for societal life does so to a greater extent when it takes the form of money. In the form of money, possession enhances its societal

---

is a well-known work of English literature that explores the lives, relationships, and social changes experienced by the Forsyte family, a wealthy upper-middle-class British family, over several generations. The saga provides a detailed and often critical look at the values, ambitions, and conflicts within this family and the broader society during the late 19th and early 20th centuries. It is considered a classic of social realism and a significant commentary on the changing mores and values of British society during that era. The term "Forsyte Saga" is often used to refer to the entire series of novels and has become synonymous with the family's story as depicted in Galsworthy's works.

[317] Lester (1907: I, 348).

effectiveness. This is especially true of its force as a means of recognition.

Money is, as must be repeatedly emphasised, originally a means of recognition. Because this is the case, a certain means of recognition is and becomes money. Primitive money is always and exclusively a means of recognition. However, not all means of recognition are money, but only those that serve a certain purpose, namely, preferably that of remuneration, although, as I have said repeatedly, I am inclined to consider certain other uses, such as regular representative distribution-goods, as having a monetary aspect. But when a means of recognition becomes a means of remuneration, that is, a means of compensation, it inevitably becomes money.

In doing so, these means of recognition acquire a new aptitude, the aptitude to be a means of payment or means of exchange. However, this in no way diminishes their role as a means of recognition; rather, it enhances it. Spending money becomes a form of expenditure that bestows recognition. [128] When complaints about luxury have tended to arise at all times, often accompanied by the accusation that the inclination towards luxury is spreading ever further, and especially affecting the lower strata, it is simultaneously a condemnation of avarice for money (*Geldsucht*) and extravagance in money. Because avarice for money and extravagance in money are the means to achieve luxury, which, in turn, is just another manifestation-form of the 'need for recognition.' Money retains its original aptitude even when it has acquired other aptitudes, meaning it has taken on other roles in social intercourses. Even then, it is often much more of a social means of recognition than a means to cover personal demand or 'household economical management' (*ökonomischer Wirtschaftsführung*). The primary purpose of money-earning is not to enable lavish enjoyment of life but to establish 'social recognition.' To be able to live better is not the primary reason why many people work; rather, it is for the sake of the social reputation that money possession bestows. Money is one of the most important means in the struggle for reputation, status, and dignity. In fact, possessing it means all of these things even more than the 'command of disposal and control' (*Verfügungsgewalt*) over consumer goods. Money is a means to achieve many goals, often the noblest ones (the acts of charity, the pursuits of art and science), but just as often, it is used for the most simple-minded and foolish purposes (when it is acquired and spent on trivial and fashionable follies). Behind this, however, there is always the 'social recognition' that actually or supposedly, generally or in a certain circle, confers a certain appearance, a deed, service, or a work.

Money-usage can also consist of merely hoarding a money-good or displaying one's money, because both hoarding and publicly showcasing money-possession provide 'social recognition.'

Just as various money-forms arise from their respective essential money-purpose, this purpose-pursuit also gives rise to its money-forms, especially showcasing-money. From the history of the emergence of money, we know that it is not just any possessions or wealth-bearing goods that perform this function but only very specific ones, such as shell rings, mats, copper plates, etc. [▶129] These items primarily serve display but also play a role in other forms of monetary intercourses (*Geldverkehr*), especially money-distribution. That is why, in contrast to other forms of goods, they are considered showcasing-money. The festival drum called "*mokko*"[318] is both a showpiece and a form of money, as unusual as this "coin" may seem to us. The Dutch government has explicitly recognised it as a "*betaalmiddel*"[319] or means of tax payment.

The philosopher Hegel, in his presentation of the system of needs,

---

[318] [tn] A metal drum.

[319] [tn] The Dutch word '*betaalmiddel*' translates to 'means of payment' or 'payment method' in English. It refers to any form or instrument used for making payments or settling financial transactions. In the context provided, it indicates that the Dutch government acknowledges the *mokko* festival drum as a legitimate form of payment for taxes.

pointed out the significance of the striving of human beings "to assert themselves through distinction (*Auszeichnung*)" (Hegel 1821:§§ 189 ff.). This will need to be revisited later. Here, it should be emphasised that it is precisely money (which Hegel does not mention in this context) that triggers the effect attributed by Hegel to that endeavour, namely, "a real source of the multiplication of needs and their dissemination" (ibid.: §193).

§16. Money as a Social Means of Power

Scientific attempts to formally define society, as is well known, move in various directions. However, in any such conceptualisation, the aim is always to determine the relation of individuals to each other within the coexistence of a group, which we understand as a society. Among the various descriptions of the content of this relation, we most frequently encounter the assertion that this relation, or as one can also say, the societal life-order, is based on power dissimilarity (*Machtverschiedenheit*), encompassing subordination and superordination. "The rulership (*Herrschaft*) of the strong over the weak," as von Schulze-Gävernitz once stated, "is the archetype of society," and P. Klöppel has even described society as "the epitome of power and dependency relations among people."[320] [▶130] One should also consider von Wieser, who placed the power-relation at the centre of his social and economic theory.[321] However, if society is a summation of power-relations, if "the struggle of [coercive] power and weakness" (von Wieser[322]) within the group or among groups is recognised as a social law in its entirety, then it is easy to understand that money can potentially play a significant role within this social legitimacy (*Gesetzmäßigkeit*) of co-living. The extent to which this is the case depends on the structure and composition of society itself.

In a society where class differences are externally marked by the disparity in assets – and this is more or less the case in every society – money serves as a means of indicating class-belonging (*Mittel der Kennzeichnung der Klassenzugehörigkeit*). At the same time, it serves as a means of maintaining classes on the one hand, and of breaking classes on the other hand. The role

---

[320] Schulze-Gävernitz, (1890: I, 113). Klöppel (1887:9).

[321] [tn] Wieser (1983/1926).

[322] [tn] Wieser (1926:65, 1983/1926:47). The quoted text reads "*der Kampf zwischen Macht und Schwäche.*" However, the original Wieser's text is "*im Kampf der Gewalt gegen Schwäche.*"

of indicating class-belonging is inherent in money even in its earliest stages of development, as has been demonstrated in various instances. This is confirmed by the fact that all money originally served as class-money. In addition to indicating class-belonging, this money, which we have come to know as hoard-money, also serves as a means of reinforcing and preserving class divisions (*Klassenscheidung*). In this way, however, money becomes at the same time the key that gives those who know how to put themselves in possession of it access to the classes based on ownership. This aptitude (among others) has made certain precious-items, which are signs of rank and honour, become money. In other words, the significance attributed to certain goods as power-symbols (*Machtsymbol*) is part of the chain of causes that turns such goods into money. Thus, money emerges in life as a carrier of power (*Machtträger*).

In a completely different way, the money of later stages of evolution of money, especially the 'general commercial-money,' or as we can also say in this context, the money of capitalist economies, has become a means of indicating class-belonging. While in the case of hoard-money, it is primarily its type (*Art*) and, to a lesser extent, its quantity that determines class-belonging, now it is solely its quantity that plays this role. [❡131] The concentration (*Zusammenballung*) of money becomes the means of expressing class status (*Klassenstellung*) or the power-status (*Machtstellung*) of classes. The size of one's money bag (*Geldsack*) determines his belonging to a class. The aristocracy transforms into a money-aristocracy (*Geldaristokratie*).

The goal of every ruling class, however, is to maintain the acquired power-status and preserve it for their children and descendants. This leads to the inclination to continually raise the barriers established by possession, that is, to increase the class-distance (*Klassenabstand*) established by possession. Naturally, this triggers counter-efforts from societal groups that do not belong to these strata. The assisting means for both [class] is money. Thus, money appears in such a society as an expression of power disparity (*Machtunterschiedlichkeit*) in society and, at the same time, as a means of both balance (*Ausgleich*) and reinforcement (*Verstärkung*) of these disparities.

This role is attributed to money not only in economic societies but also in societies that are not or are not primarily based on economic relationships, as shown in the history of the emergence of money. However, the economic society is the sphere in which the social power-effect (*Machtwirkung*) of money reaches its strongest development. Here, it proves to be the force that, like no other means, transforms the soul of the economic individual, awakening and inciting their 'orientation towards earning' (*Erwerbssinn*) and, in its excess, turning it into unbridled greed for earning (*Erwerbsgier*). For it is only through the embodiment of all possessions in money that the unrestrained development of the earning-spirit (*Erwerbsgeist*) is allowed. As it permeates economic life, it replaces the 'principle of sufficient demand-satisfaction' (*Prinzips der genügsamen Bedarfsbefriedigung*) with the 'earning principle' (*Erwerbsprinzip*). It is money that provides a leeway (*Spielraum*), a purpose, and a clear path for the exertion of this 'orientation towards earning.' Sombart expressed it this way:

> In the realm of material striving, conquering means earning, i.e., increasing a sum of money. And nowhere does the striving for the infinite (*Unendlichkeitsstreben*), the 'striving for power' (*Machtstreben*), find a field of exertion so suited to its innermost essence as in the chasing (*Jagen*) for money, this entirely abstract value-symbol (*Wertsymbol*), freed from all organic and natural limitations, whose possession then increasingly appears as a power-symbol.[323]

[p132] In a capitalist economic society, money is an unparalleled means of asserting and realising economic power. The market is the arena where the economic 'power-struggle' (*Machtkampf*) takes place. Money is the weapon in this battle, which has undergone special adaptation and

---

[323] Sombart (1919:328).

development within the capitalist economic society.[324] Among the various requirements and aptitudes for which money is prepared and oriented in this regard, the development of the **purchasing power of money**,[325] which has become unlimited only in that economic society, takes the foremost position. This will need to be discussed in more detail later.

In market price-formation, we can find the power-claims (*Machtanspruch*) of the parties involved, some offering money and others seeking money. Just as money was originally a means of expressing the status of social power-status and rank-status, it has now become a 'means of expressing economic power-authority' (*Ausdrucksmittel wirtschaftlicher Machtbefugnis*). At the same time, it becomes a means of realising power in the market. From a sociological perspective, market price-formation, as correctly observed by H. Sauermann, always appears as an expression of actual power differentials (*Machtdifferenz*).

For it is not the reproduction costs of labour, goods, etc., that are reimbursed and established in the price, nor are the subjective

---

[324] [tn] Cf. A similar observation can be found in Max Weber (1922:58):

A market struggle (*Marktkampf*) between (at least relatively) autonomous economic units (*Wirtschaften*): Money prices are the product of struggle and compromise, and hence are outcomes of power constellations (*Machtkonstellation*). 'Money' is not an innocuous 'voucher of entitlement to undefined utilities,' to be transformed into anything one might want. This would require the complete abolition of the quality of prices as an expression of the struggle of man against man (*Kampf von Menschen mit Menschen*). Money is instead and primarily a means of struggle (*Kampfmittel*), and price is the outcome of this struggle; it is a means of calculation only in the form of a quantitative expression of an assessment of *Chancen* [chances] in a struggle among differing interests.

Cf The above translation is based on Tribe (Weber 2019:201-2), with slight modifications by the translator.

[325] [tn] Refer to Translate Note at p. 354 on 'purchasing power of money' versus 'purchasing force of money.'

considerations of suppliers and demanders what constitute the price. Instead, the power differentials that exist in fact due to the 'power of disposal and control' (*Verfügungsmacht*) determine the price. Wages, interest, risk premium, rent, and quasi-rent are the actual power expansions formed in the market, gained through power-striving efforts as the winning of 'power of disposal and control.'[326]

I would like to add that money serves as both the means to bring economic 'power of disposal and control' to deployment and to reap economic success.

[P133] This function of money is linked to another characteristic that is unique to money in capitalist economic society, namely, its ability to become capital. "The money-form is," as Sombart correctly notes, "always the first and equally always the last form in which capital necessarily dresses itself."[327] By becoming capital, money transforms into a social power of the highest order because it appropriates the power of capital itself, and it continually enhances this power through its unique capital-building force.

Once money has become capital, it determines the entire production process. It becomes a dominant power that not only subjugates all those involved in the production process but also the dependent consumers. With its rulership claim, it ultimately does not stop even before the state.

Just as money proves itself as a capital-building force, it also serves as the form and force through which capital experiences its concentration, that accumulation which not only gives a character to the capitalist society but also determines its course of development, ultimately leading to a confrontation between this society and the state. The outcome of this confrontation also determines the fate of money. In the monetary regime, the state creates, i.e., in the money that is the creation of its legal-order

---

[326] Sauermann (1931:403).

[327] [tn] Sombart (1969: Vol. III.,135).

(*Rechtsordnung*),[328] the state that recognises the power claims of capital provides it [i.e., capital] with the tool to enforce those claims. It is the money of the liberal-economical state (*liberal-ökonomischer Staat*), money with unlimited purchasing power.[329]

Possession always implies power. In the liberal-economical economic state, money is the means to unfold and activate the power-function (*Machtfunktion*) of possessions in an enormous way. It unleashes forces in the social world, much like nuclear force does in the world of physics, and thus becomes a scary power that binds or at least attempts to bind the state, law, religion, custom, etc. in its chains, often with success in ninety out of a hundred cases.

The power-function of money grows in proportion to the expansion of the range of goods, the means of need-satisfaction, that can be obtained with money. [P134] This is the case in a liberal economy where "everything" is available for money; where the wealthy can satisfy all their needs with money, except for the few that cannot be obtained with money, no matter how important they may be. Even for life and health, one can bargain with money.

Money as a means of power (*Machtmittel*) brings about a goods-distribution that is not determined by the natural urgency of needs but rather by the most financially potent demand. Thus, even with a sufficient supply of goods for demand, a social scarcity of goods can arise.

Money inherently represents organised power, but beyond that, its usage tends to lead to certain institutions that amplify its power. The development of banking and credit systems, the stock market, and international payment-traffic, along with all their possibilities and consequences for politics and the economy, signify an immense

---

[328] [tn] Knapp (2023/1923:2).

[329] Cf. This will be discussed again in section § 22, "The Capital Function of Money."

multiplication of the power of money. The term 'dollar imperialism' (*Dollarimperialismus*) is an expression of this phenomenon.

The power attributed to money is also reflected in the fact that the names for money become symbols: the dollar symbolises purchasing power, the ruble symbolises bribery, the pound sterling symbolises economic stability, the drachma symbolises worthlessness, and so on.

Money is the means to mobilise possession-power (*Besitzmacht*) and concentrate it in an ever-decreasing number of hands. This makes it possible for small power groups to exert international economic control, enabling them to influence legislation[330] and significantly shape foreign policy. When a few individuals control the entire railway system of a country, when the basic industries, the world's oil and coal resources, rubber and sugar production in the major producing countries, and so on, are controlled and directed by small power groups, money becomes the most effective means of acquiring, exercising, and solidifying this power.

Money not only controls public opinion but also shapes it.

[**135**] However, the power conferred by money, or rather money possession, does not remain unchallenged. As the exploitation of classes and social parasitism grow in the highly developed monetary economy, fertile ground is prepared for modern socialism and communism. As the shift in economic attitudes takes place, leading to changes in the economic system, money must relinquish some of the abundance of power it holds in capitalist society. It is not completely dethroned but is significantly restricted in its power-authority. The absolute purchasing power that money has achieved in the capitalist economy, which will be discussed further elsewhere, is taken away from money. As a result, money loses some or most of its significance as a social means of power [obtained] in

---

[330] [tn] Cf. The wealthy can access more easily to "functions, to a centre of power in leading offices that is unattainable to the poor," so that they can attain more political power and esteem (Simmel 2011/1900:236).

the capitalist economic society. In more precise terms, this means that economic power becomes subordinate to political power. Societal life is no longer organised and evaluated purely from an economic perspective but rather from a political one. Of course, politics also values money as a means. Money becomes a political 'power instrument' (*Machtinstrument*), serving politics as a means of gaining and distributing social power.

§17. Money as an Economic Means

The purpose-change that money has undergone in the course of its development leads, as has been shown multiple times in the course of this investigation, from money as a means of recognition to money as an economic means. Money, as we have seen, does not originally originate in the economy. Of course, this is not to say that primitive money cannot also originate in the economy, i.e., in economic intercourses. This has often been the case: however, this "economic money" (*Wirtschaftsgeld*), meaning money originating from and serving economic intercourses, is not the oldest form of money, just as the earliest usage of money does not primarily serve economic purposes. [?136] However, as societal development progresses, money becomes an economic means, and the economic role it assumes becomes increasingly significant for economic flows (*Wirtschaftsablauf*) themselves. It grows into this role and adapts more and more in its appearance and effectiveness.

While it is a core idea of our societal theory of money to see money not only as a means of economic co-living (*Zusammenleben*) but also as a means and expression of human relationships in general, this should not lead us to overlook the predominance of the economic nature of money in a broad social context, namely that of the societal economy. If the economy is a form of social action (H. Sauermann), that means money in the economy is nothing but a creation of social action as well. Social action is always directed towards a specific purpose. Recognising this purpose also means becoming aware of the means-deployment used to achieve this purpose, i.e., understanding the service of money in the economy with regard to money.

In the economic societal co-living of people, money initially appears as the economical means (*ökonomisches Mittel*) of goods-procurement. This has been explained many times. However, this commonplace truth should not be understood to mean that money is an invention of purposefulness (*Zweckmäßigkeit*). The usage of money as a temporary measure

(*Aushilfsmittel*) did not arise from considerations of practical reason (*praktische Vernunft*), as has been shown, but rather from the necessity of market-intercourse, the same necessity that led to the means of transport (*Transportmittel*) or the establishment of market peace. So, for understanding the function of money as an economic means, it is not so much about its purposefulness but, as Schumpeter has stated, about "the indispensability of a money-good for the mechanism of the market,"[331] or, as we can add, for the economically rational process of goods-production, goods-distribution, and consumption.

[P137] In a capitalist economy, the fulfilment of any demand primarily occurs through societal production (not through a self-sufficient economy), specifically through the market. Such demand-fulfilment through the market and from the market requires a general means of exchange that facilitates the adjustment between the diverse offerings of commodities and services and the equally varied demands, which in rare cases align directly with the individual offers. Those integrated into this economic system are constantly in the roles of buyers and sellers facing each other. Consequently, they constantly think in terms of money because, in a free market-economy, demand can largely be satisfied only through earning with money. As mentioned, money serves as a means of exchange in this context, but this leads to another use, namely as a means of price-expression (*Preisausdrucksmittel*) and as a means of economic accounting (*Wirtschaftsrechnung*). Thus, money becomes a general economic means that serves not only in conducting exchange-intercourses but, more importantly, in controlling production and, therefore, the production and distribution of the social-product.

Although money was at first only a means of goods-exchange, the development of economic-intercourse has led to the mediating good being regarded as the essential thing and its attainment being regarded as the very

---

[331] [tn] Schumpeter (1970/1908:282).

aim of exchange activity. Economic activity becomes earning-oriented economic (*erwerbswirtschaftlich*) when it is aimed at a monetary gain. This affects the role of money in economic life in two ways. **Money becomes both an economic goal and a means of earning**. It becomes an economic goal, meaning that all economic activity seems to be directed solely towards earning money. As explained in another context (§12), this is something that Aristotle already recognised. As is well known, he strongly condemned the process which, by becoming more and more widespread and by displacing the natural-economy, as the philosopher thinks, with money-making (*chrematistic*), which is dangerous for the state, or, as we would say today, by making the 'earning-oriented economy' (*Erwerbswirtschaft*) take the place of the 'subsistence economy' (*Bedarfsdeckungswirtschaft*).

[♭138] Let's hear again, and in addition to what has already been said, what the thinker from Stagira [Aristotle] says about the emergence of this earning-spirit, which makes money the economic goal in the 9th section of the 1st book of *Politics*. However, as soon as this commodity, namely money, he explains, was introduced due to the natural 'need for exchange,' another type of art of earning arose, namely merchants and peddling (*Krämerwesen*). Likely, this art of earning was also very simple in the beginning. However, as the experience progressed, it evolved more and more into the skill of determining how and where to make greater profits through exchange.

Aristotle contrasts this art of earning (*chrematistic*), which is solely focused on money-earning through commodity-sales, with the art of acquisition (*Erwerbskunst*) which is in accordance with nature, namely, economics or the art of household management. Unfortunately, however, as the Greek sage must realise, this is also seized by the same earning-spirit (*Erwerbsgeist*). Aristotle says:

> This tendency arises because people aim solely for a life of luxury. Since the desire for mere enjoyment knows no bounds, one desires

the means to satisfy it in an unlimited quantity.[332]

To emphasise the seriousness of his accusation, he adds a few lines later, repeating himself:

> From this, this false art of earning has arisen; for since there is no end to pleasures, one seeks the means by which to acquire such pleasures endlessly.[333]

It is not the subject of investigation here whether Aristotle correctly interpreted the motives behind the development he described, but he certainly recognised the essence of the matter with unerring insight.

As mentioned, in the economic society, money is not only an economic goal but also a means of earning. The well-known Marxist formula M-C-$\acute{M}$ expresses this concept effectively.[334] The original market process, symbolised by the formula C-M-C (commodity to money to commodity), is replaced by another process represented by the formula M-C-$\acute{M}$ (money to commodity to more money). The former means selling a commodity to buy another commodity, while the latter means buying a commodity with the intention of selling it at a profit. [♪139] Therefore, the formula should be more precisely expressed as M-C-$\acute{M}$, which means money to a commodity to more money ($\acute{M}$ represents the initial deployment of money

---

[332] [tn] Aristotle (1932: Book I.iv. 1257b39-1258a4). Our translation is based on Aristotle (1872: 34-35), which was referred to by the author. The English translation (Aristotle 1932:47) reads:

> The cause of this state of mind is that their interests are set upon life but not upon the good life; as therefore the desire for life is unlimited, they also desire without limit the means productive of life.

[333] [tn] Aristotle (1932: Book I.iv. 1258a7). The English translation (Aristotle 1932:47) reads:

> Owing to this the second kind of the art of wealth-getting has arisen. For as their enjoyment is in excess, they try to discover the art that is productive of enjoyable excess.

[334] [tn] Marx (1963/1893:32ff.).

plus rent, entrepreneurial profit, etc.). In the first formula (C-M-C), M represents exchange-money (*Tauschgeld*), while in the second formula (M-C-Ḿ), it represents purchase-money (*Kaufgeld*). Whether the process in every case on the market follows this scheme does not affect the explanatory value of the formula. Also, its use should not be considered as an endorsement of its Marxist interpretation.[335] In any case, the fact that money serves both as a means of earning and a earning-purpose (*Erwerbsziel*) cannot be expressed more succinctly than through the latter formula (M-C-Ḿ).

Money as a means of earning is capital. We refer to that portion of income which is used in some form in production (in the broadest sense), thus serving the creation of goods and services. The aim of production or earning-oriented economic activity in general is a monetary gain (*Geldertrag*). The generation of a monetary gain presupposes monetary accounting, i.e., the allocation of expenditures and revenues in money. This is carried out through money itself (and not through another benchmark like labour, for example). Money primarily acquires the capability for this function through its usage as a means of exchange.

The estimation of goods in money, as it arises from the use of money as a means of exchange, gives money a new aptitude: it becomes an expression of economic value-magnitudes and value-relationships, thus becoming a benchmark for value-comparison. As a benchmark for value-comparison, money is an indispensable tool for rational economic management; because economic comparisons of costs and benefits, expenses and income, are only possible through monetary accounting. This reveals a new aspect of money as an economic means: it is a **means of account.**

As long as various means of payment coexist in a monetary community, several of these means of payment can also serve as means of account simultaneously. [ℙ140] The logic of accounting and economic reasoning

---

[335] Cf. On this point, refer to Muhs (1927: 145 ff.).

(*wirtschaftliche Vernunft*), however, leads to a selection among the various means of payment, with the result that eventually the unit of one means of payment becomes established as the unit of account for general usage.

The service of money as a means of payment, as is evident, is also of essential importance for its service as an economic means. However, it is not purely economic and must therefore be discussed in a different context. On the other hand, the service of being a means of account (in contrast to the payment service) arises directly from the economy itself; because wherever economic activity occurs, there must be accounting. Economic accounting involves numerical estimation and comparison of expenses and returns in terms of money. By using money as the unit of account in economic accounting, the 'value-magnitude representation' associated with the monetary unit becomes the benchmark for assessing the value of all economic resources, goods, and services. In this capacity, it serves as a measure of goods-distribution and becomes **the participation-measure in the social-product**, thus serving as a means of economic value-transfer and the allocation of economic values. This is the final step in the development of its functions so far.

The development of money as an economic means is closely linked to the development of its purchasing power. Only a largely unrestricted purchasing power of money can fulfil the tasks associated with its role as "being an economic means." This will be briefly mentioned here, and for further details, please refer to the following discussions on the purchasing power of money (see Chapter 4, § 27).

§18. Money as a Means of Exchange

The usage of money as a means of exchange appears to serve individual economic interests more than societal ones. In fact, its development and proliferation seem to come at the expense of the societality of exchange-intercourse.

Exchange was originally a matter of social arrangement. [P141] It did not take place between individuals but between groups.[336] There was no need for a genuine means of exchange in this case, simply because there were no chains of exchange yet, and exchange was still an isolated and individual process. This societality of the exchange-intercourse is loosened as the usage of a general means of exchange becomes established. This is replaced by a new 'social' : the interconnection of all economies involved in the exchange-intercourse through the means of exchange, creating an exchange-society that continually becomes more tightly knit. Money as a means of exchange does not satisfy any personal need, neither as a means of production nor as a means of consumption, but only, as it has been correctly understood for ages, the 'societal need' for convenient exchange.

Three sections can be distinguished, which can be schematically outlined as follows, without going into details:

Goods that are used or desired as means of distinction, as well as those demanded as means of consumption (salt, tea, tobacco), or technically useful goods (copper, iron), often serve the gift-exchange. It may be noted in passing that the possession and usage of such means of consumption and means of production often also signify distinction. The mentioned goods are those gifts through which various other goods can be obtained. During regular congregations or gift-exchange journeys undertaken specifically for this purpose, such goods are limited-use, one-sided means of exchange, meaning they have purchasing power only towards specific,

---

[336] Cf. Bastable (1888). Similarly, Simmel (1900:58).

few goods and are not further used as means of exchange by the recipients.

Another step is when goods like these become means of exchange, which the recipients can also use as means of exchange when demanded, making them two-sided means of exchange. However, the range of use of these means of exchange is still limited in such a way that a specific type of money is needed for certain goods and services. For instance, cowrie shells or glass beads may be used to purchase food, but not ivory, weapons, or slaves.

[ｐ142] A third stage in the development of exchange-money occurs when the good used as money becomes 'money as a general means-of-exchange' (*allgemeines Tauschmittelgeld*). This means that any generally available good can be acquired with the same type of money, and the primary function of this good then becomes that of an exchange-medium.

Not every good can serve as money, but some, indeed many, can, and the number of goods that have temporarily played the role of money is large and varied. Development leads to a selection process aimed at restriction of the goods that can be used as money. This is especially the case at the stage of means of exchange-money, where eventually the number of money-goods is limited to a few, if not just one. Because that is precisely the main advantage of means of exchange-money, that it is the good in the units of which not only the value of all other goods can be expressed but also, with its help, the exchange between all other commodities and service-performances can be accomplished in the simplest manner. Therefore, times of economic retreat [i.e., inefficiencies] occur when it is believed that the number of money-goods should be increased, and various things are indeed elevated to the status of money, a status that loses significance in proportion as grain, eggs, tobacco, etc., are used side by side as money or, more accurately, find a money-like use.

The developmental pathway outlined here, as mentioned in a different context, provided Karl Knies with the reason to propose a departure from the customary dichotomy of economic goods into means of consumption and means of production. Instead, he proposed a tripartite categorisation into means of production, means of consumption goods, and means of exchange.[337] This classification and categorisation not only highlight the special status of the good that has gained the aptitude as a means of exchange but also characterise a stage in economic development.

Rodbertus has placed particular emphasis on the usage of money as a means of exchange going hand in hand with the development of the division of labour. [p143] A means of exchange facilitates a division of labour, and he said:

> There must be something that each person accepts in exchange for the product they are offering, ensuring that everyone can obtain what they need.[338]

It is money.

The proposition that money, in its origin, is primarily and essentially a means of exchange is a doctrine that, based on our investigations, we repeatedly find ourselves unable to accept. Anyone who seeks the origin of money in the exchange-economy closes themselves off from insight into the beginnings of the monetary framework as well as the genesis of exchange itself. Exchange, as shown earlier, arises from gift-traffic. Initially, it does not play an explicitly economic role, or at least does so only exceptionally. Instead, it gradually grows into it. The primitive monetary intercourse emerges quite independently of the development of exchange-intercourses. Initially, it does not involve any exchange-activities at all. They are only dressed in the money-form during a long development, with the ultimate result being that money becomes the sole means of exchange, and exchange-intercourses, as in today's economy, are only carried out in the money-form. A change in economic and societal significance and semantic change of exchange-activities is the natural consequence of this

---

[337] Knies (1885a:20).

[338] Rodbertus (1842: V. §1:135 ff., §5:147, §6:152).

development.[339]

Exchange-money is the tool of exchange-intercourses. It elevates or, even more so, unfolds exchange-intercourses to a higher level, making the entire economy appear as a network of exchange relationships and exchange processes. Hence, one has probably seen the task of economics in explaining the mechanism of the exchange-intercourse or even referred to "monetary phenomena as the sole problem of economic theory" (Liefmann). Such an economy is called an exchange-economy or a commercial-economy (*Verkehrswirtschaft*).[340] Such an economy is inconceivable without money or money-usage. The exchange processes in this economy lead to the emergence of prices. [₽144] The means of exchange thus becomes a means of expressing prices and thus becomes money, i.e., a specific type of money that we have learned as exchange-money.

The needs of monetary exchange-intercourses are what determine the further evolution and ongoing development of money. Primitive money is a personal necessity commodity, a treasure, a precious usage-objective, etc. Those are the things that, as such, provide immediate demand-satisfaction as ornament, weapon, tool, etc., and only provide means of exchange services in a secondary capacity, so to speak. From this origin, the good used as money gradually detaches itself. Its other uses as ornament, weapon, tool, etc., become less important and eventually disappear completely, along with the consideration of such usability. In place of money whose substance or form allows the use of the money-good as a means of production or consumption, there comes one that, as a good, sensibly allows no other use, rather it is exclusively dedicated to circulation, i.e., to

---

[339] Cf. On this, refer to §8 of this book.

[340] [tn] We translated *Verkehrswirtschaft* as 'commercial-economy,' representing a more explicitly developed form of exchange-economy (See the notes by Tribe at Weber 2019:484).

monetary service.

This ongoing development of money, which represents a new phase in the evolution of the monetary framework, is a consequence of the development of the exchange-intercourse brought about by money itself. It is the exchange-money (and not the hoard-money) that undergoes this transformation to the perfection of its purpose.

Indeed, it is money as a means of exchange that, in progressive interactions, develops economic-intercourse and transforms the economy. Consequently, it becomes a constant driving force and constraint for adapting money as a means of intercourse to needs it has itself generated. These needs become apparent in continuously growing and densifying economic activities. Just as the economic possibilities offered by trade could only be limitedly exploited without the existence of the general means of exchange, money, progress in the division of labour and thereby the increase in individual economic performance would also be impossible without the advance of money as a means of exchange. [P145] Closed household-economy relies on the provision opportunities offered by its own production; on the other hand, economies intertwined with money in exchange-intercourses experience an enrichment of their provisions through numerous other economies. Money dissolves the so-called closed household-economy; it enables the independence of individual economic activities, their separation from self-sufficiency, and their development into distinct economic sectors, namely, enterprises as profit-oriented organisations and components of the national economy.

Thus, money, particularly as a means of exchange, is not only the facilitator of the economy but also, to a great extent, its creator and shaper. Certainly, an exchange-intercourse is possible without money; such has indeed existed, albeit with limited scope and content. However, when utopian economic reformers envision a future economic order that, in their view, could do without monetary exchange-intercourses, they overlook the fact that in an economy organised in such a manner, another means of exchange would likely replace the familiar money we use today.

In essence, this alternative means of exchange would still be a form of "money."[341] The emergence of money as a means of exchange is both an expression of the development of 'economic needs' (*wirtschaftliches Bedürfnis*) and a prerequisite for their satisfaction, as well as the expansion and spread of these needs.

While it may seem that exchange has its roots in individual aspirings, it is, in reality, a societal phenomenon, and indeed one of the most significant manifestation-forms of social relationships. In this context, money as a means of exchange plays a crucial role as a means of binding social connectivity. Exchange is not limited to economic goods-traffic, but it assumes a particular significance in this context, especially when facilitated by money. Exchange interconnects the economic activities of individuals and nations, transforming them into national economies and the global economy. Even international trade relies on money, albeit with a different role than it plays within domestic national economies.

---

[341] Cf. Compare my comment on the view of A. Marshall above on p. 147.

§19. Money as a Means of Expressing Prices

[♭146] Anthropologists have often pointed out that the transactions among indigenous peoples are governed by the principle of reciprocity and retribution or by the principle of service and counter-service. This extends to the point where the idea of compensation even permeates the closest family relationships. For example, as Thurnwald has reported, and as has been mentioned in another context, among some tribes engaged in farming, a husband must compensate his wife with a gift for any expression of affection or love.

The concept of compensation, both in social and economic intercourses, is based on convention (*Herkommen*). Equality between service and counter-service is demanded, but originally, it was not an economical principle but rather a dispositional one. Therefore, the counter-service often depends either on the status and assets of the provider or on the rank and possessions of the recipient.

Wilhelm Müller (Wismar) reports about Yap[342]:

> In one respect, Yap money differs significantly from our own. Its purchasing force is influenced by the social status of the buyer and the possessor of the commodity. If one wishes to buy something from a person of higher standing, an elderly man, or a woman, they must pay more than in other cases.

I myself have experienced such cases. When I had a half-finished handbasket made by a woman from the village of Gătšăpắr,[343] for which I paid 50 Pfennigs, the Chief Priest Rûĕpón suggested that I might want to give one mark instead, considering that it was made by a woman. I wanted to purchase a powered whale skull from the magician Iltšómăr from Omĕắn, which had no value for him, and he was entirely willing to part

---

[342] [tn] See footnote 159.

[343] [tn] A district of Gagil in northern Yap.

with it. However, when I offered 2 marks for it, he declared in utmost indignation that it was not a payment fit for an elderly man.[344]

Such price differentiations, as W. Müller seems to assume, are not a peculiarity of the 'mental landscape' (*Vorstellungswelt*) of the population of Yap. [p147] Instead, they are not uncommon among primitive peoples, and they have not entirely disappeared from the modern world either.[345]

It is a long journey from such compensations to what we now call prices today. Even exchange originally takes place according to the traditional rules outlined earlier. The exchange-ratio (*Tauschverhältnis*), or the exchange-rate (*Tauschsatz*), is customarily determined and is almost always held fixed. This remains the case even when the monetary economy has already replaced in-kind exchange, meaning that prices are discussed in economical terms. D. Varé reports on a journey through China in the year 1927:

> In Ichang (宜昌),[346] a pound of potatoes costs 20 cents, irrespective of whether the commodity is scarce or abundant. The price remains the same, but the pound itself varies in weight, depending on the circumstances.[347]

This example nicely illustrates the compelling influence exerted by conventional compensation concepts. Anthropology also has similar examples of fixed prices and price-systems from various cultural circles to report.

However, the question of how these compensation assessments, which eventually become prices, come about, has hardly been asked, let alone answered. It is certain that economical value considerations originally do

---

[344] 'Yap' in Thilenius (1929-1936: 133).

[345] This has been particularly emphasised by F. J. Neumann with reference to the motives behind price-formation. See Neumann (1896: 255, 265, and 295).

[346] [tn] A city located in the Hubei province of China.

[347] Varé (1931:431 f.).

not, or only exceptionally, play a role. These considerations are usually not only quite remote from primitive humans, but they also lack the mental capacity and life experience required for psychologically weighing demand and expenses or comparing benefits and costs. The ethnographic literature is rich in examples of the complete failure of primitive people when faced with such tasks.[348] With this statement, no expectations or standards taken from our level of civilisation should be imposed on the indigenous people. [P148] Instead, the question is simply raised – without any value judgment – about how money assumes the role that makes it a motor of the economy as a means of price-expression.

Where there is an exchange, evaluations also take place. However, as mentioned, these evaluations originally do not come from the realm of economics. The same applies to money. Is it then possible that exchange and money already intersect outside the sphere of economics? Let us recall that exchange arises from gift-traffic, and in gift-traffic, money also originates. In this sense, the connection is indeed established. The particular good that acquires the favoured status of a means of exchange in the original gift-traffic, typically becomes, to the same extent, a means of price-expression, that is, money. The price, however, is the amount of money for which a good is acquired. The question of whether prices can be expressed in ways other than money may be left aside, as we are only discussing money as a means of price-expression, which is to say, money prices. According to the perspective presented here, the price is created only through and via money. It expresses an exchange-ratio in terms of a certain number of units of a customary means of exchange. The concept of such exchange-ratios, which we call prices, arises from the use of such means of exchange. Characteristic of the role that money plays as a means of price-expression in our economy is that it led Liefmann to the statement

---

[348] I have explained elsewhere how originally price determinations are made in exchange-intercourses (Gerloff 1940: 175 f.). You can also compare the examples provided by M. Schmidt (1920: I 212 f.) albeit in a different context.

that price-formation is the only purpose of money. This claim certainly does not require refutation here. However, it should not be inferred that the means of exchange performance of money (at least money of a certain stage of development) and thus its price-formation function should be underestimated.

When money is referred to as a means of price-expression, there is more to it than it appears and is commonly understood. In a free-market-economy, money serves not only to express price-magnitudes but, above all, it serves for price-determination (*Preisermittlung*). Indeed, as is well known, money itself influences price-formation. [℘149] Due to various reasons, both the exchange-ratios of goods and the purchasing force of money continuously change in the free market-intercourse. Money serves as the instrument and measuring tool through which those changes are determined and established. The measured numbers, however, are the prices. Thus, in a free-market-economy, money is primarily a tool for price-determination or, more precisely, price-calculation (*Preiserrechnung*). It is a process similar to the determination of stock market prices. However, this process always takes place in market-intercourse, preceding both the exchange and the 'price-execution' (*Preisvollzug*),[349] which manifests in paid prices. It is easy to see that different things are meant when in one case money is referred to as **a means of price-calculation** (*Mittel der Preiserrechnung*), and in the other, money is described as **a means of price-execution** (*Mittel des Preisvollzuges*) or a means of price-payment (*Mittel der Preiszahlung*). The former is the 'measurement-unit money,' while the latter are magnitudes of purchasing force expressed in the measurement-unit, as they serve through the use of money signs or other means of transferring income portions to payments.

The usage of money as an exchange mediator (*Austauschvermittler*)

---

[349] [tn] An execution of a transaction based on a determined price.

transforms money into a means of price-expression. By gaining this aptitude from that service-performance, it simultaneously acquires a new scope of application: **based on price-representations** (*Preisvorstellung*), **it becomes a means of economic accounting, a means of income-measurement** (*Mittel der Einkommensbemessung*) **and a means of income-allocation** (*Mittel der Einkommenszuteilung*), and the registering of all economic events and magnitudes in terms of money. These monetary expressions themselves are, however, nothing more than prices. Since all economic value-calculations are done through prices, all national economic goods-distribution and income movement follows the path through prices, the full understanding of the '**price-manifestation service of money**' is the only way that leads to an understanding of the national economic process as a whole. For the function of price-manifestation, which is peculiar to money in the commercial-economy, means more to this [i.e., commercial-economy] than just a statement about trade-terms (*Austauschverhältnis*). It becomes the regulator of this economy itself. This will need to be revisited in another context.

[℘150] Just as the service of money as a means of exchange is socially conditioned, meaning it requires and also establishes societal intercourse, the 'price-manifestation service of money' is similarly conditioned and founded on societal intercourses. Free prices, meaning those not determined by governmental authority, are always a social phenomenon and an expression of social relationships, particularly social power-relations. Just as money is a creation of social action, so are prices. Social action is what brings about prices. This leads to the question of the grounds for price-determination (*Preisbestimmungsgründen*). This question can only be answered here with regard to money, i.e., in terms of what the determining factors of prices are from the perspective of money.

Money and price are mutually dependent concepts. Price-formation, as mentioned earlier, occurs only through and via money. Specifically, prices are determined by the available amounts of money, which is to say, by the incomes that enter the market. In other words, prices are determined by the utility-assessments (*Nutzenschätzung*) made by those who have incomes, within the limits and in accordance with their income. The starting point and foundation in this process are somehow legacy prices to which new prices are linked. At the same time, numerous other prices, as all prices are more or less interconnected, contribute to incorporating each new price into the existing price-system. Therefore, all price-formation occurs both in connection with legacy prices and with an eye toward certain other prices.

Money, however, not only has the role of being an expression of prices but also exerts a significant influence on price development or price changes. The Quantity Theory of Money (*Quantitätstheorie*) aims to explain the impact of changes in the circulating money quantity on the price level and price movement. The conventional view is that prices, in general, and on a broad scale (although not necessarily individual prices), move in the same direction and to the same extent as the money supply. This means that an increase in the money supply tends to raise prices, while a decrease tends to lower them. [ρ151] However, it is necessary to make a number of qualifications or additions to this. Fluctuations in the quantity of circulating money require some time to have an effect on the price level, that is, to become effective and manifest themselves. The time interval, often referred to as the "lag," between the occurrence of a change in the money supply and its corresponding effect on the price level varies depending on circumstances. Furthermore, the Quantity Theory of Money, like the theory of price-formation in general, assumes the presence of money with unconditionally purchasing-powerful (*kaufmächtig*) money or the existence of free price-formation. However, when prices that are set or determined by statute replace free prices, which might be better termed compensations (*Entgelt*) rather than prices, money loses the direct influence on price-formation that price theory presupposes. Prices then cease to be purely economic, and they become politically regulated. Certainly, even these prices do not lack a societal foundation, but they are not determined by the free play of social forces (convention, custom, economical interests, etc.) but rather by political power-relations. The unique aspect of such price-settings or, more accurately, price determinations, is that they can have a significant influence on money depending on their extent and scope, and under certain circumstances, they can even lead to a transformation of its nature. This will be explained further in the section §27, "The Purchasing Power of Money."

§20. Money as a Means of Account

In the "*Nouvelle Relation de l'Afrique occidentale*" [New Account of West Africa] published in 1728, J. B. Labat reports:

> The iron that is brought to them from Europe is in bars, and these serve as real or ideal currency (*monnoye*) in the markets they engage in.[350]

The French African traveller is describing a process that repeats itself everywhere there is economic money-usage, especially in commercial transactions: the concrete monetary unit – [P152] in the above example, the iron bars, in other cases a specifically characterised piece of livestock or a piece of fabric, and so on (Gerloff 1940: 118 f.) – becomes the ideal unit of account and, therefore, a means of account. The usage of a unit of account is by no means exclusively tied to exchange-intercourses, as is commonly assumed. Even in cases where such transactions do not exist or have not yet been established, the usage of a unit of value as a unit of account and a societal means of account for the 'value-magnitude representation' (*Wertgrößendarstellung*) is often customary. Phrases like nine-, twelve-, hundred cattle-like etc., are known from the Homeric poems. These terms were used to indicate the value of competition prizes and presents, such as a tripod, armour, a slave, and so on.[351] On the other hand, it is undeniable that money, as a means of account, i.e., monetary accounting, has its essential application in the economic sphere. In fact, one can confidently say that a modern societal economy (*Gesellschaftswirtschaft*) is not possible without calculation in money terms.[352]

Money becomes a unit of account through the habitual

---

[350] Labat (1728: II, 307).

[351] [tn] See Laum (2023/1924).

[352] [tn] See Weber (1927: Chapter XXII).

(*gewohnheitsmäßig*) usage of certain goods for various performances (*Leistung*) [of obligations], such as penances, tributes, bride-purchase, and other contributions, which are associated with 'value-magnitude representations.' These 'value-magnitude representations' are originally expressed not only in the number of units of the disbursement-good (*Leistungsgut*), whether they are cowrie shells, rings, axes, or quantities of metal by weight, but they are also objectified (*vergegenständlicht*) through these goods themselves. That is why they are also money, namely, material-money (*Sachgeld*). However, for the mere 'value-magnitude determination' (*Wertgrößenbestimmung*), there is no need for physical material-money. The value-magnitude represented by the unit of this material-money can serve purely in terms of accounting to determine the value-magnitude of goods and services. They are then used as a unit of account and as a monetary representation (*Geldvorstellung*) – accounting-money (*Rechnungsgeld*). Thus, money, to borrow a term from A. Schäffle – albeit in a different sense than he intended – is the societal means of 'value-magnitude representation' or the "societal symbol of value magnitude" (*gesellschaftliches Größensymbol des Wertes*).

The usage of a unit of account does not necessarily require a connection to a corresponding form of money. The good whose value-magnitude serves as a unit of account does not need to be money. [▶153] The unit of account 'livestock' is a good example of this (Gerloff 1940: 121 ff.).[353] Another example can be found in a report by Mansfeld. When a claim is made for two slaves among the natives residing at the Cross River in Cameroon, it does not mean two actual slaves. It means rather different objects of this [same] value.[354] The slave is a unit of account but not money.

---

[353] [tn] See also Laum (2023/1924).

[354] Mansfeld (1908: 131). One should also compare the explanations regarding monetary accounting systems in Enderlen (1929: 40 f.).

The primary application area of money as a means of account is, as previously mentioned, in the economy. However, the term 'means of account' poorly conveys what this actually entails because, in fact, money is more than just a mere medium that could be replaced by something else. It is an indispensable component of economic management and, above all, economic reasoning (*Überlegung*) and economic 'disposal and control' (*Verfügung*). Economic action in the 'earning-oriented economy' (*Erwerbswirtschaft*), especially in the capitalist economy, requires a comparison of expenses and income, which can only be done in monetary terms.

The statement that money represents a facilitation of exchange-intercourses and thereby makes a market possible is an observation that has been repeated in all discussions about the essence of money since Aristotle's time. However, this does not particularly illustrate the role of money in the economy for us. Rarely, however, have we observed that the usage of money as a means of exchange not only provides convenient facilitation but also, as a means of account, is an indispensable prerequisite for exchange-intercourses, specifically for the exchange-economic earnings by capital goods, i.e., goods of a higher order. The earnings of real productive assets, like any economic activity in the long run, require monetary accounting. Without it, rational choice among potential production paths, as characteristic of capitalist economies, would be inconceivable. [p154] Through monetary accounting, the goods to be used in the production process and the expected returns are brought together on a common basis. Subsequently, economic action is aligned with this information, meaning that economical production capabilities are determined, and the corresponding 'disposals for production' (*Produktionsverfügung*) are made. Only through the unit of account, money as the benchmark of the value of all economic goods, can one form a judgment about economic success and, consequently, the 'adequacy of means-deployment' (*Zweckmäßigkeit des Mitteleinsatzes*), i.e., capital and labour.

The more widespread the usage of money becomes, the more money as a unit of account becomes the means of expression for all commercial-economic evaluations (*verkehrswirtschaftliche Wertschätzungen*). Economic-intercourse makes use of the value-magnitude "money," thereby compelling all participants to base their decisions on this unit of account. In this way, money becomes a means for economic rationality (*Mittel der wirtschaftlichen Rationalität*); in fact, one can say that without money or, more precisely, without monetary accounting, there is no 'economic efficiency' (*Wirtschaftlichkeit*). The "in-kind accounting" (*Naturalrechnung*) if one can even speak of it in terms of strict calculability, often lacks rationality to some extent. It is not truly a calculation because it lacks the accounting-magnitude (*Rechnungsgröße*) or unit of account (*Rechnungseinheit*) and the accounting-measure (*Rechenmaß*) that money provides.

Every economy, whether it is truly economic or rational, requires control through monetary accounting. This naturally applies primarily to an 'economically oriented economy' (*ökonomisch ausgerichtete Wirtschaft*), even if the pleonasm is allowed,[355] but administrative policy-driven economic management also cannot do without it.

Money as a means of account facilitates the order of action (*Ordnung des Handelns*) that constitutes the economic aspects of earning and consumption. Especially, the rational order of earning-oriented economic actions is not possible without money or, more precisely, without monetary accounting. The extent and direction of production in a free-market-economy are determined by demand. However, demand wields this peculiar power to determine the scope and direction of production because it presents itself as a money-offer (*Geldangebot*) that promises

---

[355] [tn] The phrase "economic oriented economy" can be seen as an example of pleonasm, as 'economy' already implies an economic orientation, making the additional words somewhat redundant.

monetary gain to entrepreneurs. Based on this anticipated monetary gain, entrepreneurs align their production, the deployment of capital and labour for the production of goods for the market, and the sale of goods in the market through monetary accounting. [p155] Therefore, the development of the earning-oriented economy goes hand in hand with the development of the monetary economy. The advancement of rationalism in the realm of earning-oriented economic thinking and action, and ultimately the complete rationalisation of the entire 'earning-oriented economy' with its boundless expansion of pursuit of profit, is based on money as a means of account, which serves as the means of expression for all economic events as recorded in the bookkeeping of both private and public sectors.

The primary application area for meaningful monetary accounting is the free commercial-economy. However, even an economy with elements of central planning requires monetary accounting as a support and guidance for its commercial-economic components. Without it, economic efficiency (*Wirtschaftlichkeit*) and success with it may suffer significant losses, potentially posing a serious threat to the entire economic system. This is also one of the reasons why proponents of socialist or communist economic systems, such as Owen, Pecqueur,[356] and others, may not want to abolish money, even if they may propose or recommend a specific form of it. In fact, money, at the very least as a unit of account, is indispensable even for a collectivist economic order that does not want to perish due to its inefficiency. Money can only serve as a unit of account and remain as such in the long run if it is a means of exchange or possesses purchasing power, albeit to a greater or lesser extent, i.e., if its conversion into commodities, whether they are consumer goods or productive goods, is

---

[356] [tn] Adolphe Blanqui (1798-1854) was a French socialist thinker who played a role in early discussions of communism, advocating for social reforms and the concept of association as a means to achieve a more equitable society.

guaranteed at all times.

The usage of money as a unit of account and thus as a means of account creates a societal relationship structure for which W. Heller coined the term accounting-community (*Rechnungsgemeinschaft*).[357] He views the accounting-community as a consequence and further development of the payment-community (*Zahlungsgemeinschaft*). The accounting-community is a prerequisite for the market-economic cohesion of the elements within a national economy. [p156] However, price-formation is not only the result and confirmation of its [accounting-community's] presence through prices but also signifies its continuous reinforcement and expansion.

---

[357] Heller (1927: 99, 105).

§21. Money as a Means of Payment

Payment is the delivery or transfer of a sum of money in order to fulfil an obligation. Simply put, in the Prussian Land Law, it is stated: "If the debtor fulfils the obligation by means of money, this is called a payment" (I, 16, § 28). Payment is often predominantly or even exclusively considered a phenomenon of legal life. In reality, it means much more: it is the realisation of social purposes. It is a one-sided formalistic consideration to perceive the essence of payment solely in its legal sense. In payment, the social and legal meanings of the process are, in fact, inseparably linked; they are two sides of the same phenomenon. To be a means of payment means that a good serves a specific use in society, in social intercourses. This use is both socially and economically-technically, as well as legally significant.

Opinions are divided as to whether the function of money as a means of payment is inherent to money itself or merely incidental, whether it constitutes an independent function in its own right or is merely an inseparable accessory to others, G. Cassel goes so far as to answer the question of what should be considered physical money by saying that any generally accepted means of payment, recognised as such, is "money." Carl Menger, on the other hand, argues that there is "no justification for attributing any special function to money as a means of payment or as a general means of payment."[358] G. F. Knapp, on the other hand, decidedly places the service of a means of payment above all other services of money. To him, money is nothing more than the state-declared means of payment. In the German language, according to Knapp, money always signifies a formed (*morphic*)[359] means of payment. [157] Money, as Knapp puts it,

---

[358] [tn] Menger (1909:579, 2002/1909:51).

[359] [tn] From Greek '*morphe*' (μορφή), which means 'form' or 'shape.' It means a means of payment has a certain shape. To quote Knapp,

> Our 'legal-order' stipulates the admission of only certain shaped pieces as

is a *"chartal* means of payment."[360] On the contrary, S. Budge argues that

---

valid means of payment. The 'marks' on these pieces are prescribed by law. It is these particular pieces that are referred to in the following. The means of payment commonly used today always possess the legal characteristic of being in a 'piece format' (*Stückverfassung*). In the legal sense, they are considered '*morphic*.' Morphic means of payment, as we will see, do not always constitute money, but all money falls under the category of *morphic* means of payment. *Morphism* is a condition but not sufficient for the 'monetary regime.' (Knapp 2023:25).

[360] [tn] To quote Knapp:

Debts that are denominated in value units can be discharged by handing over marked pieces – be they coins or 'financial-certificates' – that have a certain validity in value units according to the 'legal-order' (*Rechtsordnung*). Such pieces are called 'chartal means of payment'; they are called money. The validity [of money] is independent of the contents of the pieces. The 'legal-order' emanates from the state, therefore, money is a state institution (*Einrichtung*) (Knapp 2023: 23; 1923: IX).

Perhaps the Latin word '*Charta*' has a similar meaning to 'mark'; however, if it does not, we still prefer to use the term '*Charta*,' primarily because it allows us to form a new adjective, '*chartal*,' that is easily understandable. Our means of payment have a 'marked' or '*chartal* constitution.' Only with payment tokens (*Zahlmark*) featuring *chartal* pieces can payments take place among the civilised nations of our time (Knapp 2023: 30; 1923: 32).

For the meaning of '*chartal*,' it is worthwhile referring to Max Weber's more sophisticated definition of '*chartal*'based on Knapp:

means of exchange or of payment will be called *chartal* if they are artefacts that have, within a personal or regional domain, been lent a conventional, legal, agreed on, or compulsory degree of formal validity (*formale Geltung*) and that have been broken down into specific units, that is, have a specific nominal value, or are either a multiple or a fraction of this value, purely mechanical calculation in terms of this nominal value being thereby facilitated (Weber 2019:160).

This particular word, '*charta*,' is believed to have its origins in the ancient Greek words '*kharássō*' (χαράσσω, meaning 'I scratch, inscribe') and its noun form '*khartēs*' (χάρτης, meaning 'papyrus'). However, some scholars contend that its

payment has never been understood as anything other than the transfer of money, both historically and in contemporary times. To call money a means of payment would, therefore, mean defining money as a means of transferring money, which appears to be a circular definition. K. Helfferich, in conclusion, believes that the function of money as a general means of payment is part of its fundamental functions and is on an equal footing with its function as a general means of exchange in this regard. However, K. Knies expresses the situation quite clearly:

> The process in question, when it simply involves satisfying a claim to our assets, is by no means a measurement of value – nor is it an exchange act or buying-selling act. So, if money is used to accomplish this and has been used for a long time, then it cannot be related to the function of the value-standard or the means of exchange. The function of a means of payment or a medium of exchange must be unique, and their distinctiveness and equality need to be explained in more detail.[361]

I believe that this perspective is entirely agreeable.

It is an arbitrary interpretation to wish to consider all transaction processes involving payments, such as the payment of rents, leases, penances, taxes, etc., as exchange-activities, and then to view payment services as exchange services. This does not lead to any clarification. To be a means of payment means something entirely different from being a means of exchange, without denying, of course, that the means of exchange service of money is significantly influenced by its use as a means of payment. Certainly, the reverse is also true, meaning that because money was often more of a means of payment than a means of exchange

---

etymology remains unknown. In Latin, it pertains to a sheet of papyrus or parchment employed for writing or drawing. Presently, the theory of money that stems from Knapp's ideas is commonly referred to as 'chartalism.'

[361] Cassel (1932:341), Menger (1923: 282), Knapp (1918: 31), Budge (1931: 13), Helfferich (1910:249), Knies (1885b: 221).

historically, it gained acceptance and widespread use as a means of exchange. Let's remember that money originated from the gift-traffic. [§158] The gift made in the form of money is a payment. However, even the gift that becomes money due to its peculiar and regular use (such as rings) or what we call money for that reason, is a payment. Payment by no means requires an exchange-economic intercourses beforehand. Where tributes are paid, taxes are levied, penances are imposed, and gifts are made, money can come into play long before there were any exchange-economic relations.

Most uses of money as a means of payment were already in practice before exchange-intercourses, and consequently, the use of money as a means of exchange became customary. Once established as a means of exchange, this practice continued to lead money, due to its unique 'force for exchange' (*Tauschkraft*) or stronger 'purchasing power' (*Kaufmacht*), to be increasingly recognised as a disbursement-good (*Leistungsgut*) wherever charges (*Last*) are imposed. The imposition of levies, the determination of contributions and penances, and the calculation of rents, interest, and other claims in money allow both a distribution of charges and revenue (*Aufbringung*), as well as an application of means that are independent of the natural form of goods. Just as money as a means of exchange eliminates the limitation of reliance on self-production or in-kind exchange for provisions (*Versorgung*), it also renders all exchange economies, especially the public ones, independent of the constraints that in-kind-disbursements (*naturale Leistung*) entail. Of course, this is only the case to the extent that money possesses purchasing power. The development of the payment service of money is, therefore, largely dependent on its use-potentiality (*Verwendungsmöglichkeit*) as a means of exchange.

When money is referred to as a means of payment, that is, as the medium for performing payments, the question arises as to whether one can make payments in ways other than with money. Knapp is clear on this opinion.[362] [⟨159⟩] I prefer to stick with the customary usage of language, according to which, as Heyne (1890-95) states, the concept of '*zahlen*' (to pay) in modern language is restricted to the act of counting and laying down money to settle a debt. Expressions like '*mit dem Leben zahlen*' (to pay with one's life) or '*Fersengeld geben*' (to run away from debt)[363] and the like are figurative expressions that cannot argue against this linguistically established view that making a payment is inseparably linked to the concept of money. What cannot be paid with money is not payable at all. '*Zahlen*' (to pay) means 'counting' or 'adding up' (*zuzählen*). In the true sense, it involves counting (or adding up) money pieces for the purpose of transferring them to the recipient. Just as one can 'count blows' (*Schläge zuzählen*) [or tallying physical harms done by others] and, figuratively speaking, 'pay back' (*heimzahlen*) [or seek revenge] using them [i.e., the number of blows counted], the term '*Zahlung*' (payment) is also used for the mere transfer of income portions or asset portions expressed in monetary units, even when no physical items are being exchanged. Giro-payment (*Girozahlung*) is conducted using giro-money

---

[362] G. F. Knapp distinguishes between 1. payments before the emergence of money (*autometallism*, more generally *authylism**), 2. *chartal* payment, which is synonymous with payment in money, and 3. *giro* payment, which is payment without the use of money (Cf. Knapp 1918: 2 ff.). On the other hand, F. von Wieser states, and I concur with him, "Payment can only ever be made in money" (Wieser 1924: 182).

[tn] * A neologism formed by combining the Greek words '*auto*' and '*hyle*.' It refers to the 'money system' or constitution that relies on a physical good as money, emphasising its inherent qualities. *Autometalism*, specifically highlighting the use of 'metal' as the preferred physical good in the 'money system,' is a subset of *authylism*. See Knapp (2023: 8, 430).

[363] [tn] '*Fersengeld*' is a German expression that translates to 'running away from debt or responsibility.' It essentially means avoiding a situation or escaping from an obligation, often in the context of financial matters. The term is derived from the idea of someone turning and running away, showing their heels ('*Ferse*' in German) to escape a situation.

(*Giralgeld*), so, according to our understanding, it is by no means a payment without the use of money. The measurement-unit in value-calculation (*Wertrechnung*), i.e., the means of account, is still money.

Money can be a different entity than the measurement-unit for a means of payment. There is no shortage of historical examples of the divergence between the value-calculation unit and the payment unit.

The peculiarity and, at the same time, the independence of the payment process lies in the fact that the payment process is by no means bound to exchange, as if it were only the continuation or completion of the exchange. Instead, the process encounters us, long before there were exchange-intercourses, in the form of certain unilateral services. Money emerged as payment-money (*Zahlgeld*), not as exchange-money. As demonstrated, hoard-money is payment-money, but not yet a means of exchange because it originally did not serve the purpose of exchanging. If one were to classify the phenomena observed in payment-traffic in the service of levies, penances, offerings, as well as the payment of tributes and various kinds of payments, as falling under the concept of exchange, it would signify a wholly unwarranted narrowing of the money-concept. The understanding of the historical development of money would thus be closed off, just as the sociological understanding of the monetary framework itself, and ultimately, the theoretical clarification of the monetary phenomenon in general.

[160] The situation is similar with the social, economical-technical, and legal significance of a means of payment. Each of these aspects is relevant in its usage. It represents the triple effect of a single act, but each one requires a completely separate perspective. This has often been overlooked, as the service of money as a means of payment has been exclusively considered as a legal fact. However, what needs to be presupposed or given is the societal nature of the process, which only acquires the meaning of a legal norm or rule in its regular, social enforcement. Certainly, this does not lack social significance, but what is essential for understanding social connectivities is the realisation of social

purpose-settings inherent in the usage of a means of payment.

Therefore, when money is used as a means of payment, it serves a triple function: a social, an economical, and a legal one. The social function is the most comprehensive, as it encompasses the other two since it signifies the realisation of social purposes or the establishment and expression of social relationships. These relationships can have economical content, and they usually do, and they can also be legally significant. Therefore, it follows that a payment can be a subject of consideration both as an economical and as a legal process.

Money as a means of payment, therefore, cannot be defined solely in economical terms, unlike Huppert suggests,[364] nor solely in legal terms, unlike Knapp proposes. One can only say that the legal function of money as a means of payment has come to the forefront of our economic system. As a result, it has gained significance in both economical and societal life. It is understandable, therefore, that modern monetary theory has primarily focused on the legal aspect of the means of payment function. Further elaboration on this will be provided in the discussion on "Money and the Legal-order" (§ 25).

---

[364] Huppert (1938: 36).

§22. The Capital Function of Money

[¶161]Among the various ways in which money has contributed to social development and continues to influence it today, perhaps the most powerful is the capital function of money.[365]

In everyday language, the word 'capital' is often used to refer to money capital (*Geldkapital*), meaning "a borrowed or available sum of money" (as defined by K. Knies). 'Money capital' is [based on] the idea that money, as expressed by Turgot, "represents every kind of value, just as, conversely, every kind of value represents money."[366]

The capital nature of money is a subject of controversy in theoretical national economics, as is well-known. However, from a sociological perspective of money, there can be no doubt about its capital function, as posited by K. Marx, Adolf Wagner, C. Menger, A. Amonn, W. Sombart, J. Schumpeter, and others.[367] This is not to say that the explanation of the capital function of money is unequivocal by any means. That is certainly not the case. Böhm-Bawerk includes money as a form of capital to the extent that it "serves the execution of a production process." He explains:

For the same reasons that anyone counts the wagon and horses with

---

[365] [tn] See Laum on the emergence of the concept of capital (Laum 1954/55).

[366] Turgot (1776: LIX). Cf.Also, Böhm-Bawerk (1908-1911a: 777 ff.).

[367] As evidence of the debate on this matter, consider the following references: Franz Oppenheimer once remarked in a review of contemporary writings on the theory of money that almost everywhere, even in the better and best writings, one can find elementary errors and confusion. He referred to the view that "money is somehow capital" as an "inescapable error" and added, "money is not capital in any scientific sense" (Oppenheimer 1924:399). In contrast, A. Spiethoff in his contribution (1908: Contribution IV, 28) asserts that "money has been viewed as capital with rare unanimity from Adam Smith to the present." For further reference on this topic, see Passow (1913: 40 ff.), which provides a good compilation of the ambiguous usage of the word "capital," and also Menger (1888: especially 37 ff.) and Sombart (1927: 127 ff. and 147 ff.).

which the farmer brings home the grain and wood as means of production and capital, [p162] it is also consistent to count the objects and apparatus for the broader national economic 'home-bringing' (*Heimführen*) – the products themselves, the roads, railways, ships, and money as a tool of commerce – as capital.[368]

Against this view, S. Budge argues:

> To the extent that it is an only indirectly useful good, money is on par with the means of production. However, an essential difference should not be overlooked above this similarity. All means of production, of whatever order,[369] assist us in obtaining first-order goods through technology. Money, on the other hand, has nothing to do with the production of goods in general. It certainly serves the **goods-acquisition** to a high degree, but it is not, like transport goods, a **technical** assisting means of this process, meaning it does not serve any usage in the sense of technology.

One could at most describe money as a kind of means of production in a metaphorical sense because, in a market society, it not only facilitates but indeed makes the goods-procurement possible in the first place. However, it is more accurate to consider money as a *sui generis* [distinct and unique] good. This idea is sensible (*zweckmäßig*) because the emergence and value of money are determined by laws that deviate from the principles governing other economic goods.[370]

Capital is the term for money that is allocated for specific purposes. The capital function of money is thus tied to its mode of use. Money is considered capital when it serves or becomes a means of generating monetary returns. The deployment of money for use in production

---

[368] Böhm-Bawerk (1902:70).

[369] [tn] 'Order' refers to the hierarchical structure of products, with consumption goods being the first order. Higher-order goods are positioned further away from consumption goods in this hierarchy.

[370] Budge (1933:41).

classifies that money as capital. Not all money is capital, but any money that is used in the mentioned sense, that enters into production as a cost-good (*Kostengut*), is considered capital.

I understand by the capital function of money the aptitude of money to acquire capital goods (including labour force) for productive use. [163] Money designated for such purposes is called 'potential capital' (*potentielles Kapital*) (Sombart). It arises through savings. The allocation of savings for productive purposes, i.e., for the establishment, operation, or expansion of a capitalist enterprise, signifies the transformation of potential capital into 'actual capital' (*aktuelles Kapital*).

The capital function of money is a historical-legal category, not an economical one. Like all historical-legal categories in economics, it has emerged from the interaction of economics and law and can only be explained within the context of the private economic organisation's relationship with the legal-order, from which it derives its economically and socially significant and far-reaching role.

The capital function of money is rooted in its 'exchange mediating function' (*Tauschvermittlungsfunktion*). It is, therefore, a consequence of the purchasing power of money. Carl Menger rightly criticised the conventional definition of money as a general means of exchange and a means of payment as being too narrow in his famous article "Money" (1909: 555 ff.). He argued that this definition "does not include the reference to the mediating function of money in the capital market" (ibid.: 580). And A. Amonn rightly speaks of the second primary function of money as a means of capital-amassing, which is closely related to the first function as a 'general real means of payment (*allgemeines reales Zahlungsmittel*). According to Amonn, "money amounts" mean "concentrated abstract 'power of disposal and control'," which means they directly represent capital.[371]

---

[371] Amonn (1927: 381).

The capital function of money presupposes: 1. a far-reaching possibility of goods-acquisition and goods-disposal (*Güterveräußerung*) by means of money, and 2. an equally far-reaching possibility of goods-utilisation in production. This means that to the extent that the purchasing power of money experiences contraction or expansion in relation to the means of production, its capital function also experiences contraction or expansion.

The fact that money can be used as capital, that it is, so to speak, the most perfect form of capital, gives it its tremendous social power. [p164] Karl Marx demonstrated this in a very effective, albeit somewhat one-sided manner in his work "*Das Kapital*."

The capital nature of money is thus tied to the manner in which money is used. The use itself is a technical matter and is not of immediate interest here, but it is sociologically significant. It has sociological implications, and this is what a societal theory of money is concerned with.

The journey from primitive money-usage, as sufficiently marked in Chapter 1, to the formation of money capital is quite extensive. Money-earning does not necessarily imply the use of money for capital investments.

Money becomes capital at a particular economic and legal stage of development, namely when the subjective and objective purchasing power of money[372] is not subject to significant restrictions and confinements, such that anyone wishing to participate in the economic process (*Wirtschaftsprozeß*) with their monetary assets has the legal ability to acquire and dispose of goods and services. This first occurs historically in trade. The prevailing doctrine therefore also sees the accumulation of money profits as the original source of large assets or money capital.[373]

---

[372] [tn] Refer to 234ff. and 235ff. for the objective and the subjective purchasing power of money.

[373] Cf. See also Sombart, "*Die Entstehung des Geldkapitals*," in Sombart (1927: 152 ff.).

Karl Marx expressed this situation with concise statements: "Commodity circulation is the starting point of capital," and "the final product of commodity circulation is the initial form of capital."[374] The underlying idea behind this concept is well-known: money brings about a transformation in the exchange-economy. In place of exchange focused on acquiring commodities, as explained earlier (on p. 163), there emerges exchange directed toward earning money. According to this, money possession is the starting point of exchange. Money is the means to gain more money through buying and selling commodities. Money becomes the form of appearance of capital. This marks the complete monetisation (*Vergeldlichung*) of the economy.

[165] The intention here is not to examine "the transformation of money into capital" or engage in any discussion of the explanations that Karl Marx provides under this heading in the second section of the first volume of his main work, "*Das Kapital.*" Instead, the aim is no more than a brief explanation of the capital function of money. Our study does not focus on capital itself; rather, it aims to recognise the capital function of money as a social factor. Therefore, it is not of interest at this point to determine whether the process of money becoming capital, as presented by Marx or others, is correct and complete. Instead, the sole concern here is the fact that money becomes a form of capital, giving rise to social relatedness (*soziale Bezogenheit*) of significant importance.

The purchasing power of money is the prerequisite for the possibility of large-scale and extensive private capitalist economies. By acquiring the capital function and thus becoming a means of capital formation (*Kapitalbildung*), money strongly incentivises self-interest and places it in the service of capitalist economic development. This gives rise to 'money capitalism' (*Geldkapitalismus*), which takes on its distinct form in loan-capitalism (*Leihkapitalismus*).

---

[374] [tn] Marx (1962/1890:161).

The profound transformation of economic life that money has brought about over the past two centuries, the transformation that has shifted from household-economy to a societal economy, is the result of its capital function. It is the capital function of money that has given market economic events the form commonly referred to as a capitalist economy. It opens up paths and possibilities for the accumulation of capital that prove to be of great economic and social significance. It enables the free combination of production factors, both variable and constant capital, in a perfect manner, thus paving the way for the development of the capitalist economy by unfolding all productive forces and aggregation of means of production. This is reflected not only in quantitative economic growth but also in a transformation that contains the seeds for the development of a new form of economy, namely, the societal economy.

[p166] Money in its capital function enables societal forms of enterprises and favours the emergence and predominance of joint-stock companies in production, trade, and transportation. It paves the way for what is called 'participatory capitalism' (*Beteiligungskapitalismus*), the concentrations of capital (*Kapitalzusammenballungen*) in large combinations (*Konzern*) and interest groups. The crucial fact for our consideration is that this creates a network of financial obligations, commitments, and dependencies, resulting in changes in income-distribution and possession-relations that transform the social structure of society. This fact finds its most pronounced expression in the subjugation of ever-widening segments of the population to the money power of capital (*Geldmacht des Kapitals*), in the uprooting of the population and a population movement determined by capital interests. It also manifests in the economic dependence (*Verunselbständigung*) of individual existences and the incorporation of the masses as wage labourers into capitalist enterprises. At the same time, an economic approach predominantly oriented towards demand-fulfilment is replaced by a more or less unrestrained earning-oriented economy, which Aristotle criticised and referred to as money-making (*chrematistic*). In place of a

predominantly static economy with extensive self-provision and in-kind compensation, a dynamic economy emerges in which economic returns are monetary gains, incomes are distributed in money, and it is left to the recipients to decide how they want to use this money. An economy arises and initially spreads across all states within the European-American cultural sphere, in which the majority of the population maintains its livelihood through earning money and spending money. Income generation and income expenditure are closely related to capital formation and capital valorisation (*Kapitalverwertung*), and vice versa, in this context. It is a process in which, for various reasons not discussed here, surges and blockages alternate with each other. [¶167] The result is that economic flows take place in a tidal change, in a continuous change of the economic conditions similar to the ebb and flow of the tide, which has the character of business cycles (*Konjunkturzyklen*).

The capital function of money plays a significant role in this process. Namely, it facilitates that peculiar transformation of capital that begins with the money-form and repeatedly ends with it, or, as Marx expressed it, concludes with the "money-form of the commodity." This circulation of money as capital is subject to disruptions that occur with a certain regularity. Theories of business cycles and crises have sought to uncover their causes. Their findings, which can only be obtained through a thorough examination of the capitalist economy, are, however, controversial. In any case, capital formation is of particular importance in this cycle of money and its disturbances. The problem of '**full employment of money**' (*Vollbeschäftigung des Geldes*) arises.

As money acquires its capital function and thus becomes increasingly significant in the life of nations, the appreciation of the role of money and the evaluation of its usage in society also change. For example, P. Lehmkuhl in his *Theologia moralis* (7th edition, I, 698) points out that one must understand from this semantic change of money why the Church now allows taking interest, although not in as solemn a manner as it had previously prohibited.

The emergence of the monetary economy is what makes the capital function of money valid and effective. The development of the capital function goes hand in hand with the development of the money economy. In the advanced monetary economy, the capital function of money serves as a motive for the formation of money capital, which in turn contributes to the creation of real-capital (*Realkapital*), because the reproduction and multiplication of material-capital (*Sachkapital*) typically occur through money. [168] Thus, in this sense, one can also say that money makes the capitalist mode of production possible in the first place if one understands the capitalist mode of production as "the mode of production that takes place under the rulership and guidance of the owner of capital, the capitalists," as mentioned by Böhm-Bawerk.[375]

Capital is created, as has been emphasised repeatedly, through saving and the productive dedication of savings.[376] However, as Böhm-Bawerk himself says, this is only a partial answer to the question of capital formation. The further question, according to Böhm-Bawerk, is:

> What does it depend on whether people want to save in order to produce products, want to produce, and actually do produce?"

It is not necessary to delve into this here, but what needs to be noted is something else, namely, that money is the means that people can and generally do use for saving, and it is precisely this means that enables the productive dedication of savings. This is socially significant but also not insignificant for money itself. Not all money is equally suitable for capital formation or, as one could also say, equally fulfils the capital function. This also belongs to the problem area that I have outlined with the development of the concept of the purchasing power of money (see §27).

The aptitude to be a means of capital formation gives money its strong society-shaping force. Without this aptitude, money would have had only

---

[375] Böhm-Bawerk (1908-1911b).

[376] Cf. Böhm-Bawerk (1909: Bd. 1, 209 and 139).

a minor socialising influence. However, as soon as it becomes apparent that money is not just a means to acquire goods with use-value (*Gebrauchswert*) but also a means to form capital that yields returns, and therefore a means to self-multiplication, i.e., to acquire more money than is given up, that it can yield a profit, it becomes, as previously explained in another context,[377] an earning-purpose (*Erwerbsziel*) beyond the measure necessary for demand-fulfilment. It is saved to contribute to production; capital is formed. Sombart has outlined the circumstances that determine the size of saved amounts, "the magnitude of potential capital."[378] [p169] The transformation of potential capital into actual capital, i.e., the investment of saved amounts for productive purposes, is the actual process of capital formation. It is governed by the 'law of capital valorisation' (*Gesetz der Kapitalverwertung*) because capital, according to Marx, has only one vital impulse: to valorise (*verwerten*) itself. "Capital is the surplus value that breeds value" (Marx). [379] W. Sombart sees the 'drive for valorisation' (*Verwertungsstreben*) of capital as the primarily operative causes and ultimate driving forces of modern economic development.[380]

The valorisation of money as capital initially faced hindrances and various constraints, the removal of which took several centuries. Overcoming the belief in the sterility of capital, to which Aristotle and Thomas Aquinas subscribed, is one of the greatest contributions of the late Middle Ages. It starts with the breaking of the canonical prohibition of interest and reaches its full triumph in the era of 'economical liberalism' (*ökonomischer Liberalismus*) with the abolition of all economic constraints

---

[377] [tn] Refer to p. 165.

[378] Sombart (ibid.:156-7).

[379] [tm] This remark appears to be an interpretation or rephrasing of Marx's concept of capital as a value that generates surplus value, as discussed in Volume II of "*Das Kapital*" (Marx 1963/1893:32-34).

[380] Sombart (1902: II, 7).

and the realisation of complete economic freedom of contract.[381] Money as capital creates in this course a social order that is fundamentally different from that determined by land possession, namely, the capitalistic [social order].

It is the peculiarity of money as capital that it continually sets the economy and society in motion, thus becoming a means of constantly shifting possession-relations, resulting in a society undergoing constant transformations and the major societal upheavals of the last two centuries that are rooted in the opposition between possession and non-possession.

Hegel, Lorenz von Stein, and many other social researchers have identified 'possession differentials' (*Besitzunterschied*) as a characteristic of an advanced form of society. While 'possession differentials' in society certainly predate money capital, money as capital has increased and expanded possession differentials, thereby contributing to the development of society. [P170] Indeed, while it tends to increase 'possession differentials,' it also threatens to disrupt the handed-down form of society or has already done so, thereby creating the modern class society. Money capital, and even more so, interest on capital (*Kapitalzin*),[382] have become social factors that, under certain conditions, primarily appear as bearers of class formation and class division. This is why the socio-ethical and economic discussions of the late Middle Ages were dominated by an attitude that was full of mistrust towards the art of money-earning. A different appreciation of money and capital emerged only with Calvinism, which bestowed a consecration on money-earning

---

[381] [tn] See Laum (1954/1955).

[382] [tn] It differs from 'interest on loans' (*Leihezins*) and signifies:

> 1. the calculated lowest normal possible Chance of profitability imputed to material means of acquisition by profit and loss accounting; 2. the interest rate at which commercial enterprises obtain money or capital goods (Weber 2019/1922:184).

that, if done in the right way, turned it into a virtue.

Since then, the significance of money capital in the economy and society has grown immensely. It has become essential to the capitalist economy. If modern economic theory focuses on the analysis of the phenomenon of capital as one of its core problems, the subject of this analysis is the capital function of money.

IV. The Domains of Influence by Money

§23. Money and Division of Labour

[♭171] Society has been defined as a group of people connected through the division of labour as stated by Sacher (1899) and Mises (1922). Mises argues that society is an organism, which means, "Society is a division of labour."[383] It becomes evident from his further explanations that the word 'organism' means more than the usual comparison of society to the human body (the view as an organism). Mises identifies the starting point of the societal division of labour in the individual inequality of human abilities and the diversity of external living conditions on the Earth's surface. According to his perspective, these two facts practically compel humans towards division of labour. This is undoubtedly correct. However, it is not necessary to affirm the reduction of everything societal to the development of the division of labour and the "equating society and the division of labour" and to endorse the assertion that the principle of division of labour reveals the essence of societal becoming (*Werden*). Here, it is sufficient to characterise the significance of the division of labour in a very general sense as follows: wherever it begins, it also determines societal development. It should not be overlooked, however, that while its origin may be rooted in the two mentioned facts, its further development is substantially influenced by social power-relations. Even in natural economic conditions, there is sometimes a significant division of labour. However, its expansion and prevalence are still tied to the emergence of regular money-usage.

[♭172] Division of labour does indeed presuppose society, but it also influences society by causing its continuous transformation through its own progressive development. Even the division between "urban and rural" and between "citizens and farmers" presuppose money-usage. Urban life

---

[383] [tn] Mises (1940:115).

and the "denser" urban population, which forms the basis for the advancement of production division, have become fertile ground for increased money-usage. K. Knies sees in regular and established money-usage, which facilitates exchange-intercourses, the necessary support for the emergence of new divisions of labour and the emergence of new economic groups. Money-usage not only enables a more advanced division of labour but also guides towards it.[384]

The clarification of this situation is the task of social theory. However, it has made little effort in this regard, rather it has mostly focused on uncovering the principle of division of labour. The studies associated with names like Turgot, Ferguson, Adam Smith, Karl Bücher, Gustav Schmoller, Durkheim, and others are well-known.

Rodbertus was the one who emphasised the significance of money for the expansion of the division of labour. "To conclude the division of labour," he says, "money is necessary." He illustrates this with an example and then goes on to explain:

> However, money is only conceived empirically in this way. In its essence and concept, it is the means of liquidation (*Liquidationsmittel*)[385] for the division of labour.

In this sense, he refers to money as "a voucher (*Bescheinigung*) that everyone accepts and a directive (*Anweisung*) that everyone honours."[386]

Division of labour is, of course, as numerous ethnographic examples teach, possible without the use of money as a means of exchange. However, it is equally certain that the societal division of labour experiences

---

[384] Knies (ibid.:433).

[385] [tn] 'Liquidation' refers to settling debts or exchanging goods and services. When people engage in various specialised tasks in a division of labour system, they often need to trade their specialised products or services with one another. Money serves as the common medium through which these exchanges occur.

[386] Rodbertus (1842: 146 f. & 152).

significant facilitation through the usage of money as a means of exchange. Money relieves individuals from the hardship of self-provisioning or seeking necessary opportunities for barter to sustain themselves. Consequently, it allows individuals to engage in specific professions and specialise. The exertion of professions such as artists, teachers, researchers, and others in our economic system relies on the existence of money.

[p173] With a growing population, the pressure to the division of labour arises. Karl Rodbertus stated:

> The fortunate circumstance that has made civilisation possible is the fact that divided labour is more productive than non-specialised labour.

But, as mentioned, he also recognised that money is an essential assisting means in this regard. Division of labour, often referred to as the driver of social progress, would have a meagre impact without money. In this sense, A. Forstmann describes money as the true root of culture and civilisation.[387]

It is not the division of labour that relieves people from the compulsion to work for their daily subsistence demand; rather, it is money as the means of disposal and control (*Verfügungmittel*) over the goods produced in the process of production based on the division of labour that enables people to enjoy the fruits of the division of labour and the leisure hours gained through the division of labour. Poverty and luxury are possible without an economy based on the division of labour, but broad welfare for the masses is not. The development of culture and civilisation for the large masses is hardly conceivable without the benefits of the division of labour and the medium of money that makes these benefits accessible to them. Mass welfare would certainly be much more challenging to achieve without money and would require entirely different forms of co-living than those familiar to us today.

---

[387] Forstmann (1943: I. 142).

When the division of labour is described as the great instrument of cultural progress and greater prosperity (as by Schmoller), it must be added that money is the facilitator of the cultural progress and greater prosperity made possible by the division of labour. And when the same author refers to "today's state, today's national and world economy with all its splendour and wealth" as a result of the division of labour, the role of money must not be forgotten in this context as well. As Herbert Spencer expresses it,[388] "The existence of a concurrently sustaining, regulating, producing, and distributing system of organs, [P174] and the entire collaboration of these regulating, creating, and distributing circles, the division of the regulating circles into central and local, into specialised branches, into commanding and executing organs, the separation of economic management from governance in society, the division of liberal professions from religious functions, the contrasts between city and countryside, industry, trade, and agriculture, between entrepreneur and worker, in short, this more complex cultural life is," not only, as Schmoller suggests, "a consequence of division of labour,"[389] but just as much a consequence of the possibilities for societal divisions provided by money-usage.

Money enables the division of labour in production just as it imparts broadness to the consumption of wealth, for which the former creates the prerequisites.

The organic collaboration, the cooperation of labour in agriculture and industry, in trade and commerce, must also remain limited and can only have modest effects until money enters as the mediator that establishes the connection between labour forces, both in terms of the individual's

---

[388] [tn] Since the precise source of this quote in English is not specified, we translated a German rendition back to English. Nevertheless, the fundamental concept originates in Spencer (1877: 489-568).

[389] Schmoller (1900: 1. Teil, 635).

participation in joint work and its outcomes. In this sense, Georg Simmel has said that money serves to "establish justice in the distribution of labour and satisfaction."[390] It is clearly meant that money is a means to shape *justitia commutativa* (commutative justice) according to its principles. But precisely because money is the means of distribution (of participation in the social-product) and thus a directive (*Anweisung*) towards satisfaction, it is the subject of a social struggle for its way of life, a struggle that will never end as long as there is money and money-usage.

The peculiar aspect of the division of labour is that, although it multiplies labour efforts, it does not improve the status of labour in the economic process but that of capital. The medium here, too, is money.

---

[390] [tn] Simmel (1908:63).

§24. Money and Needs

[p175] The Bible verse "You shall not covet" finds its strongest counterpart in money. Money is nothing but aspiration (*Begehr*), a claim to satisfy needs (*Bedürfnis*) and desires (*Wunsch*). In the monetary society, it is the means to fulfil virtually every aspiration.

The principle whose application enables increasingly perfect need-satisfaction and, thus, the increase of prosperity for individuals and society, was already recognised by Adam Smith in the division of labour. Division of labour places all members of an economy in mutual interdependence for the satisfaction of needs, and through this, it leads and binds those involved into a social unity.

As demonstrated, money is the means through which the products of the division of labour in society are provided as a means of satisfying their needs. The aim of all economies is human need-satisfaction. Their purpose is the satisfaction of human demand (*Bedarf*). The situation that arises from humans striving to satisfy needs is the subject of national economics, which Hegel, for this very reason, referred to as a 'system of needs' (*System der Bedürfnisse*). He considers the "system of needs" as one of the three moments characterising civil society (Hegel 1821: §188). In the examination of this system – and it is worth noting – Hegel particularly emphasises that need, for the sake of which I have referred to humans as "*anthropos doxomanés*" (opinionated human),[391] namely, the need to assert oneself through distinction. He calls this need – the desire to assert oneself – a real source of the multiplication of needs and their dissemination, which distinguishes humans from animals.

> Need and means become a being (*Sein*) – as a real existence (*Dasein*) – for others, through whose needs and labour the satisfaction is mutually dependent" (ibid.: §§ 190-193).

---

[391] [tn] See footnote 34.

They become "societal needs, means, and methods of satisfaction," and in that sense, they become societal. Money, however, fulfils a function in this regard that cannot be replaced by anything else. [P176] It serves as both a means of expression for the ideas which set certain purposes for society, as well as for the considerations that aim to realise these purposes. In other words, money is a means of expression for both the goals of demand and comparative assessments of needs.

Money is thus the most crucial means in the process of spreading, multiplying, generalising, and equalising needs. It is a means to execute that process, which continually generates new and more refined means and methods of need-satisfaction, means of both de-mentalising and spiritualising human existence.

While the progressive refinement of needs and the means to satisfy them is possible without money, their dissemination and generalisation are not. Through the development of production and the creation of means of demand-satisfaction (*Bedarfsbefriedigungsmittel*), money is the tool that makes these accessible to everyone: Food and clothing, means of intercourse, and cultural-goods are utilised by both high and low, rich and poor, albeit with certain quality differences. Thousands of pleasures, as facilitated today by things like newspapers, theatres, concerts, cinemas, etc., are accessible to everyone thanks to money. Without money, that development, which E. A. Roß has summarised as "growing unlikeness as workers, a growing likeness as livers and enjoyers," is not possible.[392] This demonstrates its significance for societal development because it does not simply serve basic sensory needs; rather, as shown in another context, it is the means that completes the process of liberation for human society, which was initiated by the division of labour. Indeed, to quote Hegel once more:

> The direction of the societal condition towards the indefinite

---

[392] Roß (1905:262).

multiplication and specification of needs, means, and enjoyments knows no bounds" (Hegel ibid.: §195).

Human 'unfolding of need' (*Bedürfnisentfaltung*) has found in money a means that, by enabling and facilitating the demand-satisfaction, greatly propels that development itself. [₿177] While the increase in needs does indeed establish a growing interdependence among people, this interdependence is, in a certain way, mitigated by money, if not entirely eliminated. As the society-forming force of money creates innumerable relationships that interweave the individual in numerous social ties, a series of needs are created that find their satisfaction again by means of money.

The introduction of money as a means to satisfy all possible needs does not necessarily entail a multiplication of the goods-possession within a society. However, by indirectly enhancing the provision of goods, it also leads to an increase in prosperity. In this sense, one can indeed say that money makes society wealthier. The promotion of the circulation of goods through money generally leads to an increase in the utility of goods. It is certain that humanity would be more needy and historically less rich without money.

In line with the development of the forms of satisfying needs which were made possible by money, whose improvement also signifies an increasingly stronger societalisation, the societal aspect becomes more and more the content of life for humanity as a whole.

So, by being a means of need-satisfaction, money is also a means to infinitely increase the number of needs. Especially concerning the process that Hegel observes with the words: "A need is not so much produced by those who have it in a direct manner, but rather by those who seek to profit from its emergence,"[393] money plays the decisive role. The "profusion of arbitrariness" (Hegel ibid.: §189)[394] in demand and the need-satisfaction is

---

[393] [tn] Hegel (ibid.: §191).

[394] [tn] The arbitrariness of needs and satisfactions in bourgeois society.

brought into order and maintained by money. It ensures better need-satisfaction compared to all other forms of provision. Precisely because it allows for more versatile and complete individual need-satisfaction than other goods, money is valued higher than all other goods, unless its functions are impaired – i.e., without 'purchasing power restrictions' (*Kaufmachtbeschränkungen*) – or exceptional circumstances exist.

[p178] In the selection and satisfaction of needs, money itself is neutral. It can equally serve the satisfaction of both moral and immoral needs. Money-usage in our societal order is always, in every case, not only an economic decision but also a moral one.[395] Critiques raised from an ethical perspective against money are based on the fact that it often serves condemnable purposes. However, this is a criticism that the tool itself does not deserve but rather those who misuse it. Nevertheless, one can certainly say that the quality of money does have some influence on the selection of needs for which it is used for satisfaction. What is meant is that inflationary money can easily lead to wastefulness and a misguided hierarchy of needs.

The luxury laws of earlier centuries reflect the efforts of public authority to intervene against excesses and degenerations in need-satisfaction. Their regulations effectively represent a constraint on the purchasing power of money.

The judgment about the role of money in shaping the need-satisfaction hinges on the answer to the question of whether the increase and multiplication of needs towards unlimited diversity are moving in a rational direction or not. However, it would certainly be wrong to consider money solely as a means for the convenient satisfaction of individual needs and the enhancement of personal enjoyment. Money is more than just a technical tool for meeting the necessities of life and enjoying it; rather, by being this [i.e., technical tool], money acquires a significance that makes it not only a tool of material civilisation but also a cultural carrier of the utmost strength.

---

[395] Taeuber (1950: 75).

§25. Money and the Legal-Order

[**179**] If we want to understand money as a creation of social action in its meaning, it involves clarifying the question of whether that social action, which creates money by utilising certain goods in a particular way, requires an *external* regulation of social life through the state and the law.

Customs (*Sitte*) – the practice (*Gepflogenheit*) of primitive money-usage can indeed be called custom – have their roots in habit (*Gewohnheit*), i.e., in the consistent behaviour of the members of a communal life. The activities and institutions associated with the customs, which become habits through repetition or constancy, establish a regulation of life. Therefore, it is not the regulation of life (*Lebensregelung*), whether one calls it custom or law, that creates money; rather, when money comes into existence, the corresponding order (*Ordnung*) in which it exists also arises. Money is always an expression of a societal fact. Societal facts consist of psychological relationships among people that manifest through interactions and thereby establish society. They objectify themselves in certain manifestation-forms, such as language and law, or in specific activities, such as rituals. Each of these social manifestation-forms itself possesses a means of expressing the social, and money is one such means. It is an expression of societal existence.

Just as society did not arise from a contract or is not founded on a contract, money is not the result of any agreement. Money is not a work tool created through hidden economic agendas; rather, it is a natural formation that has grown out of [social] conditions (*Verhältnissen*). Social and economic life together constitute money. They are what define what money is, i.e., what functions as money. The legal-order (*Rechtsordnung*) is merely the expression of this fact, or to put it differently, economic and social facts lead to a legal-order that corresponds to the needs of social and economic life, shaping and unfolding it accordingly. The creation of law from custom, tradition, and general practice presupposes habit and convention, which gain legal authority through repetition and duration.

214

[p180] However, it is not the law that creates legal facts; the act of legal creation cannot produce anything but can only recognise what already exists.

Law is a life-order established by a power that grants acknowledgement and validity to that life-order. The question of whether money is inherently part of such a regulation of life, i.e., whether to be integrated into such a life-order is part of the essence of money is thus already answered. One can also pose the question in this manner: does money come into existence only through a normative life-order that defines services and functions of money, or does money merely expand its scope of work through this order, thereby elevating itself to a higher level of existence? We lean towards the latter interpretation. While according to Stammler (1914), law and order are indeed the logical prerequisite for economic relationships and social co-living in general, it would be a fallacy to mistake something that is nothing more than a conceptual idea for the reality of life and claim that every social phenomenon exists solely through the legal-order and within it. Social phenomena can serve to explain the legal-order in terms of its origin, validity, and significance, but the reverse is not true. The legal-order cannot provide an interpretation of the original social roots and interconnections. The law can never make life understandable, but life can certainly make the law understandable. For example, it is natural that the ownership-order (*Eigentumsordnung*) can provide insights into the life that unfolds within that order, but the emergence of an ownership-order can only be explained by social conditions. The legal-order is a product of society, not the other way around. It plays a role in shaping social life but is not social life itself.

The answer to the question of whether money is an original category of social life or a derived one, i.e., created by legal-order, can therefore only be: Money is, according to its origin, an original creation of social life; it is not an institution created by statute. However, it has become 'natural' (*naturhaft*), as already repeatedly emphasised.

[p181] Every order recognised or established by the legal-order is bound

by certain prerequisites, meaning it is based on societal facts. Certain original conditions must exist to enable a legal-order or to incorporate a situation into it. Only based on such conditions can the legal-order validly establish a specific condition, that is, make it effective. However, it fundamentally cannot determine two facts constitutively, which are the 'feeling of need' (*Bedürfnisgefühle*) of social individuals and the goods suitable for this need-satisfaction. These two, though, are the foundation of primitive money. Money is an elemental or original phenomenon of social life. It is a tool or an assisting means (*Hilfsmittel*) of social exertion. In its origin, it does not differ from other tools, weapons, clothing items, etc., which can all acquire symbolic significance beyond their original practical purposes, such as a belt, a headband, a head covering, etc., or are linked to such symbolism in their origin. The original prerequisites which condition the emergence of money are not of a legal nature. It is not any legal-order that gives rise to money. The legal-order is not necessary for the emergence of money. It is not a formative or constitutive element of money. We refer to such [formative or constitutive] phenomena as original or elemental. The emergence of money is based on psychological forces. This is not to say, and it should not be said, that the legal-order has no influence on this elemental phenomenon. Not only does the legal-order appropriate the elemental phenomenon, but an existing legal-order can also under certain circumstances grant a greater or lesser scope of action or life to this elemental phenomenon.

We call a 'good money' (*Gut Geld*) when it provides certain services. It is and remains money as long as it performs these functions, completely independent of the legal-order. Only when the fulfilment of one of these functions is conditioned by the legal-order, and this function is considered essential for moneyness, must the legal-order be regarded as constitutive of money. [p182] Money is, therefore, a phenomenon that is independent of the legal-order in its origin, but not necessarily in its ongoing existence. Money is not initially a category of historical law but rather a category of historical sociology. Its legal character develops later on. The legal-order imparts to money, at a certain stage of monetary development, a new characteristic feature: the aptitude to be a means of payment. For this money, the legal-order is the enabling force. However, whether this money is genuine and vital money is determined solely by social action.

The developmental course is as follows: Money, initially and originally a general social category, becomes a specific economical category as it becomes a manifestation of the market, a means of market-intercourse, and further, when the state becomes the bearer of the order of the monetary framework, it becomes a legal category, namely a creation of the legal-order. The money that originally became natural in the social sphere becomes a creation of the market, an economical phenomenon whose existence, in the course of further development, receives acknowledgement through "statute." This transforms money into a legal category, and there comes a turning point where the money created by statute replaces what had naturally evolved. This not only opens up the possibility but, in a practical situation in general, often leads to the detachment of money from a specific substance or substance altogether. Paper money emerged alongside metallic money, and further developments led to the emergence of 'book entry money' (*Buchgeld*), giro-money (*Giralgeld*), or clearing-money (*Verrechnungsgeld*), eventually replacing the former. The material condition of being money is lost, leaving only the nominal. Money has freed itself from substantive [material] constraints. It has evolved from a category of substance into a category of function.

Society, as the bearer of social life and not the state as the bearer of the legal-order, is the prerequisite for the emergence of money. However, when the legal-order takes control of money, i.e., regulates money-usage, it imparts aptitudes to money that it owes solely to the legal-order. [p183] Money acquires certain legal functions in addition to its social and economical functions, but these legal functions are merely a specific manifestation of its social and economical functions.

The examination of the relationships between money and the legal-order presupposes an economy in which money-usage is customary. If the view has been presented here, as also advocated by scholars like W. Eucken, that "the legal-order arises to shape certain existing facts that are economically relevant,"[396] then this also characterises the status of money in the legal-order. This means that money is able to perform functions that correspond to a given economic order thanks to the legal-order. As previously mentioned, the function of being a means of payment is paramount. Some additional points have been made about this function elsewhere (see §21), which will be supplemented here.

Money serves as a means of payment wherever payments need to be made, wherever it serves interpersonal value-transfer, in other words, when it is used "as an instrument of interpersonal intercourses" (Helfferich). As previously explained, this function is not tied to the legal-order, but it gains significant expansion through the legal-order, and this expansion is retrospectively significant for the quality of money. Money thus becomes a tool for fulfilling juristical – both public-law and private-law – obligations. When the state collects levies or imposes penances, it must specify what is to be paid. It establishes the means of payment for such payments made by private individuals *to* the state (*epicentric* payments[397]). As G. F. Knapp emphasised, what matters is not the state's issuance (*Emission*) but the acceptance (*Akzeptation*).[398] The means of payment

---

[396] Eucken (1947:91).

[397] [tn] It is a neologism developed by Knapp and refers to the payments made *to* the state. Greek preposition '*epi-*' (ἐπί) carries the meaning of 'into' or 'upon.' In the context of '*epicentric*,' it suggests a condition or position that is directed or focused on a central point. On the other hand, '*apocentric*' refers to the payments made *by* the state, where the state acts as the 'giver.' The prefix '*apo-*' in the term '*apocentric*' is derived from the Greek preposition '*apo*' (ἀπό), which means 'away from' or 'separate from.' In the context of '*apocentric*,' it indicates a condition or position that is located *away from* or divergent from a centre point. See Knapp (2023:90 ff.; 1923:96 ff.).

[398] [tn] Knapp (2023:89; 1923:95).

that is recognised and exclusively designated for settling obligations under public-law achieves particularly high negotiability (*Verkehrsfähigkeit*). It is also used for *apocentric* payments (payments *from* the state *to* private individuals),[399] and the ease and frequency of such use increase as the compulsion for *epicentric* payments (e.g., taxes) intensifies.

Another reinforcement of the means of payment function is when a means of payment is declared as the '**statutory means of payment**' (*gesetzliches Zahlungsmittel*). [⁋184] This refers to the designation of a means of payment that, in the absence of any other agreement, is considered valid for settling obligations between debtors and creditors. Furthermore, if 'statutory means of payment' is declared obligatory for certain other payments, this strengthens the means of payment function of the respective money and thereby its status in the economy. An example of this is the regulation in all civilised countries that wages must be paid in the 'statutory means of payment' (prohibition of the truck system[400]).

Everywhere the 'statutory means of payment' is used, it has been granted two additional legal functions in our legal and economic system: the **enforcement function** (*exekutionsrechtliche Funktion*) **and the solution-function** (*Solutionsfunktion*).

In our economic system, it is an essential task of the legal-order to guarantee the fulfilment of obligations, i.e., the legal-order must provide the means to enforce the fulfilment of claims if necessary.

'Personal enforcement' (*Personalexekution*)[401] [to fulfil claims] is

---

[399] [tn] Refer to footnote 397.

[400] [tn] The term 'truck system' refers to a practice where employers provide their workers with goods or services instead of standard currency (money) as a form of payment for their labour. This practice can lead to exploitation of workers as they may not receive fair compensation for their work. Laws and regulations prohibiting the truck system aim to ensure that workers are paid in legal currency, which provides them with more financial flexibility and protection.

[401] [tn] '*Personalexekution*' denotes the enforcement of legal measures directly

consistently rejected by modern legal systems. 'Natural enforcement' (*Naturalexekution*),[402] or the so-called direct enforcement, is not possible in many cases (especially when the debtor does not have control over the object). In such cases, 'indirect enforcement' (*indirekte Exekution*) comes into play. This makes use of money. Through money, 'compensatory disbursement' (*Ersatzleistung*) for both *damnum cessans* and *lucrum emergens* [403] can be determined. When Frauenfelder asserts, "without money, a consistently implemented private legal-order is inconceivable,"[404] this well characterises the significance of money in the legal and economic order.

Money in the private legal-order serves yet another function. It acts as the universal last resort **means of solution** wherever there is a lack of agreement or specification regarding what is to be rendered, i.e., what form the means of disbursement-fulfilment (*Leistungserfüllung*) is. This

---

targeting an individual.

[402] [tn] This term originates from German and may not have direct equivalents in the commonly used legal vocabulary of the UK legal system. It refers to the enforcement of obligations or actions through non-monetary methods, ensuring compliance with required duties. It involves direct or indirect coercive means and aligns with the concept of 'enforcement by non-monetary means' or 'coercive enforcement of obligations' within UK law. Its counterpart is 'monetary enforcement' (*Geldexekution*), which specifically pertains to the enforcement of financial claims or debts via money.

[403] [tn] *Damnum cessans* translates to 'loss not suffered' or 'cessation of damage.' It refers to a situation where a person or entity has not suffered any actual loss but has been deprived of potential gain or profit.

Lucrum translates to 'profit' or 'gain.' In a legal context, it refers to the actual financial benefits or gains that a person or entity receives as a result of a particular action or transaction. These terms are often used in legal discussions, especially in cases involving damages, compensation, or financial assessments. *Damnum cessans* deals with potential losses that were not realised, while *lucrum* deals with actual gains or profits.

[404] Frauenfelder (1938).

requires a corresponding legal regulation. The legal-order determines the 'statutory means of payment.' This is not a concept of *jus cogens* but of *jus dispositivum*. [405] [p185] It is the 'rule of interpretation' (*Auslegungsregel*)[406] for cases where nothing else has been determined by law or contract.[407]

With the title of this section, "Money and the Legal-order," as should be evident from what has been said, it is not meant to be "money within the legal-order." The scope of the questions encompassed by this title can only be briefly touched upon here. Indeed, the previous explanations have already provided a brief overview of the title.

Another related issue of this kind should be briefly mentioned. It is the question of the nature of monetary debt (*Geldschuld*). This debate revolves around whether money constitutes an 'obligation in kind' (*Sachschuld*)[408] or a 'value-debt' (*Wertschuld*).[409] For a societal and

---

[405] [tn] *Jus cogens*, in Latin, means 'compelling law' or 'peremptory norm.' It refers to a fundamental principle of international law that is *universally accepted* and recognised as so fundamental that it overrides conflicting treaties and customary international laws.

Jus dispositivum, also known as 'dispositive law,' refers to legal norms or provisions that can be altered or overridden by the will of the parties involved through agreements or contracts. These norms are not considered absolute and can be modified if the parties involved agree to do so.

[406] [tn] It refers to a guideline or principle used by legal authorities, such as judges, lawyers, or arbitrators, to interpret laws, contracts, or legal documents. The purpose of the 'rule of interpretation' (*Auslegungsregel*) is to provide a structured approach to understanding the meaning and intent behind legal texts.

[407] Cf. See Peitmann (1941).

[408] [tn] The debate or question revolves around whether they are essentially obligated to deliver a specific tangible object equivalent to that amount when someone owes a certain amount of money. In other words, it questions whether money itself represents a specific object or if it is simply a representation of value.

[409] [tn] It refers to an obligation or a financial liability where the debtor owes a

economical theory of money, there can be no doubt that monetary debt is a 'value-debt.'

The question of the content of a monetary debt is a different matter. Of the three possibilities customarily discussed since Savigny's time, i.e., metal value, market value (*Kurswert*) and nominal value (*Nennwert*), legislation and jurisprudence have generally opted for nominal value. For the societal theory of money, this is a fact that must be considered.[410]

---

certain amount of value or monetary worth, rather than a specific tangible item or asset.

[410] From the extensive literature on the aforementioned questions, you may want to consider the following sources for further reading: Hartmann (1868), Gumpel (1914), Nußbaum (1925), Tiemann (1932), Schwander (1938), Geiler (1926:320) and Seidler (1894). Additionally, you might want to explore well-known economic presentations on the theory of money by K. Knies and K. Helfferich (1910). These sources should provide valuable insights and perspectives on the legal and economic aspects of money and monetary debts.

§26. The State and Money

Money is therefore originally not created by statute but by social action, as must be emphasised repeatedly, although it has often been emphasised by numerous older authors. It is, in its origin, a societal rather than a state phenomenon. Social action generates money, and social action can cause it to disappear. [▶186] Even at that late stage of the development of money, where the state takes control of it, makes its existence and its usage subject to its legal-order, it is social action that gives life to money.[411]

Describing money as a creation of the legal-order or as a state-proclaimed means of payment (G. F. Knapp) is misleading.[412] The statement applies only to the money of a certain time period and only to a specific form of money even within that period. A compelling example of this can be found in Franz Obermaier's account. He reports from Ukraine:

Where money is a rarity, as is the case with all small farmers in the

---

[411] Cf. The relevant explanations in Amonn (1926: Vol. I, 195).

[412] Knapp (2023:2; 1923:1). [tn] However, a common mistake is to interpret the meaning of the 'legal-order' in a narrow sense. It is often overlooked that Knapp further qualifies the meaning of the 'legal-order' later in this book (Knapp 2023, 1923), specifically referring to the legal-order "in communities (*Gemeinschaft*), whether they are state or private" (Knapp 2023:142; 1923:157). Knapp also corresponded with Bernhard Laum after the latter published "*Heliges Geld*" (Sacred Money, Laum 1924/2023), which traces the emergence of money to ancient religious rituals. Knapp mentioned that his book and Laum's book differ solely in terms of the period of application but fully agree in terms of methodology. Laum's assertion was that money is a creature of *sacred* 'legal-order' rather than *profane* 'legal-order.' Therefore, 'legal-order' should be understood as '*nomos* (νόμος),' encompassing a broader concept beyond the narrow definition of law. In Knapp's letter to Laum, he stated,

I have focused on recent history, without considering prehistory. (...) You aim to explain the oldest form of payment through erudition, while I focus on the most recent. Are we so far apart methodologically? I feel we are not (quoted from Brandl 2015: 196).

East and Southeast, it is replaced by a marketable commodity: people simply calculate in eggs.[413]

This means nothing else than that original money arises for a limited economic circle alongside the state-issued money. For one cannot deny that we are dealing with this "egg money" as a good that provides monetary services and is therefore money without any "state proclamation" (*staatliche Proklamation*)

The state-issued money is the one to which the principle of civil law applies: "*Monetandi jus principum ossibus inhaeret*," which means "The right to coin money is inherent in the prerogatives of princes." In this sense, Lord Liverpool wrote to King George III in 1805:

> There is no doubt, that the Sovereigns of most the Kingdoms and states of Europa have enjoyed and exercised from time immemorial the right of declaring, at what rate or value the Coins of every denomination, permitted to be current in their respective dominions, shall pass, and become in that respect lawful Coins, or legal tender. In this Your Majesty's kingdom, Your Royal predecessors have always enjoyed and exercised the right. Sir Matthew Hale reckons the right *inter jura majestatis*,[414] and says that it is an unquestionable prerogative of the Crown.

To want to limit the concept of money to 'money valid by the state'[415] would mean not only doing injustice to the monetary phenomenon, but it would mean depriving oneself of a full understanding of it, and thereby also foregoing an understanding of essential social processes.

[187] The State Theory of Money, as is well known, was developed by Georg Friedrich Knapp with masterful conceptual clarity and richness of thought. His contribution, which has become a permanent part of

---

[413] Obermaier (1942: 91).

[414] [tn] Among the rights of sovereignty.

[415] [tn] Money which becomes valid by state proclamation.

monetary theory, deepens our understanding of money, but at the same time, it also narrows the scope of monetary theory. An examination of the State Theory of Money is not intended here. Its strengths and weaknesses have been discussed often enough. Here, the intention is only to emphasise the broader concept of money in contrast to Knapp's view, as Sombart rightly states:

> It is impossible, as Knapp does, to use the word 'money' solely for the concept of state money or, in his terminology, for '*chartal* means of payment' (*chartales Zahlungsmittel*).[416]

Knapp's theory of money is, strictly speaking, only a theory of state-issued means of payment. Instead of "State Theory of Money," the title of his book should actually be "Theory of State-Issued Money."

It should be emphasised once again in this context: good is not money simply because it has been designated as such by law, but rather by virtue of the acknowledgement it receives in transactions (*Verkehr*).[417] However, this recognition does not solely rely on the ability conferred upon it by the law to serve as a means of payment (the law can facilitate or strengthen this, but it can never achieve it on its own). Instead, it is based on its aptitude to provide essential monetary services. Good becomes money because, in its usage, it is recognised and used as money by those connected within the monetary community. Money does not come into existence through law but rather through usage. The legal-order (laws, regulations, etc.) can indeed promote its usage in transactions, but the prerequisite is always that the economy, through its usage, transforms a good into money. Therefore, the source and benchmark of 'moneyness' is not the legal-order alone but rather a certain goods-usage within the economy. When the goods-usage and the legal-order diverge, the money created by state decree (*Befehl*) may

---

[416] Sombart (ibid.: 1 HalbBd, 402).

[417] [tn] In this context, '*Verkehr*' can also be translated more broadly as 'social intercourses.'

exist in name, but it does not truly thrive in reality. [⟨188] However, when the state decree aligns with the practice of transactions,[418] strengthens and reinforces it when the state's sanction of money-usage corresponds to legal conviction, then money is still not a creation of the legal-order, but rather a social institution supported and protected [by the legal-order] in its effectiveness to provide services.

The roots of the validity (*Geltung*) of money, as this book aims to demonstrate, are certain psychological facts that, in transactions, lead to similar behaviours and activities *without* external pressure or coercion. This does not refer to the "mass habit of acceptance" (*Massengewohnheit der Annahme*) but rather to the general estimation and aspiring for the money-good and its corresponding widespread use as a gift and reciprocal-gift. From this, the 'mass habit of acceptance' develops, to which the general practice (*Übung*) is added, where things are valued in money and transactions are conducted in money.

The state's sanction of money primarily concerns the technique of monetary intercourses. It represents a technical improvement in the functioning of money. However, at the same time, it also entails an enhancement of the capability of money both as a medium of exchange and as a means for unilateral 'voluntary gift' (*Dargaben*) and contributions (*Hergabe*). By regulating the monetary framework in detail and, above all, specifying the 'statutory means of payment,' whereby making it universally valid money *per se* – the 'national currency' (*Landeswährung*) – in which payments to the state itself are to be made, as are all monetary-disbursements (*Geldleistung*) in general in the event of a dispute, the state establishes the foundations for a secure system of accounting-traffic (*Rechnungsverkehr*) and payment-traffic.

The nationalisation of money, which is often linked to the suppression of any non-state money, does indeed represent both a significant

---

[418] [tn] See footnote 417.

strengthening and expansion of money's domain of influence. However, it also carries the risk of constitutional weakening, meaning a potential impairment of the viability and service-capacity (*Leistungsfähigkeit*) of money. This danger is given firstly by the possibility of arbitrary money-creation (*Geldschöpfung*), and secondly by the regulation of the use of money through measures (*Maßnahmen*) directing market-policy. [⁋189] If, as will be shown in another context, money as such can no longer enter the market when, where, and to what extent its possessor desires, and if its purchasing power is restricted, then money is constitutionally weakened or, as has been said elsewhere, is paralysed through those state measures that prevent its unconditional exchange for goods or services of any kind.

Then there arises the phenomenon that has been referred to as a 'monetary overhang' (*Geldüberhang*). This term is often associated with the idea that money has only temporarily lost its function as a general means of purchase (*Kaufmittel*). However, whether this loss of function is indeed temporary or not remains an open question. However, what is crucial is something entirely different, namely, that the restriction of purchasing power results in a fundamental change in the function of money. This will be further elaborated upon in the section on the purchasing power of money (§ 27).

More than the latter, which is a more recent development in monetary policy, arbitrary money-creation with its devastating consequences such as money-devaluation has led to the failure of state intervention in money matters. Despite the acknowledgement of the state's role in maintaining an orderly monetary framework and providing the economy with money, there is a viewpoint held not only by proponents of unrestricted economic freedom but also by advocates of planned economic objectives. This perspective suggests that state intervention in money matters should be limited to establishing mechanisms that ensure its proper functioning and circulation. According to the principles of economical liberalism, state monetary policy should focus on defending the monetary circulation against non-economical influences that disrupt the natural dynamics of economic forces. Any further influence on the economic flows carried out by means of money, whether through the manipulation of money or prices, means – according to this view – a weakening or even obstructing the allegedly natural function of money, which must eventually lead to money ceasing to operate.

[P190] It is certain that throughout the millennia, state monetary policies have been repeatedly abused in the exercise of monetary sovereignty. Hence, the desire for a monetary regime that significantly limits the power authority of the state is understandable. It is no coincidence that alongside state-issued money, private money has managed to assert itself for a long time. Particularly in times of deterioration of state-issued money, private money-creation, whether in coinage or the establishment of a unit of account, has often been successful. Similarly, efforts to create international money, especially since the end of World War I, have been in the same direction.

While the Bretton Woods Agreement did not materialise the plan for a world currency based on a new monetary unit (such as the *Bancor* or *Unitas*), the objective was clear. It may not have aimed to completely replace state-issued money, but it sought protection against state-led monetary manipulations. These manipulations not only endanger the domestic economy but also have repercussions on interconnected national economies in the global economy.

§27. The Purchasing Power of Money

In Aristotle's *Nicomachean Ethics*, a work on the moral behaviour of citizens, it is stated in Book V: "He who brings money must be able to obtain what he needs," and further, money is referred to as "a guarantee for the 'possibility of exchange'" (*Möglichkeit des Austausches*), through which we can satisfy our needs.[419]

Certainly, it will not need to be elaborated here that during the past few decades in most, if not all, countries, money has not been what the Greek philosopher described as a guarantee for the 'possibility of exchange.' Whether it ever was this in the past and to what extent money has once again become a guarantor for the 'possibility of exchange' in recent years remains to be determined for now.

[p191] One might think that the condition where money fails as a guarantor for the 'possibility of exchange' is a symptom of monetary illness that appears during times of war and other emergencies but disappears with the recovery of the monetary framework. However, this is precisely what requires closer examination.

I have referred to the property of "being a guarantor for the 'possibility of exchange'" as the purchasing power of money.[420] By this, I mean the

---

[419] [tn] Aristotle (1133b10). The term of 'possibility' (*Möglichkeit*) does not show up in many English translations. Instead, a particular English version (2004:91) states,

> Money is, as it were, our guarantor for *future* exchange: if we do not need a thing now, we can have it if ever we do need it, since we must be able to get it if we pay.

The original text, *'mellousēs allagēs'* (μελλούσης ἀλλαγῆς), translates to 'impending exchange.' *'Mellousēs'* (μελλούσης) is derived from the Greek word *'méllousa'* (μέλλουσα), signifying 'future' or 'about to be.'

[420] Gerloff (1944: 240, 249) and Gerloff (1947).

[tn] Here is a quote from Gerloff (1944: 248-251), providing a concise preview

of the discussion in this section:

It is obvious that in this way money has become more and more adapted to its purpose in its form and features. Money is now no longer the hoard goods which were sometimes rather shapeless, hard-to-move and indivisible, no longer treasures that are guarded and kept sacred as precious family possessions but goods that can be used for economic purposes, especially commercial raw materials and products (copper, brass, hoes, axes, woven fabrics) in manageable form. Their further adaptation to the monetary purpose then leads to the epoch of monetary and chartal money.

With its use as a means of exchange, money has gained a new sphere of services. Hitherto only as a carrier of power in the field of social power-relations, it now becomes an economic-technical means, which as such is certainly also able to exert social power effects and in fact does so to a large extent. However, in contrast to hoard-money or money of status (*Geltungsgeld*), at first only indirectly, and then, of course, to the extent that money acquires significance as an economic-technical means in economic society, it also becomes a social carrier of power (*sozialer Machtträger*) in this society. The peculiar contradiction of money as a means of exchange lies in the fact that it transforms the character of exchange so that in its usage the idea of *exchange* finally *recedes completely into the background*. Through money, the act of exchange becomes *purchase* and *sell*. Thus money, because it is a means of exchange, becomes a 'means of purchase' (*Kaufmittel*). The term 'means of exchange' *only* fits the beginnings of barter money. At the moment of its creation, however, it becomes 'purchase-money'; there is then no more *exchange*, but only *purchase* and *sell*. No one thinks of exchanging any more, but only of purchase and sell. Money acquires the *purchasing power* (*Kaufmacht*).

The further role of money in the economy and society now depends entirely on the extent to which and the manner in which it has purchasing power. The social power of money is its purchasing power. Even if this power was originally based on magical ideas and mythical connections, its origin lies in the factual use of money from the very beginning of its use: Wives, allegiance, allies, and even eternal bliss can be acquired with it, and uses of this kind already signify a profitable "capital investment" at the earliest cultural level. It is this purely factual suitability that gives the possessor of money prestige and social power, and in doing so, money

ability (*Fähigkeit*) of money to enter the market or, more precisely, the nature and extent of its usability (*Verwendungsfähigkeit*) as a means of exchange. Therefore, the purchasing power of money is something *different* from its purchasing force, which refers to the *quantity* of goods or services that can be purchased with a specific amount of money.

The possibility of using money as a means of exchange is not necessarily unrestricted, although it has been a widely held belief and an assumption of conventional theories that with money, specifically with 'good money,' one could buy whatever, whenever, and wherever within its scope of

---

becomes a social means of power, money possession means social power. Understanding the development and changes in the purchasing power of money means recognising the role of money in society and understanding the fate of money itself. The purchasing power of money is originally only of limited breadth and width, whereby 'breadth' is understood as the personal and 'width' as the objective limitation of the purchasing power. In other words, the subjective and objective purchasing power of money is more or less limited. Originally, money had no general and unconditional purchasing power at all, but only an individually determined and conditional one. This goes so far that different money is needed for different purposes. Ethnology knows numerous examples which teach that in this or that case a service can only be fulfilled, or an exchange can only be carried out if a very specific money is paid. Conversely, this corresponds to the fact that a certain money, as money, can only serve this or that purpose and no other. All primitive money is purpose-money (*Zweckgeld*), i.e., it serves certain purposes and cannot be used for other purposes. But even if the purchasing breadth of money is not so narrow, i.e., if its purchasing power is less limited than in cases where it is only entitled to a single field of use, it is nevertheless quite generally the case at the early stage of the development of money that for the acquisition of certain groups of goods or for the fulfilment of certain services quite specific money is required. This means at the same time that several types of money are in circulation side by side. These cannot originally be exchanged for each other. Such money is therefore objectively limited in its use.

validity. In his inaugural lecture in Vienna, titled "The Value of Money and Its Historical Changes" (*Der Geldwert und seine geschichtlichen Veränderungen*), for example, Friedrich von Wieser states:

> He who has sold for money attains the freest mobility to buy what he wants, where he wants, from whom he wants, in whatever sums or fractions he wants, according to the measure of his money power (*Geldmacht*).

In the classical textbook of German orthodox monetary theory by Karl Helfferich, it is stated without any reservation that "everything available at all can be obtained with certainty against money." Furthermore, it is asserted that "money is always ready and quickly responsive in all cases."

According to the American scholar E. W. Kemmerer:

> By virtue of being the most exchangeable of all goods, money gives its possessor the power to acquire any desired good from society on the market; provided, of course," Kemmerer adds, "that he is equipped with a sufficient amount.[421]

[₱192] Therefore, according to this view, anyone who possesses a sufficient quantity of money can make purchases as desired.

Certainly, statements of this kind, which could easily be multiplied, all pertain to "good" or "healthy" money. They implicitly assume a *sound* monetary framework that adheres to conventional notions. However, this characterisation only *inadequately* captures the situation. It is more accurate to say that such statements apply — and this is usually overlooked — *only* to the money of a specific economic constitution in general, namely, the *money of the liberal economic order*. It is *this order* that has conferred purchasing power upon money.

The purchasing power of money, like every function of money, is *not* an inherent characteristic of money itself but rather a *use-potentiality* of money determined by the *prevailing* social, economic, or legal-order.

---

[421] Kemmerer (1932: 351).

From this perspective, it is understandable that the money of other eras does not possess the same general purchasing power that appears so essential to us today thanks to a usage that money-expending found in the era of economical liberalism. When this purchasing power is temporarily shaken, it is considered the most important goal of monetary reform to restore the money's general purchasing power.

Johann Georg Büsch, whose work marks the beginning of the actual German monetary theory of the 19th century, characterised the essence of money in a way similar to the modern authors mentioned earlier. In his first book (Büsch 1780), he explains:

> The agreement of people has turned money into a commodity in which we possess something that we do not have with any other commodity — the certainty that we can provide ourselves with all the necessities of life with the freest choice.

He sees in it "the great magic force of money, which it exerts on the entire activity of free people." [p193] He says:

> They subject themselves to all toils when they believe: with this labour, I will earn money, which is the means to obtain all conceivable necessities. The more I work, the more I will obtain this means, the more needs I will be able to satisfy, and the freer choice I will have among all needs.

If one were to remove money from civil society, he continues, the incentive for work would also be taken away. He exclaims:

> Imagine, O man, whatever you consider beneficial for your improvement. If you have the money for it, you have the means to call upon all people who can contribute something to fulfil this specific desire to serve you. You do not have this means if your stockpiling house is full of surplus grain, wool, flax, or wine. For you may still encounter people who could provide you with the service or satisfy the need you lack for your improvement, but they will refuse because they have enough grain, wool, flax, or wine for their own needs. Offer them money (...) There is nothing as powerful as this thing to motivate people to act, that which civil

societies have given the ability to satisfy every passion. Let a person be inclined as they wish, whether noble or base passions dominate them. The means to satisfy them is money.

Büsch concludes his remarks with the significant observation that he must add an important conclusion to his praise of money:

> Money will exert its beneficial effects in promoting general activity most vigorously where the desire and prospect of improvement are least disturbed for those who acquire it. All the institutions of civil societies that infringe upon, complicate, or completely disrupt these prospects, all such disposals and controls by which one believes they can compel labour from people without allowing these prospects to remain with the workers, suppress the useful industry of people that contributes to the happiness of individuals and all. They render money, which could so easily promote these, ineffective. [P194] And even if they force a portion of what one intends for the immediate purpose, the prosperity of such a civil society will still fall far short of what it could be if these obstacles were removed, and money was allowed its full effectiveness.[422]

The effectiveness of money that Büsch has in mind is what is referred to here as the purchasing power of money. It is evident that this phenomenon has not escaped the notice of monetary theorists. Nonetheless, I am not aware of any attempt to develop the concept of the purchasing power of money and analyse the relevant facts. Expressions like those found in the works of J. G. Hoffmann, such as "The tool through which power is transferred to purchase is called money," or when the same author speaks of the "concept of a power to purchase in general, i.e., without reference to a particular purchasable object,"[423] have nothing to do with the concept of the purchasing power of money. In Hoffmann's case, it is a question of the emphasis on a mere aptitude and only on this; in our case, on the other

---

[422] Büsch (ibid.: §§ 34, 35).

[423] Hoffmann (1838: 10 f.; 1847: 531, 533 f.).

hand, it is a question of to what extent and under what conditions this aptitude can be exercised in a given social order. From the simple notion that money grants the power to buy to the development and analysis of the concept of the purchasing power of money is quite a journey.

When we talk about the purchasing power of money, everyone typically thinks of exchange-money, which serves as the medium of exchange. However, hoard-money also has purchasing power. One acquires with it – if one understands the word 'acquire' in a broader, perhaps even metaphorical sense – women and friends, promotions, impunity, favours, etc.[424] Numerous examples have been given for this. At the same time, it has been shown that both hoard-money and exchange-money do not possess unlimited purchasing power.

[p195] The restrictions can be of various kinds, namely:

1. Only certain things are purchasable, whether goods, rights, claims, or opportunities. The range of these purchasable things is initially very small. However, it expands with economic and social development. The scope and content of this range determine the 'objective purchasing power of money' (*objektive Kaufmacht des Geldes*). It can be referred to as the 'purchasing *width* of money' (*Kaufbreite des Geldes*).

The gradual expansion of the objective purchasing power of money has significant social consequences and essentially determines the 'societal power of money' (*gesellschaftliche Macht des Geldes*). Just imagine what it means when an increasing number of things are included in monetary

---

[424] [tn] This perspective is in line with Marx's viewpoint:

> Thus, what I am and am capable of is by no means determined by my individuality. I am ugly, but I can buy for myself the most beautiful of women. Therefore, I am not ugly, for the effect of ugliness – its deterrent power – is nullified by money. I, according to my individual characteristics, am lame, but money furnishes me with twenty-four feet. Therefore, I am not lame. I am bad, dishonest, unscrupulous, stupid; but money is honoured, and hence its possessor (Marx 1844).

intercourses, especially important things like land and soil. At the end of this development, the world of things *extra commercium*[425] includes very few items, mainly subject to restrictions on possession, acquisition, and exchange for reasons of public order, safety, and morality.[426]

2. Purchasables are indeed more or less numerous things with very few exceptions, perhaps even everything that is of value in economic and social life, in terms of goods, rights, claims, etc. However, if these things are subject to legal price-controls (*Preisbindung*), it follows that money can only be used to a limited extent to acquire these things. Such legal regulations have been known since ancient times, especially concerning food, wages, the use of money or interest rates, and more recently, foreign exchange. In cases where these items are in short supply, the highest money-offer does not necessarily determine the acquisition. Money legitimately has limited purchasing power in the regulated market through methods like taxes, price-ceilings, and so on.

3. Money has purchasing power only in the hands of certain individuals; in other words, the purchasing power of money is subjectively limited.

The *extra commercium* status established by law, convention, custom, etc., legally excludes the acquisition and sale of the relevant goods for everyone – both physical and legal persons. It is very common, however, that money possession and money-expending are reserved for certain individuals and only belong to them. From the perspective of money – bearing in mind that this is a quite one-sided point of view – this signifies a restriction of 'subjective purchasing power of money' (*subjektive Kaufmacht des Geldes*) or the 'purchasing *breadth* of money' (*Kaufweite des Geldes*). A restriction of subjective purchasing power of money exists when the exercise of purchasing power is not solely determined by the 'disposal and control over money' but is bound by subjective

---

[425] [tn] It means 'beyond of commerce.'

[426] Cf. Wappäus (1867).

qualifications. These qualifications can include rank, social status, class-belonging, income category, or any other benefit-right (*Bezugsberechtigung*). For whatever reasons such provisions are made and enforced, the more or less extensive restriction of the circle of those authorised to make purchases through them can have an impact on money and money-usage.

In the case of primitive societies using class-money, the restriction of the subjective purchasing power of money is characteristic. The same can be the case with 'tribal-money' (*Stammesgeld*), where it holds purchasing power only in the hands of tribal members. Thurnwald reports that the natives of Seleo Island[427] make bracelets, while those of Pultalul[428] make arrows. "For example, if a Pultalul wants to buy something with bracelets, he will be rejected with the words: 'You are not a Seleo. You have to pay with arrows'," he explains.[429]

Restrictions on the authorisation of money possession and money-usage based on class, tribe, social status, etc., are virtually non-existent in contemporary states and economies. On the other hand, as mentioned earlier, different restrictions on the subjective purchasing power of money were in force for centuries. [p197] They have not been completely eliminated even today, and there are even attempts to establish new restrictions on the subjective purchasing power of money (Soviet Union). It refers to the restriction of the purchasing power of money based on the requirement of belonging to a qualified group of individuals in some way. The qualification can be achieved through birth, age, origin, occupation, race, nationality, religion, party affiliation, etc. Examples include nobility (*Ritterbürtigkeit*) or peasant status (*Bauernfähigkeit*),[430] which were long-

---

[427] [tn] An island located in West Sepik Province, Papua New Guinea.

[428] [tn] A small settlement in Papua New Guinea.

[429] Thurnwald (1929:624).

[430] [tn] It referred to the legal and social status of being a commoner or peasant

standing requirements for acquiring land possession in German territories. In a caliphate,[431] adherence to the faith is demanded. During the era of guild systems, only guild members could purchase raw materials offered by foreign merchants. Furthermore, these merchants could often only use their proceeds to acquire a limited selection of goods. In his well-known work "England's Treasure by Foreign Trade" (1664, Chapter X), Thomas Mun mentions the "Statute of Employments," which was a regulation stating that foreign merchants could only convert their proceeds into goods specified by the authorities. The restrictions on acquiring land possession for Jews, foreigners, religious institutions, etc., are also well-known. In these cases, the subjective 'purchasing power restriction' of money, which applies to the holders of money, is combined with an objective one related to a thing. In the USSR and similarly, in the Russian-occupied zone of Germany, a 'commodity procurement system' (*Warenbezugssystem*) was introduced, which Kromphardt coined as 'market split' (*Marktspaltung*), where different prices must be paid for the same goods depending on one's membership in a particular group. In this case, the purchasing power of money is subjectively differentiated.

With regard to the subjective purchasing power of money, a fundamental distinction can be made: on the one hand, there are groups of people who are not entitled to make purchases at all, such as slaves, women in cultures with strict patrilineal organisation, and youth. On the other hand, there are groups of people for whom only specific types of purchases are reserved or denied, meaning that their money-usage is either allowed or prohibited with regard to certain objects or goods. [p198] Former are often not allowed to possess any money at all, while the latter

---

engaged in agricultural work. Individuals with *Bauernfähigkeit* typically did not have the same rights and privileges as the nobility. They were subject to feudal obligations, such as providing labour services, paying rent or tribute to noble landowners, and working the land.

[431] [tn] An Islamic state or territory that is ruled by a caliph.

may possess money but are subject to restrictions on its use. The motives for such usage restrictions are varied. In primitive economies, they usually aim to reserve the possession or enjoyment of certain goods for the dominant stratum or social group.

Indeed, it is a long journey until "all exchange counterparts, regardless of their caste, have the right to exchange with anyone." But this is the prerequisite for the full development of the exchange-economy with money-exchange, i.e., the sales of a commodity for money and money for a commodity.

> For only the *jus commercii*[432] guarantees the seller the free choice of consideration. Money-exchange presupposes the merging of castes.[433]

4. The purchasing power of money is bound to specific locations or times. Local and temporal restrictions often coincide. There are numerous examples from the history of primitive money, but such constraints are also evident in later times. A fascinating example from the Admiralty Islands was already mentioned on p. 101.

Of course, as already mentioned, this, as with the entire area of questions, does not concern an actual qualification of money, but rather "market regulations" prompted by origin, usage, custom, or authoritative policy objectives, which as such more or less affect the purchasing power of money and often decisively influence it. In other words, the majority of 'purchasing power restrictions' do not directly target money, although there are also such restrictions (e.g., restricted-money (*Sperrgeld*) that can only be used for specific and limited purposes). Instead, they are market policy measures that indirectly, namely through their effect, result in a restriction of the purchasing power of money. This is not to say that the directly related 'purchasing power restrictions' that affect money itself

---

[432] [tn] The right of commerce or the right of trade.

[433] Dobretsberger (ibid.:33).

cannot also serve the purpose of market regulation.

Max Weber distinguished market regulations as follows:

[p199] 1. A traditional one, based on the habituation to inherited exchange restrictions,

2. A conventional one, determined by social disapproval of the marketability of certain useful services (*Nutzleistung*),

3. A legal one, through effective legal restrictions on exchange, either general or specific to certain groups or exchange objects.[434]

This listing demonstrates how, as a result of such "market regulations," the marketability of goods is subject to traditional, conventional, and legal restrictions. From the perspective of money, it means that the purchasing power of money is subject to subjective or objective constraints.

Magical, clan-related, and class-based beliefs and orders tend to exclude certain objects or subjects from market exchange for a long time. Furthermore, socially or politically motivated price-regulations (price-ceilings) and consumption regulations become significant for the purchasing power of money.

The living space of money (*Lebensraum des Geldes*) is initially quite small. This applies to hoard-money as well as exchange-money. In the exchange-money stage, the power of money expands as exchange-intercourse and payment-traffic develop. Early on, as mentioned earlier,

---

[434] Weber (1925:43; 2019:169). [tn] In addition, the last one mentioned by Weber is:

> voluntaristic, that is, related to the given constellation of interests, with material market regulation in a formally free market. This tends to arise when particular parties interested in exchange, by virtue of their more or less entirely exclusive Chance of either possessing or acquiring powers of disposal with regard to specific utilities (monopoly), are placed in a position to influence the market situation by effectively blocking the market freedom of others (ibid.).

some rights (performance-rights for dances, songs, etc., or rights to use spells, recipes, and the like) become the object of 'money as a means of earning.' An important expansion is achieved in the purchasing power of money with the development and spread of the idea of composition (*Komposition*)[435] or penance (*Buße*). This refers to the possibility of compensating through a payment for a physical atonement that has been incurred. *Wergeld* is the most well-known and important example of this. "The idea of composition," as H. Trimborn has shown, "has triumphed around the world with the spread of agriculture and pastoral cultures, but it has also seen a triumph in terms of content, as more or less all types of legal violations have been encompassed by this possibility."[436] [P200] This leads to the development of "composition systems" (*Kompositionensystem*) or "penance-catalogues" (*Bußkatalog*), which means comprehensive cataloguing and pricing of the consequences of wrongdoing in terms of money.[437] The emergence of such composition systems, as Trimborn explains, is due to the richer development of means of payment that occurred in these cultures of 'producing economy'

---

[435] [tn] 'Composition' (*Komposition*) refers to a legal concept in which a penalty for a crime can be redeemed through the payment of compensation, consisting of a combination of *Wergeld* and penance (*compositio*). The exact amount of this compensation varied depending on the severity of the offence and the social status of the victim. Part of this penalty was allocated to the community, later known as '*Friedensgeld*' (peace-money), and a portion was designated for the judiciary (approximately one-third of the compensation). This concept was prevalent in the period of legal development during the Frankish era (around 500–888 AD) but declined in importance from the 10th-11th century onwards, eventually giving way to legal systems based on physical punishments, such as the principle of talion (retaliation in kind), which persisted as a significant influence on the development of criminal law throughout history.

[436] Trimborn (1950: 139).

[437] Cf. Achter (1950, 13 ff.).

(*erzeugende Wirtschaft*).[438] [439] It is evident what significance it must have for the development of the monetary framework when even the most serious offences can be atoned for with money-penances. It should be mentioned in passing that, as V. Achter (1950) has shown, this transformation was not driven by materialistic considerations but by magical or religious beliefs.

According to this, money has been a means of exchange and a means of payment with very limited service-capacity for millennia. For a long time, most of the world of goods and services was not accessible to the purchasing power of money, either because they were considered *extra commercium*[440] or because their acquisition, like money-usage itself, was limited to a specific group of people.

Furthermore, the purchasing power of money is further constrained by the fact that initially, usually multiple money-types circulate side by side, each with its limited domain of influence. Therefore, from the perspective of goods, various types of money are required to acquire different goods.

For the economic-intercourse of primitives, Thurnwald also notes:

> The purchase-price cannot be paid in arbitrary value carriers because so-called primitive money never has universal exchange force or purchasing force but always represents a specific target object.[441] Additionally, as mentioned earlier, there is the restriction of the time and place binding of the exchange-intercourse.

---

[438] [tn] It is a term used to describe the economic system in the Neolithic period. A transition occurred from gathering and harvesting wild grains to deliberate cultivation. People became settled. Instead of makeshift dwellings, they constructed permanent houses. The producing economy continued to evolve during the Bronze Age.

[439] Trimborn (ibid.:139).

[440] [tm] Refer to footnote 425.

[441] Thurnwald (ibid.: I, 122).

[p201] In the course of its evolution and development, money breaks through the constraints imposed on it by convention, custom, and law. It reaches out for all things and, by grasping them, becomes the measuring unit for all things. Its purchasing power grows and encompasses the full range of possibilities for interest and enjoyment. Money becomes the unrestricted and universally valid means of exchange, whose deployment is crucial everywhere and always.

To the extent that money acquires purchasing power, it gains social power. Because the social power of money is its purchasing power, and anything that strengthens and increases the purchasing power of money — such as the development of market-intercourse, the structure of legal-orders, and so on — enhances its social power. Through its purchasing power, money becomes the nerve centre of the economy, even of society. It becomes a formidable power that not only dominates economic life but also permeates, if not undermines, political and cultural aspects, and it does not spare religious life from its influence either. All of this, however, occurs because it finds its foundation in the purchasing power anchored in the economic aspect. It draws its force from this source.

> The purchasing power of money is what lures everything desirable to the market: goods of all kinds, whether they serve the coarsest material or the finest intellectual pleasures. Everything becomes purchasable: food and drink, women and friendships, honours and opinions. And it is precisely this, that money must have material purchasing power, i.e., purchasing power vis-à-vis physical things in life to make the psychological ones dependent as well.

> Where money guarantees material purchasing power, the spirit of venality and corruption tends to nest there, there corruption finds its fertile soil, there it serves equally for legal and illegal purposes. Only where money has material purchasing power is it possible for a handful of money to outweigh a sack full of justice and truth.

> In a society corrupted by the purchasing power of money, crimes are atoned for with money, sins are forgiven through monetary payments, blemishes of character are erased with money, and

conscientious scruples are appeased with money. Of course, the old saying still holds true here: 'Money is neither good nor bad; it depends on the one who uses it.' To those who know how to use it properly, money is a willing servant; to those who submit to it, it becomes a cruel master. This applies to individuals as well as to society. When success is solely seen in the act of making money, when the sole purpose in life is 'to make money,' a sharp division of classes emerges, with the exploitation of the weak by the strong, meaning the poor by the rich. Self-interest determines judgment. In the scales of justice, it is not the sword that is placed, but the money bag.[442]

The peak of its power-authority as a means of exchange and a means of payment, its **almighty purchasing power** (*Kaufallmacht*), is reached in that societal order founded on individual ownership of the means of production, which is often referred to as the individualistic or liberal. To realise their 'system concept' (*Systemgedanken*) of unrestricted free 'permission of disposal and control' (*Verfügungsberechtigung*) over people and things according to the principle of self-interest, it also includes the elimination of all remaining restrictions on the purchasing power of money. The monetary policy of economical individualism (*ökonomischer Individualismus*) or liberalism turns money into a tool of economic freedom by ensuring its unrestricted usage. When the freedom of ownership is proclaimed and every ownership is declared to be freely transferable, when all barriers of trades, of inheritance, of sharing, of disposal are removed, so that everyone can acquire and enjoy without hindrance, when free competition in production and sales, freedom of the market, of supply and demand, of price-formation, of investment and of choice of consumption are demanded and enforced, then behind this stands money in its highest unfolding of purchasing power.

---

[442] Cf. Gerloff (1947:17 f.). [tn] See also, Marx (1844) with strikingly similar observations.

But the moment this economic system is called into question, the moment its institutions are no longer seen as expressions of immutable claims of innate human rights, but are attacked and tampered with, the status of money is also shaken. [℗203] It is not a question here of the exchange-economy being eliminated and money as a means of exchange thus becoming superfluous. Instead, it concerns restrictions on free exchange-economic intercourses, which can be imposed from various angles and for various reasons, and which hinder the exercise of the purchasing power of money. These restrictions can lead to a situation where the control over money no longer ensures the ability to exchange it at any time for a variety of material-goods and service-performances of any choice. It is the planned economy that undermines the omnipotence of money as a means of purchase and exchange by its order of demand-fulfilment and thus economic intercourses. Its measures do not necessarily target an immediate influence on money-usage and often do not; however, they almost always result in a significant restriction of the purchasing power of money.

Interventions in the free exchange-economic intercourses usually occur in order to achieve certain economic, social, or political goals. The customary means are measures of 'price policy,' especially government regulations and price-controls, which supersede free price-formation. Instead of competitive-prices (*Konkurrenzpreis*), regulated-prices (*gesatzter Preis*), i.e., prices determined by statute (*Satzung*) take their place. The regulated-prices can be market-near (*marktnahe*), which is why the term 'market-complied tariffs' (*Ordnungstaxe*) have been suggested for them, or they can be 'market-distant prices' (*marktferner Preis*), also known as 'authoritative tariffs' (*echte Taxe*).[443] The former refers to prices

---

[443] [tn] 'Market-complied tariffs' (*Ordnungstaxe*) means prices set at the market equilibrium level. Cf. The distinction between 'well-arranged tariffs' and 'authoritative tariffs' is made by Mises (1929:123) in a similar vein.

In the context of terms like '*Ordnungstaxe*' (market-complied tariff) and '*echte*

that do not significantly deviate from those that would form in a free market exchange. The latter, on the other hand, are those that significantly deviate from the prices that would form based on supply and demand in the free market. The market-near regulated-prices, as is evident, hardly affect the purchasing power of money. It is different with market-distant regulated-prices. These come in two types: underprices (*Unterpreise*) or overprices (*Überpreise*). The latter are not of interest in this context. While the latter do affect the purchasing force of money, they do not directly affect its purchasing power, i.e., the ability (*Befugnis*) to buy. The situation is different with underprices.

Regulated-underprices are prices that are set lower by statute than the prices that would form for the respective goods in the free market. [𝔭204] They result in an increase in the purchasing force of certain incomes and income portions. That is also their purpose. However, achieving this must be accompanied by a reduction in the purchasing force of the money used in the free market, which comes at the expense of diminishing the objective purchasing power of money. Because goods are bound by prices to this extent, money cannot be used at will in competition for a limited supply of goods. It no longer provides the guarantee that it can be exchanged at

---

Taxe' (authoritative tariff), the use of *'Taxe'* (tariff) instead of *'Preis'* (price) is specific to certain technical or legal contexts in the German language. *'Taxe'* (tariff) typically refers to a rate, fee, or charge, often in regulated or standardised contexts. It is commonly used in German legal and regulatory language, especially in fields like healthcare and insurance. So, when discussing regulated prices, especially in industries like healthcare or insurance where fees and charges may be standardised or regulated, the term *'Taxe'* (tariff) is used to emphasise the specific nature of these charges. It is a matter of linguistic convention in these particular domains. In everyday language or more general contexts, the term *'Preis'* (price) is indeed used to refer to prices. So, *'Ordnungspreis'* (market-complied price) could theoretically be used instead of *'Ordnungstaxe'* (market-complied tariff) to convey a similar meaning, but in certain industries and contexts, *'Taxe'* (tariff) has become the preferred term.

any time for any goods and services, which is actually a prerequisite for its existence as a means of exchange. It is no longer the greater money offer that determines the allocation of goods, which are not naturally available in sufficient quantity at the firmly regulated-underprices (scarce goods), but rather various circumstances – custom, law, chance, arbitrariness, or affiliation with some group (party, race, etc.) – decide who get a chance in the market.

The significance of this objective restriction of the purchasing power of money for money itself or for the evaluation of money depends on the number and nature of goods and their price-control. If the prices for a large number of goods, perhaps even for most essential goods and services, are fixed at a given level (stop-prices (*Stoppreis*), price-ceilings) as a result of official orders, this does not impair the purchasing power of money as long as these prices correspond to the market situation. However, this is usually not the case, or it does not last long. Price-ceilings or stop-prices are either initially regulated-underprices or tend to become so very quickly. This means that the purchasing power of money cannot be exercised across the entire spectrum of price-controlled goods and services. Its purchasing power can only be exerted in the domain of non-price-controlled goods and services. The narrower this scope, the greater the apparent disempowerment of money. At the same time, it should be noted that a reduction in its purchasing force is associated with the money operating in this domain.

[₽205] A number of other measures have a similar effect on the purchasing power of money as the regulated-prices in the managed economy. Think of prohibitions on sales and purchases, prohibitions on investments and operations, as well as all those restrictions on economic intercourses that have practically the same effect as those. International economic agreements with their compensatory-transaction (*Kompensationsverkehr*) [to maintain a more balanced trade relationship] also limit the purchasing power of money. One only has to imagine how many things and purposes are prescribed for in such a managed economy with constraints in money-expending to see how much the purchasing power of money is impaired. An economic system in which one needs not only money but also other forms of identifications to buy bread and other food, textiles, soap, coal, etc., and where one requires not only capital but also other legitimations to establish and operate businesses, signifies, a restriction of the purchasing power of money and thus a dethronement of money itself in all these conditions.

It is easy to see that such a development has an impact on the function of money. In short, it signifies a **de-functionalisation** of money. In a liberal societal economy, money serves as a means of exchange, a means of expressing prices, a means of payment, and a means of account. Money is used in transactions and serves as the basis for economic accounting, assuming that its purchasing power remains unchanged. In the context of the system of liberal economics, this means that money is essentially unlimited in its purchasing power. That is the meaning of money in the liberal societal economy, that it is taken as a counter-value in transactions in order to acquire any desired good, any aspired service, according to demand and opportunity. The more goods are removed from the free market, subject to supply restrictions and price-controls, the more money loses its aptitude to serve as a means of exchange, and its primary function diminishes. If money fails in this regard, it not only has significant implications for its function as a means of exchange but also for the structure of economic relations itself. [p206] When money is no longer an unconditional means of exchange, the 'disposal and control over money' or income no longer solely determine participation in the social-product and the ability to participate in the economic process.

Furthermore, if the use of money as a means of exchange is restricted, it also affects its impact on the market and price-formation, as well as its aptitude as a means of price-expression. Competition in the supply and demand for goods and services in the market is highly influenced, and even determined, by the extent of the subjective and objective purchasing power of money. The expansion of the purchasing power of money, accordingly, signifies an expansion of the market with all its well-known economic advantages. The influence on price movements is evident. Prices will correspond more closely to market conditions and, thus, to the given economic conditions (*Verhältnissen*) the more unhindered competition is asserted through the purchasing power of money. They thus become not only the regulator of the market but also the impetus of the economy itself. A restriction of the purchasing power of money, however, has the opposite effect and leads to a narrowing of the market in terms of both supply and demand, thereby inhibiting market function and, especially, economic price-formation. Indeed, this may be the intention behind an administrative restriction of the purchasing power of money, but one must not ignore the consequences of such interference in economic flows. Additionally, it should be noted that money with restricted purchasing power tends to enter the market in a very specific direction and affects supply and demand. This leads to a decrease in the purchasing force of that money, the use-potentiality of which is limited to the circle of goods and service-performances that are not subject to purchase restrictions.

A money that cannot enter the market or can only do so in a limited manner cannot make a universally valid statement about the exchange-ratios in the market, which means the prices. [p207] Therefore, money loses its function of regulating the course of the market-economy through prices. In a free market-economy, the goods-production is regulated by the prices of goods in the market. The relationships are well-known. However, this automatic control of production can only be exercised by prices if they are flexible. This is not the case when money can only buy in conjunction with restricted benefit-rights; in that case, it loses the crucial function it plays in a free-market-economy as a regulator of goods-procurement and goods-distribution. Only money with unrestricted purchasing power can fulfil this function through prices, meaning that rising prices encourage production while falling prices act as a brake or constraint.

Furthermore, 'purchasing power restrictions' of money also question its aptitude as a means of economic accounting. The deployment of cost-goods, income determination, and profit calculation can only be based on money with unrestricted purchasing power if they are to be rational. This is related to the fact that money with restricted purchasing power cannot make unconditional statements about the possibility of goods-procurement because, as explained, the provision in the market depends not simply on the disposal and control over monetary resources. This means that the rationality of economic management is at risk. Monetary accounting, as a compass for economic control and a means of controlling economic events, presupposes money with purchasing power. Therefore, it must fail to the extent that the purchasing power of money is subject to fluctuations and, in particular, differentiations [in the purchasing power of money for different goods and services depending on factors such as government regulations and price-controls].

The effect of the 'purchasing power restriction' of money on the monetary function depends on the nature and extent of the restrictions. Depending on the goods to which the 'purchasing power restrictions' apply, they can aim for either guidance for consumers or productions. [♭208] However, they can also affect or even halt the capital function of money. What this means in economical and social terms should be clear from the explanations provided about the capital function of money (§22, 193 ff.).

The 'purchasing power restriction' of money thus signifies a de-functionalisation of money. This, in turn, means that it challenges the prevailing economic and social order and ultimately transforms it.

The various methods and means of 'purchasing power restriction' of money, some of which have already been mentioned, will not be further explored here. Likewise, there is no intention to examine the 'purchasing power restrictions' with regard to specific market domains, as important as such investigations may be. Think not only of the commodity market but also of the labour and capital markets. It is only intended to be noted here that as long as free price-formation is restricted in any way and as long as there are restrictions on purchasing capabilities, such as for the acquisition or use of foreign exchange or funds from specific sources, or for the price of capital, i.e., interest rates, and the price of labour, i.e., wages (not to mention the commodity market), the purchasing power of money is subject to restrictions, and money's function is impaired. On the other hand, let's examine the main effects and accompanying phenomena that tend to occur as a result of such profound measures.

The development of the capitalist 'earning-oriented economy,' focused on monetary gain, goes hand in hand with the development of the absolute purchasing power of money. Money-earning makes sense in our societal order only to the extent that money guarantees purchases, meaning that it enables the acquisition of all desired means of demand-satisfaction. However, if the purchasing power of money is restricted, it becomes clear very soon that money-earning is only seemingly an end in itself but, in reality, it is a means of obtaining everything that is required by demand. If money cannot ensure the demand-fulfilment, a return to a self-sufficiency economy and direct barter trade becomes an immediate consequence. [p209] However, both of these are forms of demand-fulfilment that are significantly less in their service-capacity compared to demand-fulfilment based on the division of labour and monetary economic intercourses.

The goods-traffic in a free-market-economy requires unconditionally powerful money for its most efficient execution. Having disposal and control over such money typically ensures unrestricted disposal and control over any material-goods and service-performances at all times. That is why this money is, in the market itself, the good for which there is a constant and general demand. From the perspective of commodities, this means that where it can be used without restriction, it elicits the largest possible supply. To the extent that money is restricted in its purchasing power, it also loses its force to stimulate supply and thus diminishes its general desirability to some extent. The market's ability for demand-fulfilment becomes less flexible and is ultimately seriously threatened. This necessitates defensive measures such as compulsion in supply and delivery and orders of allocation. Each step along this path almost inevitably leads to further restrictions on free monetary economic market-intercourse until complete rationing seizes the production and distribution of entire groups of goods. The sovereign rulership (*souveräne Herrschaft*) of money in the market is then broken. In addition, there is something else: "When the honest citizen," as O. Veit once expressed it, "can hardly acquire essential goods for his hard-earned money and the commands of the state are constantly at odds with one's own interests, then inevitably every civic morality must waver."[444]

In a free-market-economy, "full employment of money" (*Vollbeschäftigung des Geldes*) is a prerequisite for its satisfactory function. However, it is readily apparent that to the extent the purchasing power of money is restricted, its marketability, as C. Menger called it, must suffer. [ᵱ210] The money, "which is normally the embodiment of the highest liquidity,"[445] loses its liquidity content to the extent that it loses its aptitude to carry out exchange-intercourses. Its dominant status as a generally accepted means of exchange is undermined, and it may well be that other goods that are not money acquire a special role as intermediaries in exchange, leaving open the question of whether they might not become money in this process. "However, with this, the monetary economy falls into agony" (O. Veit). In the free capitalist 'earning-oriented economy,' money is the means of generating income. Incomes are in the form of money. If the purchasing power of money is obstructed, it, seen as a whole, means a devaluation of incomes, which cannot remain without repercussions on the economic interest of income generation. Economic and social policy restrictions on the purchasing power of money have their limits. If these limits are consistently exceeded, it must inevitably lead to a reduction of the earning-interest and ultimately also of the social-product.

The distribution of the social-product in our economic system is carried

---

[444] Veit (1948:9).

[445] Veit (1947:28).

out through the use of money. The purchasing power formation of money is a means to guide the distribution of the social-product in specific directions. In the case of a 'purchasing power restriction' of money, the purchasing capability is no longer determined solely by the price mechanism of the free market-economy. Instead, it is influenced, to a greater or lesser extent, by both the subjective and objective purchasing power of money. 'Purchasing power restrictions' of money, therefore, function as measures to alter the income-distribution.

The intended restriction of the purchasing power of money brought about by administrative policies typically aims to preserve and safeguard the purchasing force of money by inhibiting or rendering inactive its unconditional purchasing power. It aims to prevent an excess of money from entering the market or the undesirable consequences of unrestricted 'disposal and control over money,' which could lead to unwanted demand affecting price levels and the value of money. The most familiar case to us is when the free disposal of money is restricted with the intention of raising or preserving the purchasing force of smaller incomes or income portions to meet social subsistence demand by limiting the free use-potentiality of a portion of the income. [p211] Under certain conditions and with the right choice of means, as experience teaches us, this goal can indeed be achieved.

However, one must be clear about the consequences of such measures for our economic and social order. 'Purchasing power restrictions' tend to weaken and undermine the social and economic status of money possessors and income receivers; on the other hand, they strengthen the power-status of the possessor of material-values. The recipients of small incomes are usually favoured because the restriction of the purchasing power of money generally only applies to areas that are more or less outside their areas of interest. But this preferential treatment is therefore kept within the rather narrow framework of a purchasing breadth and purchasing width, which as a rule only extends to the essential subsistence demand. It therefore affects a relatively small circle. For all those for whom this money-expending is not sufficient due to their income situation, 'purchasing power restrictions' mean a disadvantage. The same applies to all creditors who have claims based on money with purchasing power, which are then paid and settled with money with restricted purchasing power. Conversely, their debtors benefit from this situation with corresponding gains.

The **purchasing power** of money is therefore just as much a subject of economic and social power-struggle in society as the purchasing force of money. Restrictions on the **purchasing power** of money are sometimes demanded for social and economic reasons, but they are also fought against and rejected for similar reasons. If, as shown, a restriction of the unconditional purchasing power of money – in the sense of eliminating or narrowing down the free competition for essential life necessities through money – corresponds to the desires of small and lowest income receivers, [p212] then all those who have an income exceeding the minimum for existence are consequently interested in the unrestricted purchasing power of money. As a result, in the societal struggle over the power of money, there are always efforts to restrict the purchasing power of money competing with those aiming to expand it. Certainly, there may be a public social interest in ensuring that small incomes provide the guarantee of satisfying life's necessities on the market, but it is equally important that attractive use-potentiality for private income aspirations are preserved for income portions that go beyond that. Both large and small income recipients feel disadvantaged by restrictions on the purchasing power of money, and they often call for the restoration of the purchasing power of money. Both large and small income recipients will be encouraged by too extensive restrictions on the purchasing power of money to engage in uneconomical expenditures and to forgo prudent saving. Their earning-interests are being paralysed. In addition to this, there is the well-known phenomenon of asserting the purchasing power of money by bypassing regulated-prices. The supply of commodities is withheld from legitimate trade and diverted to the black market. This already implies that even temporary restrictions on the purchasing power of money may encounter significant resistance under certain circumstances. However, if there were to be permanent restrictions of this kind, it would certainly not eliminate money from the economy, but its status would indeed become significantly different.

Such a transformation of the nature of money would be both a consequence and a contributing factor to a complete transformation of the handed-down economic system, in which conventional money has played a decisive role in its development and expansion. Only money with a highly developed purchasing power could bring about that transformation of the economic life that led to the dissolution of the natural-economy (*Naturalwirtschaft*) and the transformation of service-performances and in-kind-disbursements (*Naturalleistung*), and of patrimonial obligations into monetary-disbursements (*Geldleistung*), [₵213] as well as to a substantial division of labour and occupational division of the population with an exchange-economic interconnection of all individual economies, to the dissociation of urban and rural areas, and the creation of a society entirely dependent on income derived from money, be it wages, profits, or rent.

The organisational principle of a market-economy is only compatible with money that does not have restricted purchasing power. The 'purchasing power restriction' of money is a characteristic of a planned economy, a centrally managed economy, or an economy that aims for differentiated demand-fulfilment and enforced consumption restraint based on some social or political principle.

When one considers that individual self-responsibility and an 'orientation towards earning' are the psychological aspects, individual ownership of the means of production and free disposal and control over goods and labour are the legal aspects, and division of labour is the technical foundation of this system, and that it has been money that has made it possible to build the modern economy on this basis, then it appears to me that the answer to the question of how the purchasing power of money will be in the future is given. It will certainly have some constraints compared to the money of the era of economical liberalism that correspond to the social and political demands of the time. However, primarily, it will remain objectively and subjectively unrestricted. Because only money that is essentially unrestricted in purchasing power is capable of serving as a means of exchange, fuelling the economy, and functioning as a tool for social action in providing the services upon which our civilisation and culture are based. Therefore, in our economy, only such money is conceivable.

V. Money in the Social Order

§28. The Right Money

[ρ214] Money is a peculiar thing. There is probably no one, that is, no adult in our cultural sphere, who has not been concerned about this at some point; many, especially when money was lacking at the right time and place or was too scarce; but likely everyone when it is necessary, every day, this is the case every day when it comes to dispose of monetary resources in a sensible and responsible manner, whether they are limited or abundant, sensibly and responsibly. That is why a witty Frenchman, Jules Renard,[446] once said, "Finally, I know what distinguishes humans from animals: money worries."

However, it would be incorrect to only associate the concern that money brings to people with the worries of the common man. The worry over money has preoccupied statesmen, philosophers, and theologians of all times, from Lycurgus[447] to Roosevelt, from Plato and Aristotle to Fichte and Simmel, and from Thomas Aquinas to Leo XIII.

What is the concern that has preoccupied them? It is the concern for the 'right money' (*richtiges Geld*). Money is a means for specific purposes. Considered as a purposive institution (*Zweckeinrichtung*),[448] there is 'good money'[449] and 'bad money.' The 'right money,' however, is something

---

[446] [tn] French author (1864-1910) known for poignant and concise observations on life through his *"Journal."*

[447] [tn] A legendary figure in ancient Greece, traditionally credited with the establishment of the Spartan Constitution and way of life. He is said to have lived around the 9th century BCE.

[448] [tn] To rephrase the sentence: "When a functional aspect of the institution called money is considered." See p. 117 for 'purposive institution.'

[449] [tn] Refer to p. 215 for 'good money,' which is characterised by its efficiency in functions.

different from 'good money'; it is money that provides the assurance that its services or performances align with certain concepts or perhaps even convictions, such as a certain legal belief. The 'right money' is 'just money' (*gerechtes Geld*). Indeed, as we read in Aristotle, as quoted in another context: "He who brings money must be able to obtain what he needs."[450] Significantly, we find these words in his *Nicomachean Ethics*, specifically in a chapter that contains an examination of which activities are to be considered 'just' (*gerecht*) or 'unjust' (*ungerecht*).[451]

[📖215] A medieval commentator on Aristotle, none other than Thomas Aquinas, says in clear reference to the Stagirite's[452] explanations:

> Money must have a purchasing force so that the one who offers it immediately obtains what he needs. However, it is a fact that the same applies to money as it does to other things: you do not always get as much for it as you want because it does not always have the same force, meaning it does not always possess the same value. However, it should be designed to maintain a more constant value than other things. The 'right money' is the money that is as value-stable as possible.

If we add to this that Thomas Aquinas, in his work *De regimine principum* (On the Government of Rulers) dedicated to the King of Cyprus, places a moral obligation on rulers to align the nominal value of the money coin they determine as closely as possible with its exchange value, we have the Thomistic monetary doctrine's response to the question of the 'right money.'

What the *doctor angelicus*[453] taught was embraced by later Scholastics.

---

[450] [tn] Refer to footnote 419.

[451] [tn] Aristotle (2009:1132b20-113a15, 88-91).

[452] [tn] It is a reference to the philosopher Aristotle, who was born in the ancient Greek city of Stagira.

[453] [tn] A Latin title that means the "Angelic Doctor." It is an honorary and reverential title given to the philosopher and theologian Thomas Aquinas.

In addition to the authority of the head of the canonist-scholastic economic doctrine, scholars like Buridanus[454] and Oresmius,[455] to name just the most important ones, were also influenced by the monetary disruptions of their time. Given the constant debasements of coins, often bordering on fraud, which were a common tool of public financial policy at the time, the answer to the question of the 'right money' could be no different than the one Thomas had given: the 'right money' is the one that maintains its value as much as possible, and according to the prevailing understanding of the time, that was the fully minted and issued coin.

In the subsequent period, the question of the 'right money' seemed to recede somewhat. While previously it had primarily been philosophers and theologians who had provided certain fundamental considerations about economic matters, it was now statesmen, administrators, and men of business who addressed immediate and practical questions within their spheres of influence. [⁋216] The total of their quite different economic doctrines, all aimed at promoting the prosperity of the ruler, the state, and the people, is commonly referred to as mercantilism. What characterises the era of mercantilism is the increased significance of money as a means of circulation, as the lifeblood in the cycle of the rapidly developing economy. At that time, a new phase of monetary economic development began. Therefore, the mercantilist writers directed their interest primarily towards acquiring sufficient reserves of money, which, according to the

---

[454] [tn] Jean Buridan (c. 1300-1360), often referred to as Buridanus, was a prominent French philosopher and logician in the late Middle Ages. He made significant contributions to various fields, particularly in logic, physics, and philosophy.

[455] [tn] Nicolas Oresme (c. 1320 – 1382), often referred to as Oresmius, was born in France. He made substantial contributions to various fields, including mathematics, natural philosophy, and economics, and he's particularly known for his work on the nature of money and the theory of value. He served as an advisor to King Charles V of France and played a crucial role in shaping economic ideas during his time.

prevailing monetary regime of that time, meant precious metals. M. Saitzew coined the word *chrysohedonism*,[456] a fortunate term for this attitude of mercantilism, namely, as he puts it, *"auri sacra fames"* [the sacred hunger for gold], its insatiable greed, its centuries-long cry for precious metals.[457] According to this *chrysomania* of theirs, the 'right money' for the mercantilists is full-value precious metal money.

Even among older proponents of natural law, one can find remarks that relate to our subject in a certain sense. Just as they have specific ideas and convictions founded on natural law for all essential institutions concerning human co-living, so too in the case of money, they hold convictions about how the 'right money' should be structured, or rather, how it should prove to be the 'right money' through its effects or services. However, this thought does not necessarily lead to a clear conception even among them. One can, however, say that behind their discussions about money, albeit somewhat unconsciously, lies the 'idea of the right money.' This is particularly the case when there is mention of the false image of money *"que le corruption en a établie dans le monde"* [that corruption has established itself in the world] as with Boisguillebert, a precursor and Physiocrat, or when the same author laments the serious shortcomings that arise from the use of the money that was circulating at that time. He refers to the first legislator of antiquity (Lycurgus)[458] who recognised this and, as a result, introduced a different form of money (the 'right money'!) in his republic. [↩217] In certain passages of Montesquieu's famous 22nd book of *De l'esprit des lois* (The Spirit of the Laws), particularly in sections (II and III) on "Nature of Currency" (*Nature de la Monnaie*) and "Ideal Currency" (*des Monnaies idéales*), the idea of the 'right money' seems to resonate, although it is not explicitly stated.

---

[456] [tn] Hedonism for gold, where *chrysos* (χρυσός) means gold in Greek.

[457] [tn] The reference source is likely to be Saitzew (1941).

[458] [tn] See footnote 447.

Classical economics has assigned to money the role of a mere technical means. Money is just *"une petite richesse intermédiaire"* (a small intermediary wealth), as Quesnay expressed in the analysis of *Tableau économique* (Economic Table). It fulfils its function by facilitating economic flows. As John Stewart Mill has said:

> It is a machine for doing quickly and commodiously, what would be done, though less quickly and commodiously, without it.[459]

For classical economists, the 'right money' is therefore that which is confined to its technical function, and its role as an intermediary, and thus does not inherently influence exchange-ratios. It is understandable when John Stewart Mill says of such money:

> There cannot, in short, be intrinsically a more insignificant thing in the economy of society than money.[460]

According to classical doctrines, money is or should be an indifferent or, as it is often said, a neutral element of economic flows. Its role is to facilitate the goods-distribution but not to inherently alter the magnitude of the shares of economic output that accrue to individuals.

For the classical economists, this gives rise to the problem of the right currency regime (*Währungsverfassung*) that ensures the 'right money': that is, **neutral** money that does not disrupt what is perceived as natural price-formation by its presence in the economy or, better put, by its entry into the economy. Therefore, the monetary and banking discussions that dominated the first half of the previous century in England, the homeland of classical economic doctrines, primarily revolved around the question of creating a monetary and banking system that would ensure indifferent [neutral] money, which does not inherently influence what was

---

[459] [tn] Mill (1871: Book III, Chapter VII §3). The sentence is followed by "and like many other kinds of machinery, it only exerts a distinct and independent influence of its own when it gets out of order."

[460] [tn] Mill (ibid.).

considered the natural flow of goods. The famous Currency Theory and Banking Theory[461] are the fruits of these discussions.

From this concept of the 'right money,' which is just one application of the classical idea of the natural order and self-regulation of the economy, arises the task of the proper monetary or currency policy: the right **money-creation**. [p218] The nature of this, in the sense of the classical economists, is evident. What is meant is a provision of the economy with money in such a way that the money-creation does not affect commodity prices or the equilibrium of the price-system. The money created in this manner is called **classical money** (*klassisches Geld*).

The classical economists' notion that the 'right money' must be neutral is based on the fact that in the system of classical economics, money is primarily viewed as a means of exchange. However, if the role of money in economic flows changes, meaning that another function becomes significant in economic-intercourses besides its function as a means of exchange, then the requirement for the 'right money' must take on a different meaning. This is the case as soon as credit transactions (*Kreditverkehr*) become more prevalent in economic life, transforming the monetary economy into a 'credit economy' (*Kreditwirtschaft*).

Money is assigned a new role in this context. It becomes, as English literature calls it, a "standard of deferred payment" or a measure for postponed payments. Naturally, as a means for settling deferred obligations, it is expected to be as stable in value as possible. Additionally, there is another aspect to consider. Money has also served as a **means of saving** (*Sparmittel*) from the early stages of exchange-economic development. At that time, money served as a means of storing value (*Wertaufbewahrungsmittel*) to secure a livelihood in times of need. Later, capital formation (*Kapitalbildung*) and capital-amassing

---

[461] [tn] On the currency school and banking school (and related debates between them), see Schwartz (2018:694).

(*Kapitalansammlung*) came more to the fore as a purpose of saving (*Sparzweck*). Stability of value (*Wertbeständigkeit*) is also required for such savings.

The idea of stable-value money did not originate solely from the credit economy. Whenever significant money-devaluations occurred, whether due to debasement of coinage or an influx of 'paper means of payment' (*papiernes Zahlungsmittel*), there naturally arose a desire for money that maintained its value. Merchants and classical economists believed that this desire could be fulfilled through full-value money or good coins. [p219] However, the fact that even this money was by no means stable in value was hardly noticed during the mercantilist and early classical periods, or the fact was at least accepted as unchangeable. What people desired was a monetary regime that prevented any change in the purchasing force of money due to influences from the monetary side. According to their belief, the metallic monetary regime best met this requirement. According to this doctrine known as metallism, metallic money minted at a full value appeared as the 'right money.'

It was the evolution of the relations of production of the precious metals, gold and silver, primarily during the 19th century, that shook this perspective. Those two metals had almost always been in usage side by side as money since the official adoption of the money coin as money, indeed even before. While the occasional significant fluctuations in the production quantities of gold and silver had previously led to economic disruptions, it was in the 19th century, when the monetary and credit economy based on metallic monetary regimes reached its zenith, that significant monetary reform movements emerged. These movements aimed to address the causes of crises inherent in monetary regimes. The dispute that arose regarding the single domination or dual domination of monetary metals[462] is well-known. Is the 'right money,' as advocated by

---

[462] [tn] Monometalism versus bimetallism.

proponents of the gold standard, gold money alone, or is it, as bimetallists argued, both gold and silver money, or perhaps, as was less frequently demanded, silver alone? These were the questions at hand.

Those who advocated for bimetallism as a currency system (*Währungssystem*) did so primarily believing that the quantitative money demand could not be satisfied by one of the two metals alone. Additionally, they believed that they could best address the value fluctuations of money, mainly caused by varying production yields, by coupling the two metals into a unified currency system.

[P220] This doctrine, known as the "parachute theory" (*Fallschirmtheorie*) according to an example cited by Wolowski[463] and widely discussed at the time, also regards as the 'right money' that which is least subject to fluctuations in value arising from the money material or money-creation — essentially, those occurring on the monetary side.

It is noteworthy that around the same time, both bimetallists and monometallists raised the question of stabilising the value of money, but in a different sense — specifically, in terms of the purchasing force of money, or its stability in relation to commodities. The 'right money' is

---

[463] [tn] Wolowski (1870:100, quoted from Ljungberg & Ögren 2021:6-7, emphasis and brackets added):

> I would not like to impinge on a question that has been submitted to another commission, the issue of the two metals gold or silver, but in passing I will emit the opinion very firm, very clear, that the stability of prices has meant that many countries, and France in the lead, have maintained the two metals to fulfil the role of [monetary] circulation. The coexistence of silver and gold used as intermediaries in trade has prevented the violent [price] variations that necessarily would have occurred in one way or another if one of the two metals exclusively had served all over the world as intermediaries for transactions in trade. One metal has served as the **parachute** to the other.

Cf. Gabriel Wolowski (1824-1896), also known as Gabriel Wolff was a French economist and advocate of bimetallism during the 19th century.

considered to be the money of intertemporally constant value, whereby value is understood to mean the purchasing force vis-à-vis goods.

While the question of the 'right money' had previously been predominantly considered from the perspective of the monetary material, a new perspective is now being opened up. The new perspective had, in fact, been hinted at since Bodin,[464] who in his famous response from the year 1568[465] to Malestroit's paradoxes,[466] had pointed out that changes in the value of money were determined by changes in the money supply. Some others had adopted and, in part, deepened this doctrine.

The conclusion was evident: to ensure the stability of the value of money through the regulation of the money supply or the circulation of money. In Currency Theory and Banking Theory, and in their application to the organisation of central banks, efforts of this kind found their

---

[464] [tn] Jean Bodin (1530–1596) was a French jurist, philosopher, and economist who made significant contributions to political thought and economics during the Renaissance period. Bodin is notable for his early insights into the relationship between changes in the money supply and fluctuations in the value of money, which is one of the earliest formulations of the quantity theory of money.

[465] [tn] Bodin (1568). See footnote 466.

[466] [tn] Malestroit (1566). The "Paradoxes of the Lord of Malestroit Regarding the Matter of Money" (*Les Paradoxes du Seigneur de Malestroit ... sur le faict des Monnoyes*) was a treatise published in 1566, arguing that commodity prices had remained constant in terms of precious metals over the past 300 years. Malestroit's central argument was changes in the unit of account, resulting from debasement (adding low-value metals to coinage), explained any perceived price increases. Jean Bodin published a response (Bodin 1568), refuting Malestroit's arguments. Bodin challenged the validity of Malestroit's data, questioned whether certain commodities existed in the fourteenth century, and identified other causes of inflation, with the abundance of gold and silver being the most significant. Bodin's response laid the groundwork for the quantity theory of money, suggesting that an increase in the money supply could lead to rising commodity prices. For details, see Achilleos (2022: 431- 432).

expression and reflection, although not necessarily the realisation of their goals.

Efforts and discussions regarding the 'right money' received a new impetus during the crisis period that began in 1873 and extended through the 1880s. This period was characterised by falling prices and significant economic upheavals. The need to account for changes in the value of money when fulfilling long-term obligations has led to various proposals and attempts for quite some time. However, these initially did not aim directly at creating a different, namely, a value-stable money but rather focused on determining the amount of payments due in consideration of price changes that had occurred in the meantime using a table. [▶221] This system was called the table-currency [*Tabellarwährung*].[467]

The proposal to replace the conversion required by this currency emerged, as far as I can see, in the 1870s. Since then, the problem has been discussed extensively.[468]

In his *Théorie de la Monnaie* (Theory of Money, 1886), Léon Walras describes the goal that the scarcity value of the 'value-standard commodity' (*Wertmaßstabware*) and 'commodity as a means-of-exchange'

---

[467] W. Stanley Jevons discusses it in his book (Jevons 1875), which was published in numerous editions and translations. He also mentions various precursors.

[tn] *Tabellarwährung* (table-currency) is a monetary system in which the values of different currencies or monetary units are linked to a table or schedule. In this system, the exchange rates and values of currencies are fixed in relation to each other according to a predetermined table or set of rules. The purpose of this system is to provide stability and predictability in currency exchange rates, making it easier for businesses and individuals to engage in international trade and financial transactions. By establishing clear conversion rates between different currencies, it reduces the risks associated with currency fluctuations.

[468] Some sources credit the American astronomer S. Newcomb as the originator of the idea, but the authorship of the concept is also attributed to other earlier authors. For a comprehensive examination of the entire problem area, refer to the excellent work by C. M. Walsh (1903).

(*Tauschmittelware*) (also money) must change in such a way that a certain average price, which expresses these economic goods essential for societal well-being in this commodity, remains unchanged. This goal is aligned with the ideals of income distribution and justice. He comes to the request: "Money must have a value as regularly changeable as possible."[469]

Approximately at the same time, Alfred Marshall, the leading figure in English national economics in the generation before the turn of the century, advocated for the creation of money whose purchasing force or value should be continuously adjusted to the movements of commodity prices.[470] This idea was then further developed both theoretically and in terms of practical implementation by Silvio Gesell and Irving Fisher about two decades later. J. M. Keynes also incorporated this idea into his currency proposals.

[p222] Internationally, the money reform proposal (*Geldreformvorschlag*) by Irving Fisher has become the most well-known, thanks to a number of clever promotional pamphlets. Like Keynes and some others, he also starts from the premise that gold is poorly suited for the monetary service due to its value fluctuations. He aims to achieve a stable price level, which is also his goal, through a fixed currency based on continuous price-determinations, expressed in the form of an index number, hence also called an **index-currency**. It should not be a specific quantity of gold but rather a bundle of commodities that should serve as a means of monetary accounting, namely a selection of 200-300 commodities in small quantities, such as 2 ounces of butter, 1200 pairs of shoes, 2 pounds of hay, etc., because the idea is to create a **commodity-dollar**. But this bundle of commodities should not be a means of payment; instead, a quantity of gold, adjusted approximately every two months to

---

[469] Warlas (1886). Compare with Walras (1884).

[470] Marshall (1887) and also in his statement before the Royal Gold and Silver Commission in 1888 (Third Report).

reflect changes in the average price of the commodities in this bundle, will be officially determined.

In practice, this would take place in such a way that the central bank would increase the purchase-price for gold or, which is the same thing, issue a smaller quantity of gold when redeeming the notes if the price level of the bundle of commodities falls, and lower the purchase-price if the price level rises. This proposal aims to compensate for any changes in the purchasing force of money, hence the name "**compensated dollar**." The idea is to devalue money when the price level falls and revalue it when it rises.

Silvio Gesell's ideas differ from those of other monetary reformers, even though some of his thoughts align closely with the goals of business cycle policy shared by Fisher and others. What Gesell criticises about conventional money is that it is used as a means of saving, meaning it can be held back and stored for the purpose of capital formation. That is a misuse of the means of exchange. "If we want to adapt our money as a means of exchange to the needs of trade," he says, "we must significantly impair our money as a commodity."[471] [P223] The question of how money must be constituted so that it fulfils its purpose (meant as a means of exchange) in a perfect way without side effects is answered by Gesell with the proposal of '**free-money**' (*Freigeld*)[472] or **rusting-money** (*Schwundgeld*).[473] This refers to a type of money whose calculating unit is kept stable by regulating the money supply in such a way that prices neither rise nor fall, but its money signs are subject to a certain devaluation (depreciation) from week to week. According to Gesell's analogy, they age like a newspaper, spoil like potatoes, or rust like iron and are forced into

---

[471] [tn] Gesell (1906b:94, *A. Die Geldreform in der Praxis 1. Allgemeine Orientierung*).

[472] [tn] 'Free' because it is free from hoarding and from earning interest.

[473] [tn] Gesell (1958:265ff.).

circulation. According to this doctrine, only free-money, i.e., an **index-money** with a 'compulsion to circulate' (*Umlaufszwang*),[474] is considered the 'right money.' Supporters of this doctrine believe that such money guarantees the "full employment of money" and, consequently, the full employment of all labour. The 'right money' should not possess any characteristics that could encourage idleness.

Two different hidden agendas underlie these monetary reform considerations. One intention is to create money that, for its possessor, whether used immediately or in the future, for consumption or capital goods, always allows the acquisition of an equal measure of goods. The other hidden agenda starts from the consideration that the fluctuations in the rise and fall of businesses, with all their accompanying crisis phenomena (economic collapses, unemployment), are attributable to the fluctuations in the purchasing force of money. If these could be eliminated by somehow stabilising the internal value of money, that is, the general price level, it would mean controlling the business movements, eliminating crises, etc. The goal is similar to the one mentioned earlier: money with a constant purchasing force or even one whose purchasing force can be regulated according to the specific needs of the economic situation at any given time.

It is primarily English and American authors who have addressed this issue, including Irving Fisher, J.M. Keynes, R.G. Hawtrey, E.A. Bellerby, W.T. Foster, and W. Catchings. [p224] A publication by the latter two is titled "Business Conditions and Currency Control" (Foster & Catchings 1924), which aptly describes the focus of these discussions.[475]

---

[474] [tn] Gesell (1916:182,1958:217).

[475] Here, where we are only discussing the fundamental concept of the 'right money,' we will not go into the specifics of various plans. For that, reference should be made to relevant literature. In addition to those already mentioned, the following works are notable: Gesell & Frankfurth (1909), Gesell (1906), Hauser (1920), Kleinschmitt (1922), Christen (1920) and Langeluetke (1925).

The means proposed to achieve the two purpose-settings range from simple measures of discount policy to the creation of a new currency, i.e., a different form of money.

The 'right money,' as it is often reiterated, must always have the same purchasing force, just like the measure tape. To solve this problem, **stabilisation of the dollar** is proposed in such a way that its gold content (i.e., the current gold value of the dollar notes) is regulated based on the index figure determined officially from 300 commodities.

The proposals of monetary reformers for creating the 'right money' derive their appeal more from deficiencies that become particularly noticeable during times of crises and often have a significant impact on customary monetary regimes. They also rely on utopian promises of transforming the capitalist social order through monetary reform rather than highlighting genuinely practical possibilities. This statement is not intended to diminish the importance of the problem, as it has been taken seriously by prominent scholars and respected figures in the economic sphere of the United States, leading to the founding of the **Stable Money Association** for its thorough examination. [**225**] One should be aware that there is no such thing as absolutely 'right money,' just as there is no absolute right law or fixed, unchangeable content in a legal-order. The connection is easy to understand: wherever the question of the 'right money' is raised, it involves money that is bound by law in its existence and validity, and whose social functions are supported by the law. The question of the 'right money' thus becomes a question of the right law.

The Scholastics viewed money as an institution within the divine order established by God, which should be shaped and managed in accordance with divine custom law. This perspective is similar to that of the

---

Furthermore, the works of Irving Fisher are significant in this context: Fisher (1911, 1920, 1928, 1935). Additionally, you can refer to Haber's article (Haber 1927), which lists relevant literature on the subject.

Romantics, who saw money as a *donum divinum* [divine gift], a gift from divine providence. To enlightened liberalism, on the other hand, money is an invention of contemplating minds, a creation of reason, arising from agreements or implicit contracts. Kant, the great proponent of reason, also views money as a creation of reason. However, in his work *Metaphysische Anfangsgründe der Rechtslehre* [Metaphysical Foundations of the Doctrine of Right],[476] he answers the question "What is money?" as "a 'legal means of intercourse' (*gesetzliches Mittel des Verkehrs*) of the diligence (*Fleiß*) among [monarchy's] subjects themselves."[477] This confession of the nominalist monetary theory essentially means nothing different from what the defenders of princely coinage authority had always asserted in contrast to the Thomistic doctrine: money is, as Pothier[478] perhaps expressed it most bluntly around the middle of the 18th century, the ownership of the king, which is only left to individuals as a "*signe de valeur des choses*" (a sign of the value of things).[479]

When Kant refers to money as a legal means of intercourse, he is simply expressing an idea that has surfaced repeatedly, both before and after his time, ultimately leading to the belief "that true money is created by an act of legislation,"[480] a doctrine that was not only embraced by Fichte for his "*Geschlossenen Handelsstaat*" [The Closed Commercial State][481] [p226] but also found some adherents elsewhere, although it did not gain significant prominence for a whole century until it found an exceptionally

---

[476] [tn] Kant (1797).

[477] [tn] Kant (1797: §31).

[478] [tn] Robert-Joseph Pothier (1699-1772) was a French lawyer and legal scholar known for his contributions to civil law.

[479] Quoted from Sieveking (1933:278). Also, compare with the reference above at p. 222.

[480] Kudler (1856: 163f.).

[481] [tn] Fichte (1800).

skilled advocate in G. F. Knapp (2023/1923). This has been discussed in a different context earlier.

Like other authors of state utopias, Johann Gottlieb Fichte also wants to create his own money for his state, the "Closed Commercial State": money of unchanging value, with a constant purchasing force. This money, created by the state and, as he says, "introduced through wisdom," should retain its value for grandchildren, great-grandchildren, and even for all eternity. This is the concept of 'right money.'

With this money, however, Fichte meant and intended something else than the 'right money' of the liberal-economical theory of money: the money of the classical economists is the money that facilitates the economic flows but does not change their proportions, thus leaving the economic order untouched. The 'right money' in the sense of the social money reformers [like Fichte], however, is money that is intended to fundamentally change the economic order and thus the existing income-distribution.

All great social reformers from Plato to Ruskin[482] and Tolstoy have grappled with money in their programs, even if it was only in the form of condemnation, rejection, and repudiation of this institution. Just as P. Proudhon says:

> Money is the despot of circulation, the tyrant of trade, the head of commercial feudalism, the symbol of ownership. We must destroy money.[483]

In utopias, however, which have never been lacking from antiquity to the present day, this goal is not, as one would assume, badly sought to be achieved by abolishing money, but much more frequently by

---

[482] [tn] John Ruskin (1819-1900) was a Victorian writer and critic known for his influential works on art, architecture, and social criticism, advocating for ethical economics and the dignity of labour.

[483] [tn] Quoted from Diehl (1888-9: II 53).

transforming it, improving it. Therefore, in Plato's state, money should be a mere symbol that has no value itself. Plato's monetary regime, however little the philosopher elaborated on in his state designs both in *The Republic* and *Laws*, is the archetype of the monetary framework in Fichte's state. [p227] Thomas More, on the other hand, wants to abolish money in his utopian vision and to rid the utopians of their love for money. He suggests using gold and silver, the precious metals used for money, to make slave chains and chamber pots.

However, we will not delve into all the proposals of social and, in particular, monetary reformers for the introduction of the 'right money.' It can only be a matter of mentioning a few examples. Most of the time, these were simply projects or plans that remained unexecuted. All the more attention, however, are practical attempts that aim to either eliminate conventional money from circulation or replace it with another, allegedly social money. The great philanthropist Robert Owen, an employer who sacrificed his accumulated assets from successful business activities for social reform experiments, is the one who made such an attempt.

He says in a report he wrote around 1810:

> Through money, a society has introduced an artificial system of exchange, through which one class of people becomes enriched while the other falls into poverty. The workers are subjected to a remuneration system through this exchange system that makes them dependent on market valuations and is more cruel in its effects than any form of slavery.[484]

The amount of labour contained in each commodity must therefore serve as the benchmark of its value and for the value-comparison of all other commodities.

Following this idea, Owen founded the Labour Exchange Bank in London in 1832, after previously attempting to establish communist

---

[484] [tn] The source of this quotation is not identified.

communities. This bank issued notes for the products delivered, which were denominated in labour hours. In exchange for these notes, the noteholder could obtain products from the bank's warehouses of equal labour-hour value. This enterprise was intended to help realise "The New Moral World," which was the title of a magazine founded by Owen. [p228] It initially enjoyed great success but ultimately failed because the bank's warehouses became a storage place for unwanted or less desired commodities, while the useful and highly sought-after ones were quickly depleted.

If K. Marx meant that Owen's money was no more money than a theatre token, then that is a mistake. It was an attempt to create a labour-currency (*Arbeitswährung*). However, since labour itself is not an exact measuring unit, and there is a lack of benchmarks to equate various qualities of labour, this attempt had to fail, apart from other valid reasons.

The history of socialism includes several other attempts at such monetary reforms, although they were often intertwined with different objectives. However, none of them achieved lasting success.

These reformers viewed the question of the 'right money' as the question of the right share of the social-product to be allocated to individuals through money. The socialism of the German philosopher Fichte had attempted to address this question in a utopian context, while the English entrepreneur's [i.e., Owen's] socialism had made a practical attempt to solve it.

That was the scene at the beginning of the 19th century. Apart from such relatively remote attempts, the debates about money during the following decades followed the paths set by classical national economics, which were based on the natural scientific-mechanistic perspective of the economy. Specifically regarding money, it remained within the older rationalistic-evolutionary interpretations. The abandonment of this method is credited to historical jurisprudence and legal philosophy. It took some time, of course, for the new path of understanding the phenomena of economic life to establish itself. For our question, it means the realisation that each era, based on its historical context and the prevailing forces and needs within it, has its own perspective and objectives regarding the right economy, the right economic system, and therefore also the 'right money.'

[p229] In the field of monetary theory, the result of this approach is the aforementioned "State Theory of Money" by Georg Friedrich Knapp, which, as he himself stated, "is the dogmatic summary of the legal-historical facts that have developed during the 19th century regarding payment systems in the most important civilised states."[485] Knapp answers the age-old question of whether money derives its value from "nature" or through "law" in favour of the *nomos* (νόμος).[486] His thesis is that "money is a creation of the legal-order."[487] The question of whether state authority can confer existence and value upon money, even against the power of economic interests or ethical convictions, is not even raised. The 'right money' is money sanctioned by state statute. But it was precisely in the field of monetary theory, where formalistic considerations had reached their peak, that their overcoming began. This was closely related to the crisis in legal science, which was expressed in the question: is 'what law is' also right? Must 'what is' considered or proclaimed as the law also be regarded as legally binding simply because it has come into existence in a formally valid manner? The major money-devaluations that nearly all nations have experienced since 1914 have played an important role in this discussion. They were almost a textbook case that fuelled doubts about whether 'what is formally right' is also 'substantively right,' that is, whether

---

[485] [tn] Conrad et al. (1909:610 ff.).

[486] [tn] 'Nature' corresponds to the Greek term *'physis'* (φύσις), while law corresponds to the Greek term *'nomos'* (νόμος).

[487] [tn] Knapp (2023/1923: 2).

it is right.[488]

The state established the principle that one Mark is equal to another Mark and upheld it in jurisprudence for a long, perhaps too long, time. Meanwhile, economic thinking and sound legal reasoning rejected it and described its application in the redemption of old debts as downright money fraud.

In relation to our question, the result is that the "State Theory of Money" is unable to provide a satisfactory answer to the question of the 'right money.' That is, of course, not its task; but it has been perceived as a deficiency by most critics of this theory,[489] and it is for this reason that it has largely led to its rejection, [⁌230] namely, that it cannot provide an answer to the question of the determinants of the value of money or the trade-term between money and other goods.[490]

It is a twofold problem contained in the question of the 'right money.' On one hand, it concerns the issue of the changes in goods prices caused by money, or more precisely, from the perspective of money. On the other hand, it involves the question of exchange rates, i.e., the value relationship

---

[488] [tn] Cf. See Weber (2019.: 159-160) on the 'formal' and 'substantial' (or material) validity of money.

[489] [tn] Cf. Weber's comment:

> G. F. Knapp's *Staatliche Theorie des Geldes* — the greatest achievement of monetary economics — brilliantly fulfils its formal demands, but for material issues related to money, it is incomplete (Weber 2019: 163).

[490] [tn] Cf. Weber (2019: 288-9):

> The orientation is primarily to the place of money as a means of exchange — hence: the Chance that in the future it will in some way be accepted in exchange for goods thought to be defined or undefined, but at an estimated relative price. (...) It is here that the incompleteness of G. F. Knapp's otherwise quite "correct" and simply brilliant book *Staatliche Theorie des Geldes* begins, notwithstanding its permanent and fundamental importance

between one's own currency and foreign currencies. Since the famous report of the Select Committee on the High Price of Gold Bullion in 1810, primarily the latter question, concerning exchange rates, has been at the centre of all currency discussions and, accordingly, the measures of state monetary policy. This fact found its visible expression in the general transition of all major states involved in international goods-exchange to the gold standard, primarily in the second half of the previous century. However, since the First World War, the other question, the question of price movements caused by money, has come to the forefront of public discussions and adoption of measures. In short, **inflation**, which afflicted all countries to varying degrees, was what shifted the question of the 'right money' in this direction. It became a question of stabilising the purchasing force.

The various efforts in this field cannot be detailed here. Their spokespeople were mainly American politicians and scholars. Irving Fisher and his circle have already been mentioned. However, one of the political leaders in this regard must be mentioned, and that is President Franklin D. Roosevelt. He deserves credit for having designated the question of the right money, i.e., 'just money' as one of the foremost tasks of economic policy in his country and for having tackled it.

His stance on this issue is best characterised by a few remarks from his famous message to the London Economic Conference on July 3, 1933. [231] In this, it says:

> The sound internal economic system of a Nation is a greater factor in its well-being than the price of its currency in changing terms of the currencies of other Nations.

This expresses the turn in the question of the 'right money' that I already emphasised clearly. Then it goes on to say:

> Let me be frank in saying that the United States seeks the kind of dollar which a generation hence will have the same purchasing and debt-paying power as the dollar value we hope to attain in the near future.

Although these words are clear on their own, two paragraphs from a radio speech by President Roosevelt on October 22 of the same year should be added, which clearly demonstrates what is meant. The President said:

> Finally, I repeat, what I have said on many occasions, that ever since last March the definite policy of the Government has been to restore commodity price levels. The object has been the attainment of such a level as will enable agriculture and industry once more to give work to the unemployed. It has been to make possible the payment of public and private debts more nearly at the price level at which they were incurred. It has been gradually to restore a balance in the price structure so that farmers may exchange their products for the products of industry on a fairer exchange basis.

It goes on to say:

> When we have restored the price level, we shall seek to establish and maintain a dollar which will not change its purchasing and debt-paying power during the succeeding generation.

Is not it strange: what the German philosopher J. G. Fichte planned for his "The Closed Commercial State," the American President wanted to bestow upon his people exactly one and a third centuries later. Various measures in this direction were indeed taken in the United States: a new banking law and a new monetary policy are the milestones. However, the problem itself has not yet been solved!

The question of the 'right money' remains open. It is not the state that can answer it, as nominalist monetary theory believes, but only those who use money. [P232] The state can determine what is legally considered money or what should be money. Whether this state or legal money is indeed real, vibrant money is determined solely by the transactions that use it. Money that is rejected in transactions is economically not money at all. It is at least not 'right money,' by which is meant the economically 'right money' in the sense of the transactions or the money-purpose.

If one were to ask the public what money actually is, the various individual answers would all come down to the idea that money is something with which one can buy, pay off debts, or pay taxes. On the other hand, if one can no longer buy with money or can only do so in a limited way if creditors refuse to accept it for debt repayment, or if the government itself does not accept its own money at its nominal value for tax payment, as was the case at times, one must say that such money is not 'right money.'

Here, as I already hinted, the question of the 'right money' and the struggle for the 'right money' is a question of the right law and is the struggle for the right law. It is the struggle for the right of the creditor and the debtor, for the worker and the capitalist and for the farmer and the saver. The struggle is about creating money that does not cheat the worker out of the wages of their labour and the saver out of the fruits of their saving activity.

The desire for a different and better form of money than the conventional one tends to become more pronounced, especially in times of significant fluctuations in the purchasing force of money, such as when inflation or deflation disrupts economic flows. There have been various approaches — I could not outline them all within this context — that have been taken to solve this problem. One approach is to replace conventional money as a means of account with another price or value-standard. Frequently such alternative value-measures include commodities like grains, but also sugar, coal, and other goods. [P233] The advantage of choosing a measurement-unit for such goods as a means of account is that it creates an acceptable relationship between creditors and debtors, buyers and sellers, in a given situation. However, the disadvantage is that money based on such material-value is much more susceptible to much greater fluctuations in purchasing force within the ups and downs of business activities compared to conventional money.

The other way to find the 'right money' is not to replace conventional money with another but to refine it in terms of its usage or quality. That is the idea behind **table-currency** and **index-currency**. However, even they offer no guarantee that the dispute between debtors and creditors or buyers and sellers was fairer than by means of conventional money.

The success of a monetary accounting system based on a table or an index entirely depends on the selection of goods that are used as the basis for the table or index. However, there is no selection that can satisfy equally all the various conflicting interests of producers and consumers, those with possessions and those without. It is as Keynes once expressed it:

> Hitherto no official authority has compiled an index number which could fairly be called an index number of purchasing power [force].[491]

But that is not all. The questions that arise here are whether such refinement of money, which aims to create money with a stable purchasing force, is theoretically possible and practically desirable. Both of these, as will be explained in more detail, should be answered in the negative.

If the pursuit of creating a phantom of stable-value money persists, it is based on the idea of a static economy, even if often unconsciously. In such a static economy, stable money is not only conceivable but a prerequisite for the system. It is quite different in the dynamic economy in which we actually live. Its element is the continual change of all economic factors in quantity and quality, brought about by economic dispositions and expressed in the constantly shifting relationship of supply and demand and thus prices. [℘234] In such an economy, fluctuations in the value of money are not only the inevitable expression of the ups and downs of economic flows but also the necessary consequence of economic progress and growth.

Of course, this is not meant to suggest that all fluctuations in the value of money should be viewed as such or accepted as inevitable. Money must not and cannot be stable in value, but it must and should be valuable. Therefore, the 'right money' is the '**recoverable money**' (*werthaltiges*

---

[491] [tn] Keynes (1930:50).

Geld) whose value is continually controlled. Of course, even then, there is still considerable leeway for differences of opinion, as the judgment regarding how the 'right money' should be structured is determined by the prevailing interests. If a majority regularly and sufficiently has access to money as income, this majority demands money with a high and consistent purchasing force. However, if broad segments of the population are burdened with significant financial obligations and struggling with high interest rates and taxes, they are interested in the devaluation of money, which is synonymous with rising prices for commodities and services.

Raymond Patenôtre, undersecretary in the Herriot government in the early 1930s, wrote a book with the significant title: *"La crise et le drame monétaire"* [The Crisis and the Monetary Drama, 1932]. In his book, he states:

> If we have to choose between two evils, namely the rise or fall of the value of money, then give us money with diminishing value.

A dangerous word, indeed! Because money that reduces debt also makes it easier to incur debt. It leads to careless economic management, discourages the willingness to save, encourages wasteful spending, and ultimately jeopardises the overall prosperity of the nation.

The 'right money' can only be that which promotes the development of the national economy and allows everyone to participate in the growing social-product. [P235] It must be so stable that faith in the money is not shaken, that it does not become unsuitable for performing the functions that it has in our economy. In other words, it should be sufficiently stable not to hinder the orientation to save and, consequently, capital formation. The 'right money' should not deceive the public about the economic situation or give them a false feeling of security when the economical situation is different. The 'right money' must reflect the economical situation in prices and price movements. It should be such that the public does not lose confidence in money during both economic downturns and upturns. It should not encourage speculation in money or a flight from money.

This means that the problem of the 'right money' is a problem of monetary policy that cannot be solved by the creation of a specific 'money sign' but only through the proper management of what we call currency.

It is the great fallacy of most monetary reformers and the naive crowd that follows them to believe that the right economic order, i.e., a desired economic order, can be created by the way related to money. However, money is only a means to serve the purposes of the national economy. Just as 'bad money' is detrimental to the economy and the realisation of its goals, 'good money' can undoubtedly be beneficial to its objectives. However, money can do no more than that. It can pave the way towards the prosperity and wealth of a nation, which is the ultimate goal of all economic activities, but prosperity and wealth themselves can only be generated by the hard work of a nation.

I understand that this conclusion may be disappointing for some. People are often too inclined to provide or expect an answer to the question of how something should be according to their interests or their social ideals.

In this sense, proponents of economical liberalism call for neutral money, American currency reformers supporting the New Deal demand money with a stable purchasing force, socialist money reformers seek money that realises the right to the full product of labour, and various other goals are set forth by different groups. [₽236] The demands and interpretations are as numerous as the concepts of what is understood as right and justice in the relationships between people. Indeed, as mentioned earlier, it is often the idea of 'just money' that underlies the demand for the 'right money.' However, one would misinterpret and overestimate the role of money in the economy if they believe that money can be designed in such a way that it can accomplish much more than facilitating the highly complex goods-traffic resulting from extensive division of labour. The social tensions and differences that pervade our economic order cannot be dissolved and made to disappear by any technical means, including any form of money. They are based on social power-relations that are constitutive within the social structure. Money and the monetary framework have always had significant shortcomings. Therefore, the best minds throughout history have repeatedly strived for its reform. However, these efforts do not address the root of social problems.

An old saying goes, "As money, so the world." This saying, whose stark meaning becomes clear to us in the present, also holds true in its reverse: "As the world, so is the money." If we succeed in making the world different and better, then the world will also find its way to a different money, the 'right money.'

§29. The Money-Orientation

The German language associates various meanings with the word '*Sinn*.' Firstly, '*Sinn*' refers to the ability to perceive external things, specifically things of the sensory world. Examples include: '*Tastsinn*' (sense of touch), '*Geruchsinn*' (sense of smell), '*Hörsinn*' (sense of hearing), but also '*Farbensinn*' (sense of colour), '*Formensinn*' (sense of shape), '*Zahlensinn*' (sense of numbers), '*Ortssinn*' (sense of direction), and so on. Furthermore, in a narrower sense, the word '*Sinn*' signifies as much as 'meaning' or 'opinion,' namely, the meaning of words, representations, activities, etc.

[237] Finally, as word research teaches us, the word '*Sinn*,' derived from the verb '*sinnan*,' which means "to make a path, to travel, to go somewhere," was already used in the Old High German language in the metaphorical sense of an active *mental direction* or *orientation*. This meaning of the word has been retained to the present day. Thus, according to Moritz Heyne,[492] '*Sinn*' refers to "the striving inside of a human being directed towards something." With the word '*Geld*' (money) in the composition '*Geldsinn*' (money-orientation), it evidently denotes something towards which the inclination (*Sinnen*) is directed.

Therefore, when we speak of '*Geldsinn*' (money-orientation), we are *not* referring to the 'meaning of money' (*Sinn des Geldes*) as a purposive institution (*Zweckeinrichtung*), a means of expression, or a work tool (*Werkmittel*) under certain circumstances, e.g., at a certain stage of societal or economic development. Instead, money-orientation (*Geldsinn*) refers to the psychological attitude of an individual or a societal group, a class, or even of an entire nation or people of an era towards money, expressed in corresponding behaviour. Money-orientation is the *psychological attitude* associated with an evaluation (*Wertung*) and corresponding behaviour towards money.

---

[492] Heyne (1890-95).

Money-orientation is *not* just an 'orientation towards earning,' let alone greed. Money-orientation arises or is formed through the experience of 'suitability of money' (*Tauglichkeit des Geldes*) for specific purposes or to satisfy needs. This experience forms the appreciation of money (*Wertschätzung des Geldes*). A corresponding attitude arises, giving human activities and thus societal life a particular character. Money-orientation is formed based on the experience of the 'suitability of money.' Money-orientation guarantees a certain order, consistency, and continuity of behaviour in monetary matters.

When Jakob Grimm, in his speech "On Old Age" (*Über das Alter*) speaks of the "love of money (*Geldliebe*) in old age," which, as he says, can be understood most easily when we observe "men accustomed to strict order in a household gradually allow 'praiseworthy accuracy' (*lobenswerte Genauigkeit*) turn into 'blameworthy frugality' (*Kargheit*)," [493] he is referring to this money-orientation. [494]

[P238] Following on from these words of our famous linguist Jakob Grimm, we can now already state one thing: namely, that the money-orientation of the elderly is evidently different from that of youth or mature men. This statement hardly needs any proof.

The love of money is the passion of old age, the passion that increases with age. The elderly person of Salas y Gomez [495] refers to *Mammon* [496] as

---

[493] [tn] Schneidewin (1893:103).

[494] [tn] It means the admirable quality of meticulousness and care in managing a household, when taken to an extreme, can lead to a negative manifestation of excessive thriftiness or stinginess. It highlights a shift from a positive trait to a potentially detrimental one when dealing with money.

[495] [tn] A small uninhabited island in the southeastern Pacific Ocean.

[496] [tn] *Mammon* is a term often used in literature and religious texts to refer to the pursuit of wealth, material possessions, or money, often associated with greed or the worldly pursuit of riches at the expense of spiritual values. It originates from the New Testament of the Bible, specifically from the teachings

the "earthly power in which old age loves to sunbathe" (Adelbert von Chamisso,[497] "Sonnets and Terzains" (*Sonette und Terzinen*)).

The money-orientation of old age finds its fertile soil in the function of money as a means of storing value, a "*réserve de valeur*" (store of value). The idea of precautionary-measure (*Vorsorge*) for the future through hoarding does *not* originate, as one might think, in the 'mental landscape' (*Vorstellungswelt*) of the anxiously cautious shopkeeper and bourgeois. Instead, concern for the future likely begins with the awakening (*Erwachen*) of the human soul. Of course, it is *not* the precautionary-measure (*Vorsoge*) for [this] life in this world, but for the afterlife, that fills the thoughts of primitive humans. For this purpose, they amass their treasures and save money. Money is not only "the bridge between the present and the future" (*le pont entre le présent et l'avenir*) (Charles Rist)[498] or "the link between the present and the future"[499] (Keynes) but also the

---

of Jesus Christ in the Gospel of Matthew (Matthew 6:24). It is derived from the Aramaic word '*mamona*,' which means 'wealth' or 'riches.' In religious contexts, *Mammon* symbolizes material wealth.

[497] [tn] Adelbert von Chamisso, original name Louis-Charles-Adélaïde Chamisso de Boncourt (1781-1838) was a German poet, writer, and botanist, best remembered for the Faust-like fairy tale "*Peter Schlemihls wundersame Geschichte*" (1814; Peter Schlemihl's Remarkable Story).

[498] [tn] Rist (1938:90):

> The thought of the future is constantly on the mind of the industrialist, the merchant, the businessperson. They are primarily occupied with creating a representation of the future in terms of prices, markets, sources of supply, and sales possibilities. Now, stable money, metallic money, serves as the bridge between the present and the future. Thanks to it, and when it is lacking, thanks to other stable and precious objects, the economic actor can wait, reserve a choice, and calculate their chances. When it disappears, everything becomes uncertain.

[499] [tn] Keynes (1936:293): "For the importance of money essentially flows from its being a link between the present and the future."

bridge from this world to the afterlife. This is taught by the role of money in the funerary cult (*Totenkult*) of numerous peoples.

Charles Gide,[500] the renowned French economist, speaks about the impression that discovering money makes on the youthful mind:

> I remember very clearly that during my high school years, the mystery of money first directed my attention to economics, and I still see the place where this thought came to me.
>
> Since I was a child, I was completely absorbed by the tales and knew by heart the story of Aladdin and the magic lamp, that lamp which you only had to rub to obtain all the riches. I told myself: with money, you can get everything that the lamp provided: sumptuous meals, gemstones, a royal palace, black or white slaves – [p239] as many as you want, and even the hand of the princess.[501]

He continues: "The child soon knows that with a few pennies, one can obtain what one desires," and he believes that from a psychological perspective, it would be instructive to mark the age at which a child no longer enjoys a present in its natural form alone but experiences the same or even greater joy when receiving a monetary coin, thinking to oneself, "With this, you can buy whatever you desire."

One could pose the question: is it the 'meaning of money' (*Sinn des Geldes*) that begins to dawn on the child, or is it the money-orientation (*Geldsinn*) that has awakened? If, as mentioned earlier, money-orientation and the 'meaning of money' must be distinguished, the question just posed shows that it would be erroneous to assume that they have nothing to do with each other. The opposite is true. Money-orientation and the 'meaning of money' are closely related to each other. This becomes most apparent when, as can happen, a condition arises in which money has lost

---

[500] [tn] Charles Gide (1847-1932) was a prominent French economist, who advocated for social reform through cooperative movements and emphasized the ethical dimensions of economics.

[501] [tn] The source of this quotation is not identified.

its meaning. In such a case, there is a lack of an object against which a mental attitude involving perception (*Vorstellung*) and dispositions that would justify us in speaking of a money-orientation could occur. When money has lost its meaning, it results in the withering, decay, and eventual death of money-orientation.

Conversely, when the 'meaning of money' expands or, to put it better, when the significance of money in society increases in intensity and extensiveness, this certainly has an impact on the development of money-orientation. This also means that there is a close connection between the development of money-orientation and the evolution of the functions (*Funktion*) of money because it is these functions that determine its usage in society.

The function most commonly associated with money is its role as a means of exchange as already explained in another context, although experience has taught us that it may not perform this service well or only to a limited extent under certain circumstances. [P240] The form of the primitive goods-traffic is, as is known, always the same, namely that of the gift, which, linked to the events of social life, accompanies the life in its course. All of this does not need to be repeated here. What matters is the observation that primitive money consists of certain objects, often precious-items, that serve as means of distinction, turning the money of that time into **ornament-money**.

That a money-orientation develops around objects of such significance (*Bedeutung*) is evident. There is no shortage of testimonies and evidence for this. In the Germanic cultural sphere, for example, rings were known to signify higher status and also served as precious-items and, to some extent, as money. What rings were to the upper class, certain fabrics, wool and linen textiles, as well as garments, were to the peasants. They served as money. The esteem in which these items were held is illustrated by a charming anecdote recounted by the "Monk of Saint Gall" (*Monachus*

Sangallensis) in *Gesta Caroli*.[502] The story dates back to the time when Christianity was spreading in the Germanic North. The zealous missionaries of that era, much like it might be the case with pagan peoples even today, sought to convert their flock not only through words but also with earthly temptations. Those who were baptised received the baptismal garment as a present after the baptism. This practice had spread to Scandinavia. Therefore, one day, 50 Normans arrived to be baptised. Since the existing linen baptismal garments were insufficient for this influx, they had the baptismal shirts made from ordinary fabric. However, when the Normans saw these garments, their leader indignantly rejected them, saying, "Twenty times they have bathed me, and I have always received a good, white garment. This sack is not suitable for a warrior, but at most for a swineherd." It is unlikely that this honest Norman had such a great demand for underwear, but it becomes understandable that he was systematically baptised when we know that in those times, garments were highly desired both for the treasure chamber and as a means of payment.

[p241] Similar stories are told about missionaries in East Africa. The native catechumens received a small metal cross as a sign of their conversion. These crosses were soon used as a form of money by members of the tribe, leading to a situation where many people attended the catechesis not out of religious fervour but in hopes of obtaining these crosses.

Such a pronounced money-orientation does not surprise cultural historians. Wilhelm Grönbech, as mentioned in another context, has described how the joy of possession could escalate among our ancestors from "heroic inclinations to strive for gold and bronze" to "long-fingered

---

[502] [tn] The "Monk of Saint Gall," likely a pseudonymous medieval chronicler, authored the historical narrative "*Gesta Caroli Magni*" or "The Deeds of Charles the Great," chronicling the life and accomplishments of Charlemagne, the medieval Frankish king and Holy Roman Emperor.

avarice (*langfingrige Habsucht*)."[503] Certainly, he says, "greed assumed heroic forms; so its counterpart, generosity, was no less generous in those times."[504] These two conflicting Nordic traits in the perception of gold and treasures, Grönbech believes, "cannot be balanced by individual psychology."[505]

The matters are not so entangled, though. Money-distribution and money-squandering (*Geldvergeudung*), as depicted in the imagery and expressions of Germanic poetry where the king is referred to as a ring-spender (*Ringspender*) or ring-distributor (*Ringverteiler*), as previously elaborated upon, and also called a 'treasure squanderer,' are not unique to the Nordic peoples. Anthropology can provide examples of this from all around the world. The underlying motive for both generosity and greed is the same. It is the reputation, the 'social distinction,' that can be conferred by squandering possessions just as much as by their collecting and stockpiling. Here lies the root of the money-orientation of people in that era.

These are basic forms and expressions of the universal human condition, manifested in the perception and behaviour regarding money-goods. When Odysseus woke up after being brought ashore by the Phaeacians,[506]

---

[503] [tn] A figurative expression that refers to a strong desire for wealth or a tendency toward theft using long fingers. It suggests that the joy of possession among ancestors could escalate to the point where they eagerly pursued material wealth, even resorting to theft.

[504] [tn] It means generosity (*Freigebigkeit*) was equally or no less generous. In other words, it implies that while greed took on heroic forms, the counterpart, generosity, was also notably abundant and generous during that period. It emphasises that both extreme greed and extreme generosity coexisted during that time.

[505] Grönbech (1939:14).

[506] [tn] The Phaeacians are depicted as generous and hospitable people, and they assist Odysseus by providing him with a ship and safe passage back to his

his first thought was to count his copper cauldrons. "And then he counted," it says, "all his splendid tripods and cauldrons, the gold, and the woven magnificent garments." [ℙ242] Note that all the items mentioned here are indeed money-goods. With a certain satisfaction that even reveals some 'joy of possession' (*Besitzfreude*), the poet adds, "And behold, not a single piece was missing" (Odyssey, XIII, 215).

The same 'joy of possession' is expressed in the Anglo-Saxon epic Beowulf.[507] When the hero senses his approaching hour of death, he desires to feast his eyes once more on the precious-items he gathered in his life filled with battles. He wishes to see the treasure he won for his people once again.

> Quickly run, Wiglaf,
>
> that I may see the old wealth, the gold possession,
>
> securely behold the shining gemstones,
>
> so that I may then more easily depart from my treasure hoard,
>
> life and land, which I have held for a long time (Beowulf, 2745 ff.)[508]

We find this 'joy of possession,' the money-orientation, of the ancient Germanic peoples again in the depiction of the Victorian era that J. Galsworthy provides us in his well-known novel series *The Forsyte Saga*.[509]

---

homeland.

[507] [tn] Refer to footnote 106 on *Beowulf*.

[508] [tn] In these lines from the epic poem *Beowulf*, the hero Beowulf is on the verge of death after his battle with a dragon. He instructs his loyal companion Wiglaf to hurry and show him the ancient treasure (gold possessions) that he had acquired in his lifetime. Beowulf wants to see the shining jewels one last time before he dies, hoping that doing so will make it easier for him to depart from his life and land, which he has held for a long time. These lines reflect Beowulf's attachment to his accumulated wealth and the significance of treasures in the epic.

[509] [tn] Refer to footnote 316.

The poet reverses things when he says, "The folks of the old Sagas were the Forsytes' assuredly in their possessive instincts." What he means is that the respectable men of the Victorian age – the Forsytes – are nothing other than the people of the old sagas in their "possessive instincts." He is referring to the "possessive world and the sense of property."

Let's hear some more examples from ethnology. In a fascinating study titled "Beginnings of Currency," Temple (1899) says:

> The most valuable possession of the Karen[510] in Burma is their drums, called *Kyee-Zee*. Possessing these drums signifies wealth. The passion to acquire these drums goes so far that they even give up their children and relatives for them. The drums are used for the resolution of their disputes, redeem prisoners, and make penance-payments, in short, they are used both to make large payments and to represent wealth, especially during festivals.[511]

---

[510] [tn] An ethnic group primarily residing in Southeast Asia, with a significant population in Burma (Myanmar) and neighbouring countries.

[511] Temple (1899:110).

[tn] The full text reads:

> Among the most valued possessions of the Hill Karens is the kyee-zee, ..., To such an extent does the passion for the possession of these instruments predominate [among the more secluded tribes], that it is said instances are by no means rare of their having bartered their children and relations for them. The possession of kyee-zees is what constitutes a rich Karen. No one is considered rich without them, whatever may be his other possessions. Everyone who has money endeavours to turn it into kyee-zees, and a village that has many of them is the envy of other villages, and is often the cause of wars to obtain their possession.

These Karen drums, then, are of varying sizes, are used in making large payments, and represent wealth. If they are put to domestic use, as for feasts and what not, they must be classed as currency; if they are to be looked on merely as tokens of a certain value and kept only for making large payments when due or only as representatives of wealth, then they are money. They are in fact just on the line between currency and money.

[p243] *Gongs* are equally popular among various Indonesian indigenous tribes, used as home ornament, bridal dowries, sacrificial gifts, as well as means of tax payment and penances. Similarly, South Sea shell-money known as *Diwarra* is highly valued. The explorer George Brown observed the remarkably developed money-orientation among the indigenous people of New Britain. He claims that they exhibit the most advanced money-orientation among all indigenous people and goes on to explain:

> Even husband and wife were economic competitors. Their language has words for buying, selling, lending, interest, pawning, to get on trust security, extortionate, underselling, and a phrase meaning compelled to sell, sell at a sacrifice. They had regular markets and trading expeditions in which various articles were bought and re-sold at a considerable profit.[512]

Indeed, an early and strong, and sometimes excessively developed money-orientation is evident in all of these examples. Now arises the question of the psychological roots of this attitude and, at the same time, the other question: is money-orientation perhaps just a form of the 'orientation towards earning' (*Erwerbssinn*)? The answer will have to be left to psychology, but even though we should not pre-empt the psychologists, we may still be able to contribute some insights from the domain of other sciences to interpret these matters. This is how the following remarks should be understood.

Certainly, the 'orientation towards earning' takes on a distinctive character with the introduction of money into society. However, the money-orientation appears to me to be something different, despite their inherent similarities. The money-orientation, I believe, can only be explained by those psychological facts that generally determine social behaviour. Just as money is a creation of social action, so is money-

---

[512] Brown (1911: 297). Similarly, examples at Codrington (1891: 297) and Kloss (1903: 308).

orientation a product of social life, which naturally does not imply that its roots cannot be found in *a priori* given predispositions. [p244] Money, as a work tool for *homo ambitiosus*, has grown in its usage from deeply rooted primal forces within the human soul to which it satisfies. The contemplations and aspirations of *homo ambitiosus* or *anthropos philótimos* (recognition-seeking human), as has been repeatedly emphasised, constitute the strong undercurrent in the societal conduct-process; for not only the life of the Greeks is conditioned and characterised by *doxomania*[513] and *agon*,[514] but human life in general. The *anthropos doxomanés* (opinionated human)[515] rules the world, and in money, he has created his great assisting means, the most perfect tool for satisfying his cravings.

Everything we know about the beginnings of money-usage confirms that primitive money is a means of distinction, means of accentuation, and thus 'social differentiation.' It is on this basis that money-orientation develops.

This drive is given content and direction by two other drives, the 'drive for amassing' (*Sammeltrieb*) and the 'drive for adornment' (*Schmucktrieb*).

Both serve the 'drive for distinction,' as hoarding valuable things and adorning oneself with the aim to accentuate one's status before others.

The exertion of these two drives seems to be peculiarly linked to the emergence of money and the development of money-orientation. The 'drive for amassing,' also referred to as the 'drive for appropriation' and 'drive for possession,' is, as some psychologists suggest, seemingly more developed in the male gender than in the female. Therefore, perhaps that is why Goethe introduces one of the characters who appears in the imperial

---

[513] [tn] See footnote 34 for *doxomania* (δοξομανία).

[514] [tn] *Agon* (ἀγών) refers to a contest, competition, or struggle.

[515] [tn] A man who craves recognition.

palace in the second part of "Faust" with the words: "I am of the male gender, the greed."[516]

Regarding the 'drive for adornment,' one might be inclined to assume the opposite, that is, to consider the female gender as more inclined towards enjoying adornment. Here arises the question: What is the contribution of the two genders to the emergence of money as a creation of social action, when this social action is determined by those drives peculiar to the two genders in different degrees? [p245] The answer to this question is not easy to provide and should be given with reservations. Unfortunately, as far as I can see, we lack a comprehensive individual examination of the emergence, usage, and significance of adornment in the lives of individuals and peoples. Even what is found in the major works of anthropology, cultural history, and psychology on this topic is extremely limited. According to Westermarck (1891), the ornament in its emergence and development is a means of courtship (*Werbemittel*) in the service of the 'gender drive' (*Geschlechtstriebe*), or, to use a fashionable term, a means of sex appeal. Meanwhile, ethno-sociologists like J.G. Frazer and Elliot Smith seek to explain the emergence and use of ornament through magical beliefs, aligning with the thesis of J. Bachofen that "the beginning of all development lies in myth" in the Preface to *Mother Right* (*Mutterrecht*) (Bachofen 1861).

Both perspectives, which do not necessarily exclude each other but can contain the fact of both, seem too narrow to me. The significance of ornament is derived from its usage. Adornment, as mentioned earlier, always aims for accentuation. The wearer of ornament is highlighted or

---

[516] [tn] Goethe, Johann Wolfgang von (1831), *Faust. The Tragedy*. Part Two, First Act: "Graceful Landscape" line 5665. Mephistopheles, the demon, is expressing his disdain for the female gender and how they no longer conform to traditional frugality. He mentions his former name, '*Avaritia*,' which means greed or avarice. The lines highlight the idea that his relationship with women has soured over time, and he now identifies himself as avaricious.

seeks to stand out, whether it be to attract the opposite sex, to signify their rank or status, or to emphasise their dignity.

Two main types of ornament can be distinguished: ostentatious-ornament (*Werbeschmuck*) and dignity-ornament (*Würdeschmuck*). The boundaries here are certainly not sharp. One can only say that ostentatious-ornament primarily serves embellishment, while dignity-ornament serves social differentiation. In nature, the courting part is always the wearer of ornament, which in the animal kingdom is mostly the males. In exceptional cases, however, where the female is the one courting and the male is the one being courted, the female is the more adorned one.

We do not have complete knowledge of how things were in primitive human society. Many indications suggest that originally, ostentatious-adornment was primarily a female activity. [P246] This often involved simple body ornamentation achieved through painting, tattooing, creating decorative scars, or modifying specific body parts such as the head, feet, waist, and so on.

The use of the mentioned means of adornment (*Schmuckmittel*) is indeed a common custom among both genders, but it appears to be more widespread among women. There are numerous tribes, for example, where tattooing is exclusively reserved for women. Even more so, body modification, except for the artificial shaping of the skull,[517] is a means of adornment predominantly used by women. The motive behind such beautification or adornment of the female body is always also the erotic effect on the opposite sex, as indeed the ornamental-usage (*Schmuckgebrauch*) of jewellery by women generally applies to. This aligns with what Schopenhauer generally states about women: "It is in the nature

---

[517] [tn] Techniques like head binding or cranial deformation, where external pressure is applied to the skull during infancy or childhood to alter its natural shape.

of women to consider everything as a means to win over a man."[518]

On the other hand, when painting or tattooing is practised by men, it is not done for the immediate purpose of sexual attraction but rather for the purpose of indicating rank and status or as a means of adornment and battle decoration (war ornamentation). The same applies to the general ornamental-usage by men. Adornment, in its society-building force, indicating belonging to a tribe or class, a symbol of rank and status, has always been the domain of men, even when the emblem of dignity is occasionally worn by women.

In addition, there is another aspect to consider. Alongside the simple embellishment ornaments created through painting, tattooing, and similar methods, there emerges early on a certain form of 'ornament for possession' (*Besitzschmuck*). Its impact is significantly based on the social significance of the possession of rare goods. These means of adornment, which typically represent both rank and wealth, have primarily been the domain of men. Westermarck provides a number of examples in his book (Westermarck 1891) regarding the participation of both genders in ornamental-usage. Upon careful examination of this compilation, one will surprisingly find that in cases where ornamental-usage is more prevalent among men, it almost always involves 'ornament for possession.' This distinction may not be readily apparent in Westermarck's presentation. [p247] It is this 'ornament for possession' that evolves into money.

Just as according to the views of anthropologists and ethnologists, the contribution of both genders to the origin of human labour varies, a similar statement can be made regarding money. Both genders love and use ornament. However, in the hands of men, the means of adornment, the ornamental-good (*Schmuckgut*), becomes money. I have expressed this with the thesis:

The cultural significance of women as inventors of agriculture finds its

---

[518] [tn] Schopenhauer (1851).

counterpart in the service of men for asset-amassing, goods-traffic, and capital formation.[519]

At the same time, this also suggests or explains that the money-orientation of the male gender is generally more pronounced than that of the female. Certainly, there are exceptions. But just as chess is predominantly aligned with male aptitude, it seems to me that men are gifted with a trait that is not generally as pronounced in women or is significantly less common.

The use of money as a gift for various purposes brings the significance of money into economical awareness. This signifies the 'fall from grace' (*Sündenfall*),[520] indicating that money is recognised as the most perfect means of economical interests (*Mittel der ökonomischen Interessen*). It awakens that passion for earnings that Aristotle condemned as a deviation and degeneration of society and as the corruption of the state. With the introduction of money, the natural form of acquisition focused on household demand is replaced by another form of earning, which, in the words of the philosopher, "is a work of skill and practice, but not of nature. It is practised by those who aim for the enjoyment of life and understand only sensual pleasures among them."[521] This shift signifies a transition from subsistence-based work to work motivated by the pursuit of pleasure and luxury. [p248] The money-orientation takes on its pecuniary character, and *chrematopoie*,[522] money-earning, becomes the great means

---

[519] Gerloff (1940:205).

[520] [tn] It draws a parallel to the biblical concept of the "Fall of Man" in which Adam and Eve's disobedience led to their expulsion from the Garden of Eden, symbolising a loss of innocence and a departure from a state of harmony.

[521] [tn] See Aristotle (1932: 1256b40 - 1257b35).

[522] [tn] The term *'chrematopoie'* (χρηματοποίη) refers to the study or theory of acquiring wealth or riches. It is related to economic or financial matters, particularly the process of wealth accumulation. It is derived from the Greek words *'chrema'* (χρήμα), which means wealth or money, and *'poiein'* (ποιεῖν),

of satisfying human *doxomania*.[523] Alongside many other issues, there arises that particular problem expressed in a sober English saying: "A fool may make money but it takes a wise man to spend it." Even a fool can amass money, but it takes a wise person to spend it wisely.

The significance of this development, which touches upon all human relationships, cannot be overestimated. It brings about the greatest revolution in society, which has been repeated so and so often, namely, in every person when, in its thinking or the thinking of one of its strata, money as a *thing* has become a *concept*: the value concept of the general commodity equivalent. With this metamorphosis of money, the money-orientation takes a turn that Aristotle had already recognised, but to which the Stagirite [Aristotle] could not give due appreciation.

The money-orientation approaches things with a specific 'feeling of value' (*Wertgefühl*); people, relationships, and events are all reduced to a common denominator, namely the money-denominator, which lacks any other emotional emphasis than that of money calculation. In its image, money is transformed from being a means to an absolute value, to a measuring unit for a system of evaluations, into which an increasing number of things are categorised, indeed even life itself (as demonstrated by '*Wergeld*').

The expansion of the money-purpose over the course of economic development significantly strengthens the inclinations toward purely monetary valuation of all things. When money transitions from being a mere means of exchange for facilitating goods-traffic to a means of capital formation (*Mittel der Kapitalbildung*), it naturally has an impact on the money-orientation, its development, and its exertion. With the transition from agrarian self-sufficiency to division of labour and the goods-production with a national and global economic supply, this new role of

---

which means 'to make' or 'to create.'

[523] [tn] See footnote 222 for its meaning.

money – money as capital – becomes prominently evident. The relationships to things that are now extended through money possession encompass a new and significant field. This gives the money-orientation a turn and a new content of particular strength and colour.

[249] Where this money-orientation takes hold, life becomes infused with a peculiar calculative quality that initially extends to all economic evaluations, but then also reaches beyond, affecting other social relationships, and hardly stopping at any sphere of social existence. Money becomes the benchmark of a strict economical rationalism (*ökonomischer Rationalismus*) that subjects all economic behaviour and actions to the 'earning principle.' This money-orientation, directed toward earning and making money, generates capitalism, the economic system that has brought about a fundamental transformation of society.

This very economic system, in turn, affects the money-orientation that gave rise to it and causes it to undergo almost rampant development, even degeneration.

Every stage of culture, every nation, every social stratum, and ultimately every individual, they all have their own money-orientation, which means their particular attitude toward money. One knows no one whose money-orientation is unknown. The character of a people, a nation, a class, or even an individual is determined in no small part by their money-orientation.

However, merely stopping at this observation would be nothing more than stating a commonplace. It would be superficial if one did not see that money is merely a means, and the money-orientation thus finds its imprint through the purposes to be realised by means of money, that is, through the interests it serves. The money-orientation assigns its sociological status to money. This orientation appears to be most pronounced in the realm of the monetary economy, but even in the life-sphere of indigenous peoples, money sometimes plays an extraordinarily significant role. The acquisition of *Diwarra* money, the aforementioned shell-money, also called '*tambu*,' which means 'sacred,' fills the entire contemplations and aspirations of the

Kanakas, the indigenous people of the Gazelle Peninsula,[524] as has been demonstrated in another context. Their ambition is to amass as much of it as possible so that after their death, their surviving relatives can organise lavish funeral ceremonies and large money-distributions. [p250] The money-orientation can be at its peak in no trading society more than among these and other tribes mentioned earlier (see p. 53 ff.). It determines their conduct in their transactions with each other, as would naturally be the case if they were economically living in purely monetary economical relationships.

The development of a monetary economy also presupposes a money-orientation. Where it is lacking, a crucial prerequisite for its development is absent. Without a pronounced money-orientation, the management of an economic enterprise or any administration, up to and including the modern state with its finances, is not possible.

In the economical world of things, the evolution of money-orientation goes hand in hand with the development of the purchasing power of money. This purchasing power, as has been elaborated in detail, reaches its full development in the era of economical liberalism. It is the age of unrestricted use-potentiality of money.

It is only when and to the extent that the individualistic economic order is abandoned that the purchasing power of money experiences a restriction once again. The discussion pertains to the previously mentioned restrictions on income use (234 ff.), introduced across the civilized world during the war, but the Soviet Union has always attempted as a part of its economical system. In such an economic order, one requires not only money to make purchases but must also present a benefit-right perhaps belonging to a specific societal group, among other such restrictions.

---

[524] [tn] A long, narrow peninsula located on the northeastern coast of the island of New Britain, part of the Bismarck Archipelago in the southwestern Pacific Ocean.

Whether the money-orientation, as it has developed in the last millennium, undergoes any change in such a context, is a matter I leave open to discussion. It is evident that the money-orientation may wither if the role of money in the economy undergoes a significant and lasting reduction. Some may believe that in such a case, nothing ethically is lost, and perhaps much is gained. It is undeniable that money changes human relationships, giving them a different colour and valuation. Its introduction, as mentioned earlier, signifies a fundamental transformation in economic management. [ᴘ251] The original distribution economy, in which gift, 'voluntary gift' is the vehicle of exchange, transforms into the exchange-economy in private life and into the tax economy in the public sphere, with money serving as the vehicle of goods-circulation.

The money-orientation is driven by teleological thinking that incorporates money as a means into its array of purposes, and indeed, one can say the money-orientation is teleological thinking itself. The teleological determination that is associated with money spending and underlies every money-earning leads to an absolutisation of the instrumental character of money. Money, originally a means for a specific purpose-pursuit, becomes a general purposeful means (*Zweckmittel*). The not-uncommon process in technology of creating a means for a specific purpose that then gains significance for other purposes beyond its original purpose-pursuit has found its most fitting expression in money. Simmel expressed this once by saying, "Once a purpose has engendered the idea of means, the means may produce the conception of a purpose."[525] Applied to our topic, this purpose is called money-earning. From this purpose-setting perspective, a rationalism develops that extends far beyond the realm of the economical things. Money is seen as the measure of all things. Two sayings, "Money spoils friendships" and "When it comes to money matters, comfort ends," express a sociological radiance of the money-

---

[525] [tn] Simmel (1900:207, 2011/1900:227).

orientation, the money-directed sense, rooted in this rationalism. The well-known statement by Vespasian,[526] "*non olet*" (not tainted),[527] goes even further. It not only expresses the indifference of money as a technical tool but also the indifference of the disposition it arouses when using a technical means. Just as technical means often bestow upon the one who uses them a distinct demeanour alongside their intended purpose, so does money. Its usage as a technical means carries the risk of making the person who employs it like itself: cold-hearted, even characterless.

[p252] Money signifies bondage, not only the bondage of others but one's own psychological bondage, which is especially felt by sensitive individuals as pressure, even as a curse. Hence, the yearning for liberation from this curse. Thus, the pursuit of finding a balance for cold money-making in an exertion that warms the soul encounters itself. It is found in charity (*Caritas*) and the cultivation of culture. Stefan Zweig, in his book (Zweig 1941), saw the role of Jews in the cultural life of Vienna in this light. But this is not specific to Vienna or Austria any more than it is a characteristic of Judaism. Even the puritanical money-earner seeks emotional relief in a different sphere.

The nineteenth century is the era of the highest respect for money, and that is why it is also the century of saving money. For most people of that time, money possession was something that had to be hard-earned and diligently saved. Handling money carefully was, therefore, a matter of course. Those who did not do so were subject to moral condemnation. To the people of that era, money possession was more desirable than to those of earlier times who had other general asset values; but talking about it was considered plebeian. Those who have money tend not to talk about it at

---

[526] [tn] A Roman Emperor who ruled from 69 to 79 AD.

[527] [tn] The quote '*non olet*' is attributed to Vespasian and is often associated with the Roman practice of taxing public urinals, where even the money collected from such a source was considered valuable and not tainted. The phrase '*non olet*' is Latin and translates to "it does not stink" or "it is not tainted."

every opportunity.

The more money becomes a component of economical existence, the stronger the money-orientation unfolds; to the same extent, the sociological role of money grows, becoming increasingly significant. The mental faculty that currently drives the money-orientation is 'intellect' (*Verstand*). This has not always been the case. Another mental force that guides our life, i.e., emotion (*Gefühl*), also drives the money-orientation, but it is a different money-orientation, whose object is different money or money of a different function than the money of the present. The attitude of the primitive towards money is driven by emotion, while that of the modern person is driven by intellect (*Verstand*). Where intellect prevails and rationality determines values, money rules (*herrschen*). But it would be wrong to be led by a purely rationalist assessment of money as a means for the convenient need-satisfaction and the enhancement of demand-satisfaction towards a purely eudemonic[528] interpretation of the money-orientation. [₽253] That would mean ignoring the culture-creating force of money and, consequently, underestimating the role that money-orientation plays in the construction and life of society. To assess the role of the development of money-orientation (*Ausbildung des Geldsinns*), we must consider what money, i.e., its reasonable usage, means for the cultural development of existence. Certainly, the liberation through money from the constraints of self-provision is what stands out most conspicuously to contemporary humans as the tangible result of the monetary economy. However, to stop at this impression would be like contenting oneself with a view of a fence without seeing what lies beyond it.

Because a handful of people were seized by the passion to earn money, more or less, as Sombart once said, and by this is meant that they were seized by a certain money-orientation, an economic and cultural life of

---

[528] [tn]From '*eudaimonikós*' (ευδαιμονικός), which relates to the concept of well-being, happiness, or flourishing.

such magnitude, size, and powerfulness has arisen as no earlier period has witnessed. Hundreds of millions of people who were not there before have come into existence, have found bread and education, fortunes have been built and destroyed, magical realms of technology have been constructed, and the earth has been transformed in its appearance. The driving force was the money-orientation. What money was from the beginning, a means of expressing social power and rank-status, it has remained so to this day. Thus, it is also a means of realising power in the market, the economy, and society. It is the means to endow with power. By granting power, money also grants independence. In the money-orientation, there is therefore a sense of independence. If it is correct, as has been said at times, that money is the *Magna Carta* of personal freedom, then it is the money-orientation that directs thinking, feeling, and willingness towards realising the freedom that money can provide.

Indeed, such a money-orientation carries the risk of misjudging or disregarding values that cannot be expressed in terms of money, and underestimating or even destroying bonds that are more significant than formal freedom. [p254] When great social reformers from Plato to Tolstoy address the human relationships with money in their critiques of society, mentioning the money-orientation as a human weakness or passion, the underlying idea is that independence from money guarantees greater moral freedom than the independence conferred by money possession.

All major religious founders praise voluntary humbleness, warn against the spiritual dangers of wealth, and oppose money as the means of unjust wealth more than any other possession. The Church condemns money and, therefore, money-earning more than anything else because money, as the general means of exchange, more easily arouses greed, leads to indulgence, and distracts from the Christian quest for salvation. "You cannot serve both God and *Mammon*": these words of Christ determine the attitude of the Church towards the money-orientation. The money-orientation is suspicious, though it means only the unhealthy money-orientation spoken of by the Apostle Paul in his first letter to Timothy when he says, "For the greed for money (*Geldgier*) is the root of all evil." The healthy money-orientation (*gesunder Geldsinn*), on the other hand, will use money but not serve it. It will need it but not misuse it.

The healthy money-orientation certainly also presupposes healthy money. However, where the poison of inflation corrupts the monetary framework, the money-orientation tends to corrupt as well, as history has repeatedly shown.

Thus, the issue of money-orientation leads to a larger problem, namely a task for politics, specifically economic policy, and a task for education (*Erziehung*). The task of economic policy is to give money in the economy the status that ensures healthy development of the money-orientation, i.e., to create an economic order in which there is no room for either the money-centered individual or money-domination (*Geldherrschaft*). The task of education, however, is to make people aware that it is the intrinsic value of things, beyond their monetary worth, that makes life worthwhile, and that true values in life cannot be measured or expressed in money but transcend all monetary value.

§30. The Societal Theory of Money

[P255] *Money is a creation of social action,*[529] meaning its emergence and functions are the result of similar actions and behaviours of a group of people who are connected by certain relationships into a unity. This is the conclusion of this investigation. Money is not a human invention or a deliberate creation by people with a purposeful intention (*Zweckabsicht*); rather, it has evolved and emerged from the nature of human beings and their relationships with one another. It is a means of expression of human relationships, a means for accomplishing human co-living in specific forms.

However, money is not a means of expression or instrument of a *specific* economic order. That means it is *not*, as claimed by von Wieser,[530] a

---

[529] [tn] Comparing this statement with Knapp's assertion that "money is the creation of legal-order" (Knapp 2023/1923:2) highlights the fundamental distinction between Knapp and Gerloff.

[530] [tn] The passage lacks clarity regarding Gerloff's stance on Wieser's view. Wieser, aligning with Menger, emphasizes the significance of the pioneering *'alert'* individual and elucidates money's origin within the *economic* sphere. Nonetheless, Wieser doesn't presuppose an 'entrepreneurially organized economy' within this economic framework. To quote Wieser:

> Explanations throughout history, up to the present day, have interpreted money, like many other societal formations, as a purposive institution that is a creation by the state or the free agreement of citizens. However, money, in its essential form, existed before the state, and even today, it extends beyond state borders as a world money. The idea that people entered into an agreement to create money should be entirely ruled out. Money has gradually evolved from small beginnings into its final form. This happened in such a way that one or another particularly alert (*findig*) economic agent in a particular situation recognized the benefits of dividing their exchange intention (*Tauschabsicht*) into two acts of placing and acquiring. They accomplished this by inserting an intermediate-exchange good, whose usage was not their primary concern. In the first act, they received this intermediate-exchange-good only to give it away again in the second act. The example of the benefit they gained in this way

creation of an entrepreneurially organised economy. As J. Dobretsberger (1946) correctly observes in his excellent study "Money in the Transformation of the Economy" (*Das Geld im Wandel der Wirtschaft*), "We cannot attribute money to a specific form of production organisation."[531]

The task of the societal theory of money is to examine money as a cultural 'formation of meaning' (*Sinngebild*),[532] interpret this 'formation of meaning' as a social phenomenon and present its existence and function in reality. This task is *not only* about making the embeddedness (*Einbettung*) of money in the social cosmos visible or investigating the 'totalities of life' (*Lebenszusammenhang*) in which money is integrated *but also* about demonstrating that money itself is an element of the social. This is done to emphasise the significance it holds for *shaping* social relationships. The subject of the societal theory of money is, therefore, the social relationships that are expressed through money-usage and that *result from* money-usage. [🅿256] This means that money is not only seen as an expression of societal relationships but also as a *creator* and *generator* of such relationships. This perspective essentially means applying the sociological method, as developed from Pareto to Max Weber, to the cultural realm encompassed by the concept of money.

Society is a state of relationships among people that finds its expression in perceptible manifestations. The means of expression are of various kinds, some are naturally given, such as gesture and expression, and some are

---

inspired imitation. These alert hosts (*Wirt*) became the leaders for others who followed them in using money, until the 'mass habit of acceptance' of money was formed (Wieser 2023/1927:7-8).

[531] Dobretsberger (1946:43).

[532] [tn] 'Formation of meaning' (*Sinngebild*) refers to objective structures or formations of meaning that arise from intentional consciousness, playing a fundamental role in understanding the world and human experiences, particularly in Husserl's phenomenological philosophy.

created, such as language and writing. Language, writing, cultural symbols,[533] and ornament[534] are the most significant original material (*sachlich*) means of expression of societal conduct (*Gehaben*). In addition to these, there is money. Money is functionally related to the latter two and partly rooted in them, but it extends far beyond their functional scope and gains its own functional force. Its function is to express certain facts or situations.

The emergence of such means of expression is not conceivable through isolated actions (*Handeln*) but only as a social act (*Akt*). The purpose of these means of expression is to objectify a state, specifically the inner state of self-esteem within the context of money, particularly focusing on hoard-money initially. Self-esteem thrives on the resonance of one's personality in others! This resonance is not only sought in people but also in things, in the objects with which special relationships exist or are felt. This is what is meant by the objectification of an inner state.

The object used for objectification, through the facts of objectification, establishes a relationship with the individual, or more accurately: the individual establishes a relationship with the object. Money is such an object that, as a carrier and symbol of certain representations (*Vorstellung*), has the ability to nourish and enhance self-esteem in a special way. It is one of the most significant examples of the process described here. [ℝ257] Growing from original drives as a social creation, it acquires its own life and effectiveness and is capable of exerting a transformative influence not only on the societal group from which it has emerged but also significantly extending its reach beyond that.

Money is originally always something representative; something that can be a highly outward means of expression, as are or can be some rare

---

[533] Cultic representations, cult objects, and cult devices are understood to be included in this category.

[534] Ostentatious adornment and status adornment.

goods, ornament, festive clothing, weapons, and so on. The display of money possession signifies the rank, reputation, and distinction of its possessor. Insignificant things do not have the aptitude to become primitive money. The emergence of money always connects to certain conspicuous objects. The path that leads from such particularly perceptible and appealing items as money signs to sometimes completely inconspicuous money signs, and even to a mere book entry in a ledger, is the path of the transformation of the essential service of money.

The objectification of a factual situation through a tangible means of expression is associated with an important process: the detachment of the expressive function from its *personal* carrier and its transfer of the expressive function to a *material* entity. This achieves the fact that the expressive function becomes independent of the individual person and can be transferred to others.

Money serves as a means of expression with particularly strong resonance. It expresses a personal relationship among members of society. These relationships have been designated as specific communities characterised by their money-usage, such as the 'payment-community' (Knapp) or the 'accounting-community' (Heller[535]). In addition, I would say 'community of recognition' (*Geltungsgemeinschaft*). This means that the existence of money is based on a specific societal usage. Without such a usage, money does not emerge, and with its cessation, money itself ceases to exist.

The societal theory of money reveals to us the contribution of money to the system of social integration. Humans are beings that live socially, act socially in their activities, and affect the 'social.' They cannot live without sociability, and everything that strengthens this 'social' also strengthens themselves. [❡258] As has been elaborated in detail, money enhances sociability. Although the essence of money-usage is the social, it also

---

[535] [tn] See footnote 357.

reinforces the individual by strengthening a person's self and uniqueness. It is both a requirement for intense sociability and a guarantee for asserting individuality within sociability.

Instinct, habit, and intellect (*Verstand*), the primal forces behind all cultural creations, have collaborated in the creation of money. They have, in this sequence, determined the development of money, indicating three distinct levels or stages of the evolution of money. The primal drives, the 'drive for distinction,' and the 'drive for amassing' lead to hoard-money. The habit of using it as hoard-money transforms this money into payment-money (penance-money, feud-money, bridal-money). Rationalisation, without implying continuous development, turns it into exchange-money and further into the 'general commercial-money' (*allgemeines Verkehrsgeld*).[536]

The answer to the age-old Sophist question, whether money originated in '*physei*' [φύσει, by nature) or '*thesei*' [θεσει, by convention or agreement],[537] is that money is a product of nature, it did not arise from a mere 'statute.' However, the development of money demonstrates that this opposition between two concepts is not an enduring one. Instead, over the course of its development, the statute (*Satzung*) necessarily arises from the nature of money. It is the same with money as it is with the state, which, although originally arising from nature, has become a legal institution. The money that originally emerged as a social category by nature becomes, in its further usage, a means of market-intercourse, and thus a specifically economical category. Its existence, as it continues to develop, is ensured and receives acknowledgement through 'statute' (*Satzung*). In this way, money becomes a legal category; it reaches the turning point and division, as explained in another context, where the

---

[536] Refer to the detailed presentation in Section 19, Stages of Evolution of Money (*Stufen der Geldentwicklung*) in Gerloff (1940:178 ff.).

[537] [tn] Refer to footnotes 6 and 7.

money created by statute replaces the money that had originally emerged naturally. This transformation is certainly associated with a change in function and is only possible through such a change.

[p259] The circumstances of the emergence of money are only significant for the essence of money at the first stage of its development. As money acquires functions other than the original ones, the essence determined by its substantial existence fades, and another, formal essence, shapes its character. Money without material (*stofflich*) substance can never be an original social means of distinction. However, as a means of exchange and a means of value-comparison (*Wertvergleichsmittel*), it can function without being tied to a material substance.

Money is originally a general societal means of recognition, as has been explained in detail and in various contexts here and in my book (Gerloff 1940). It comes into existence through a certain goods-usage aimed at societal 'validation' (*Gelten*). However, as the monetary functions undergo ongoing development and transformation over time, the means of recognition becomes a means of remuneration; money becomes the societal equivalent for exchange-goods in general. By being widely recognised as an expression (representative) of possession, power, and wealth, and being desired and entering into circulation for that reason, certain goods gain the aptitude to become money. At a further stage, which is part of this development, these goods become generally accepted and, therefore, universally valid equivalents for other goods, including a multitude of commodities. The good that attains this characteristic of equivalence becomes money, or to put it differently: at this stage of money's development, money is that good which acquires the property of being the generally accepted and universally valid equivalent for all other goods entering into exchange-intercourses.

Thus, money becomes simultaneously the "representative of wealth-power (*Vermögensmacht*)" (Savigny).[538] Money is of crucial significance for societal structure when the development of the monetary framework (*Ausbildung des Geldwesens*) leads to a situation where the land possession or the land possession *alone* is no longer the sole representative and bearer of wealth-power.

Money is a social institution. [p260] Its nature and effectiveness are determined by the society that uses it. However, because the actions of society always rely on individuals, money gains its vitality and effectiveness through individual actions and behaviours.

All primitive money-usage is ritualised. Ritualisation involves adhering to *forms* to which magical or spiritually religious significance is attributed.[539]

In its early form (*Frühform*), money is often seen as a bearer of a magical life-force (*Lebenskraft*) that elevates the possessor to a higher being and provides him with assurance of access to the afterlife and the attainment of a rank-status among the departed. This belief in the supernatural qualities of money can explain the intense greed for money and the seemingly shameless greed observed in some indigenous tribes. Indeed, the belief in

---

[538] [tn] Friedrich Carl von Savigny (1779-1861), a German jurist, vehemently opposed the doctrine of nominalism and developed the theory of monetary value in his book (Savigny 1851). This theory remains relevant today and is often echoed by people, even if they are unaware of its origin. Savigny's theory revolves around the concept of 'wealth-power' (*Vermögensmacht*), which denotes the abstract wealth-power or purchasing power inherent in money. It represents a distinct and subjective right embedded within money, enabling it to fulfil various obligations, including future ones. This concept underscores the significance of money's capacity to function as a unit of account, possess purchasing power, and require an embodiment or carrier to materialise its value. These attributes collectively enable money to effectively serve as a medium of exchange within an economy.

[539] [tn] Refer to Laum (2023/1924) for insights into the importance of forms in rituals.

the sanctifying force, in a mysterious force that guarantees bliss through money, transforms money-earning into a virtuous work and a religious activity, not just within Calvinist sects but more broadly across various religious systems.

However, when we talk about the ritualisation of money-usage, we mean something different. It refers to the fact that money-expending initially occurs only on specific occasions and always in a particular, formal manner. If monetary payment is meant to acquire women, atone for transgressions, seal peace treaties, or accomplish any other 'transfer of possession' (*Besitzübertragung*), then this means must be applied correctly in a formal manner to have the magical effect and fully fulfil that intended purpose-setting.[540] This is to be understood as the formal and proper execution of payment often reflecting the semblance of a sacred or ritualistic activity.

The crucial question is: what is the social function of money? The answer: it consists in bringing about a certain behaviour pattern that imparts a specific character to society. However, this behaviour pattern is by no means always the same everywhere and at all times. In eras characterised by a feudal or military societal structure, money plays a different, and often a lesser role than in times when the character of society is determined by economical traits. Natural-economy always implies small, self-contained economic circles. [p261] In contrast, a monetary economy signifies an expansion of trade, not only in the economic sense but also in the intellectual and cultural sense, across unlimited spaces.

In a capitalist society, the character of social life is significantly shaped by money. Money determines the "community of views" (*Gemeinschaft der Anschauungen*),[541] the 'business society' (*Unternehmungsgesellschaft*),

---

[540] [tn] See Laum (2023/1924: 81ff.).

[541] [tn] The term '*Gemeinschaft der Anschauungen*,' translated as the 'community of views,' refers to a shared set of perspectives, beliefs, or ideologies held by a

and the 'political society' (*politische Gesellschaft*), following the classification provided by A. Eleutheropulos. [542] The evolution of the monetary economy goes hand in hand with the advancement of technological civilisation. The earth becomes an economic sphere, and the world of intellectual interests is connected to form a cultural world.

Money is not only an economic means but also a cultural instrument of the highest order. It is certain that just as there can be a culture without writing, there can also be a culture without money. However, a moneyless culture, like a culture without writing, will be impoverished, as the absence of money as the cultural-good imposes significant limitations.

Primitive money serves as a means of distinction and means of accentuation, as well as 'social differentiation.' For this reason, all money, initially, is referred to as 'elite-money' (*Herrengeld*) or 'class-money.'

Congregations (*Zusammenknft*), both among tribal members and with outsiders, play multiple roles in the emergence of money. They not only provide an opportunity to showcase distinctive possessions but also contribute to a gift-traffic that contributes to the development of money.

$$A means that grants societal recognition also inherently bestows societal power; it determines the behaviour pattern of the socialised. The sequence: societal recognition leads to societal power, and this connection is inevitable. Money, as a means of expressing societal recognition, is therefore also a means of societal power-exercise (*Mittel gesellschaftlicher Machtausübung*). This function is particularly relevant to money in cases

---

group of people within a society. In the current context, it suggests that money plays a role in shaping the common perspectives or values held by individuals and groups within a capitalist society. Money can influence the way people perceive the world, their priorities, and their shared understanding of economic, social, and cultural matters. It implies that the prevalence and significance of money in a society can contribute to the formation of a collective mindset or worldview among its members.

[542] Eleutheropulos (1923:189).

where it represents the disposal and control over economic means, which are marked in money as a ratio of magnitude. In the realm of economics, money serves as the denominator that expresses 'power-relations' (*Machtverhaltniss*) and, consequently, 'power dynamics' (*Machtrelation*) and 'power differentials' (*Machtdifferenz*). [?262] However, in doing so, it also becomes a *carrier of power* (*Machtträger*) itself. By granting the 'power of disposal and control' (*Verfügungsmacht*), money becomes more than just a means; it embodies the 'realisation of purpose' (*Zweckverwirklichung*) within itself.

In money, wealth is transformed into power, including societal, political, religious power, and so on. However, this power is a means of wealth-acquisition again. The formula can be stated as follows: Wealth is converted into power through money, and power, in turn, creates wealth through money. This has been the case throughout history, although the triggering of this interaction is certainly influenced by economic and societal structures. Above all, the age of capitalism creates "that world where one buys power for money and then turns power into money again" (Zweig 1929: Chapter 4).

Every expansion and enhancement of the use-potentiality of money increases its effectiveness as a means of power. Civilisation amplifies the power of money by increasing the number of pleasures and sensory delights that can be purchased with it.

Money is the intermediary of goods-distribution. The ordering (*Ordnung*) of goods-distribution is not determined by money itself, but it exerts a powerful influence on it. From the perspective of the overall economy, the question arises whether money is merely a mediator in the exchange of goods and services or whether it also stimulates the supply of goods and services. The answer is that a distinction should be made between its usage and its effect (*Wirkung*). In its usage, money is nothing more than a measure or a means of transport that does not change the quantity of the goods it measures or transports. However, in its effect, it has the power to bring water forth from the rock.[543] So, it can never distribute more than what exists, but it entices offers of services and thereby increases goods-production. This effect is a consequence of the role of money in private or individual economies. For the individual entrepreneur, money represents the 'capability of disposal and control' (*Verfügungsmöglichkeit*) over material-goods and services to satisfy any desires. Money, by its ability to stimulate services and performances (*Darbietung*), leads to a tremendous multiplication of useful goods, improvement in their quality, and enhancement of technological, artistic, and scientific services. [P263] All of this simultaneously signifies the continued growth of the power of money.

Rudolph von Jhering, in his famous work "The Purpose in the Law" (Jhering 1877 – *Der Zweck im Recht*), succinctly described the "advantage of money over 'non-compensation' (*Unentgeltlichkeit*)"[544] with a few words. In this context, he particularly emphasises the "absolute non-requirement of prerequisites of money." He says:

> Favour (*Gefälligkeit*) requires many prerequisites, money requires none other than itself. Favour needs to be addressed with care and skill; it has its moods, its whims, and antipathies. It might turn away from the one who needs it the most or at the very time when it is most necessary. Even if it were always willing, it still has its narrowly defined limits. Money, on the other hand, knows nothing of all this. Money knows no respect for the person, it suffers from no moods, it has no times when it is less accessible, and it knows no limit at which its willingness ends. Self-interest has the most vivid interest

---

[543] [tn] This metaphor originates from a biblical story in which Moses, the leader of the Israelites, was instructed by God to strike a rock with his staff, and water gushed forth to provide for the thirsty people. It means that money has the extraordinary ability to produce significant effects or outcomes, much like the water miraculously flowing from a rock.

[544] [tn] It refers to 'favour,' which is not contingent on the principle of compensation. The following quotation provides further clarification.

in serving **everyone at all times, to any extent**; the more one expects of it, the more it delivers, the more one desires from it, the more willing it becomes. A situation where we had to depend on favours for all our needs would be extremely burdensome, akin to the plight of a beggar. Our personal freedom and independence are based on our ability and necessity to pay. In money lies not only our economical but also our **moral independence**.[545]

It is essentially the same as what James Stewart means when he says that the main characteristic of what we call freedom lies in the circulation of a corresponding equivalent for every service.

The economic power of money is most evident in the class formation. The dependencies created by the contrast between possession and non-possession are amplified through money. Money, or the possession of power, generates a different social order compared to material goods-possession, land possession, or occupational possession. [ᵖ264] Money-domination shatters the feudal lordship based on possession of weapons, the caste-based dominion founded on conquest, and the hierocracy stemming from religious worship.

In the modern state, money is an excellent means for providing the state with possession-power. When the state collects levies in money, pays its officials and soldiers in money, when the church grants masses and indulgences for money, when social hierarchy is based on money possession, when opinions or votes can be bought, and rank-statuses and privileges can be acquired through monetary payments, then the power of money becomes dangerously significant.

The moral dangers of the power of money are well-known. They are counterbalanced by an ascetic way of life that views money-earning only as a means in service to the community.

The 'disposal and control over money' lead to a change in the status of

---

[545] Jhering (1877:128).

societal strata among themselves. Formerly leading strata are displaced. In primitive society, the strong have the leadership, i.e., the members of the middle age groups. Later, when the societal structure (*gesellschaftlicher Verband*) [in a tribe] is well-balanced, the council of elders also plays a role, contributing their experience and insight to the decision-making process. However, when possession and ownership have gained significance, the elderly can make use of it [i. e., the power from possession and ownership]. Money gives them leverage (*Einfluß*); it incarnates possession in its potential for impact (*Wirkungsmöglichkeit*), in other words, in its purest social power-function. This change significantly alters the status of the elders, who are typically money possessors, both in terms of their influence on public affairs and the respect owed to them. Just as they are the subject of "affectionate, familial care" within the family, they are also granted a special status in society that ensures them respect and influence. Polygyny practically becomes a privilege of the elders because the increased bride-price makes it more difficult or even impossible for young tribe members with limited means to acquire a wife. [₽265] Money becomes a powerful means of societal transformations and destratifications, as it sometimes works in conjunction with established claims and positions and at other times gives rise to new groups opposed to the existing ones.

One will have to wonder whether money serves this function [of societal transformations and rearrangements] or serves possession, i.e., the disposal and control over possession. The answer is certainly 'possession.' However, money represents the mobilisation of possessions and thereby enhances the effectiveness inherent in possession. While it may not create social order itself, it does influence it by helping to destroy old orders and establish and shape new ones.

The social order of the monetary economy is different from that of the moneyless society. Money transforms the social meaning of possessions and also that of the individual acts of 'transfer of possession,' such as gift, exchange, tax, etc. The sociological effect of a process is in any case different when it is directed towards money than when it is directed directly towards a material-good. The attitude of giving as well as of taking is expressed in the object that is given or taken, whether it is an immediately useful good or whether it is money. The relationship among people is different when their 'engaging with each other' (*Miteinander-in-Verbindung-Treten*) are centred on goods compared to when they revolve around money. The relationships established through monetary intercourses entail a dehumanisation and depersonalisation of these relationships. Their reification (*Versachlichung*), as it is commonly referred to, is, in reality, a de-reification (*Entsachlichung*).[546]

This development is associated with a purpose-change of money and a modification of money-usage. It represents a transformation that is peculiar to various cultural areas, shifting from a spiritually-magical and irrational purpose-setting to a technically-rational one. The ritualisation of money-usage is replaced by its rationalisation, which means the development of forms of secular purposefulness. This evolution is inevitably driven by the expansion of the economic organisation that characterises the era of individualistic capitalism.

The transition from ritualistic money-usage to rational money-usage involves a change in the function of money. [P266] What is lost in terms of its original effectiveness along this path is replaced by an expansion of its domain of influence that extends far beyond the initial, magical-religious, and class-tied functional realm. However, one aptitude remains with money throughout all functional changes: it remains a means of power. If this function is taken away from money, i.e., the function of representing power in society, in the economy, and especially in the market

---

[546] [tn] It might imply that in exchanges involving tangible goods, a more personal and human element is present, as these goods often possess specific qualities, uses, and meanings. However, when exchanges are facilitated with money, the relationships tend to become more abstract, standardised, and impersonal. This shift can be seen as a form of 'de-reification,' moving away from the direct, tangible attributes of goods.

(understood in the broadest sense), then it ceases to be money.

The money-usage determines the power of money. Money becomes a social means of power to the extent that money-usage becomes customary, establishes itself. Especially in exchange-economic intercourses, money acquires purchasing power. Money serves as a carrier of power in quite different societal domains. In the societal economy, it functions as a means of payment, a means of exchange, a means of purchase, a calculating unit, a means of price-formation, a means of price-expression, and finally, a means of price-statement (*Abrechnungsmittel*).[547]

The term means of price-statement refers to the function of money in a regulated economy where regulated-prices, better described as fixed consideration (*Entgelt*) or charges (*Taxe*) than prices, replace free market prices. In that case, money serves as *not* a means of price-formation (*Preisbildungsmittel*), but *merely* a means of price-statement.

Which monetary service takes precedence and must be considered as the essential service of money in the money-concept of a given social constitution depends on the respective monetary society, i.e., the society that uses money, or in other words, on the stage of evolution of the monetary economy. The differentiation of various stages in the evolution of money is observed through the diverse monetary services within the respective successive epochs of the monetary framework.

The question of *which* service of money is the original one, which has led to the development of "money" as a 'purpose category' (*Zweckkategorie*) is a matter of debate. I believe it should be answered that it is the social 'recognition-function' (*Geltungsfunktion*). Money as a 'purposive institution' (*Zweckeinrichtung*)[548] does not originate from the

---

[547] [tn] Means of price-statement (*Abrechnungsmittel*) specifically refers to a means of finalising or concluding transactions by calculating and determining the final regulated price, especially in the context of a *regulated economy*.

[548] [tn] Refer to p. 117 for 'purposive institution' (*Zweckeinrichtung*), a term

exchange-economy, indeed, not from the economy at all. However, as societal development progresses, money becomes an economic means, and the economic role it assumes becomes increasingly significant for economic flows themselves. [₽267] It grows into this role and adapts to it more and more.

In the exchange-economy, money serves as a means of evaluating goods and services. Simultaneously, it acts as a means of 'value-magnitude representation,' meaning it serves as the benchmark for the value of all economic goods. It functions as both a means of representation (*Vertretungsmittel*) and a means of communication of the values of various goods (Schäffle 1906: 221). Precisely because of this, it is the most effective means of organising economic intercourses. Just as language serves as the tool for organising intellectual intercourse, money functions as the instrument for structuring economic intercourses. What the hand or tool means for the execution of mechanical processes, money means for the flow of economic intercourses. Money becomes a means of more or less reasonable management of economic affairs, and not only that but to a considerable extent, of life as a whole. Society transforms into a monetary society, and the economy into a monetary economy. The latter is one whose relationships receive their character through money, while the monetary economy wants to claim that the economic process in all its stages finds its expression in money, that money becomes, so to speak, a measure and control (*Maß und Steuer*) of the economy. The care for the best satisfaction of human ends (which is what we mean by the economy), pursued with purposeful use of means, has found in money a tool for the meaningful conduct of production and consumption. Its application creates not only economic forms and ways of co-living but truly societal ones. It is, as Jhering says, the practical dialectic of purpose that has created the step-by-step progress of wealth in the forms and configurations that

---

devoid of rationalistic implications.

money itself and money-usage have found and gone through in their historical existence up to the present day.

In its earliest appearance, money is characterised by being a 'carrier of services' in three ways: it is a social means of recognition, a social means of power, and a means of expression of social relationships. [p268] These three services remain inherent to money throughout its further development, even though the external forms of their effectiveness may change.

The socialising force of money cannot be overestimated. However, this should not be understood to mean that the spread of money-usage leads to a societal levelling[549]; that is not the case. There are few things that can cause such a significant expansion of self-awareness and self-esteem as money, to the extent that it is often pursued solely for its own sake, meaning it is desired not for any other or specific purpose but for its own sake. This statement is not a contradiction but rather an explanation of that process, meaning it highlights a motive that is effective (among others) when it is pointed out in this context that the form that money especially takes in the form of coin often acquires a significance for the society using money that goes far beyond the immediate money-purpose. Form becomes a symbolic entity in which the group (the nation) perceives itself objectified. The money of the Greeks, the Greek coin, was the subject of representing the deity in an ideal human form.[550] It was "first developed somewhat unintentionally, and then often entirely consciously into a work of art."[551] Greek money, as Kerényi says, "acted no differently than a small sanctuary next to the great temples of the city: sanctuaries and coins express the spirit of the polis — the spirit, in turn, of a small, distinct

---

[549] [tn] It refers to a situation where societal differences or hierarchies become less pronounced or less extreme, leading to a more even or equal society.

[550] [tn] Laum (2023/1924).

[551] Regling (1924: 1).

world."[552]

Similar principles apply – although in a different and adapted manner depending on the form and measure – everywhere money is created and money-usage becomes customary, depending on the circumstances. Particularly characteristic money pieces that, in a way, represent the monetary system of a country, such as the Louis d'or, the Friedrichsdor, the gold crown, and the gold piece with the emperor's portrait, become national symbols. [p269] The national coinage, as Mommsen has said, "draws the bonds of the community closer together; it increases, if the expression is allowed, the centripetal or the communistic element, which is just as necessary to any state as the antithesis [to the centripetal element]."[553]

But even the mere currency unit is something entirely different for the members of the country using that currency unit than for foreigners who also use it, of course. It holds a similar significance to the national flag. The battle for the supremacy of the dollar or the fate of the pound sterling is more than just an economic matter. The currency unit represents the unity of the country; however, the quality of currency is an expression of its economic and political power, and thus its social reputation. "The silver is only good enough for second-rate nations," said the lawmaker Bamberger[554] when advocating the introduction of the gold standard in the newly established German Empire.

All of this is an expression of the social and socialising force of money. In money, the spirit and soul of a people are shaped; they find their reflection in the money-form. One can say that the money of a group,

---

[552] Kerényi & Lanckoroński (1941, quote 21).

[553] Mommsen (1863:256).

[554] [tn] Ludwig Bamberger (1823–1899) was a prominent German economist and politician. He played a key role in advocating for the adoption of the gold standard in the newly formed German Empire during the late 19th century.

especially the state's money – but not only this – is the symbolic expression of the existence of a society.

Conscious social interacting action uses money as a means of social co-living and collaboration. However, money does not only signify association but also dissociation, not just bonding but also separation. With the penetration of money into society, the social bonds of communal life loosen, mutual support and care lose their original strength, weaken, and in some areas may even come to a complete halt. In exchange, other values are traded. Money makes individuals independent or at least reduces their dependency, leads to economic self-sufficiency and self-accountability, and fosters the thinking and activity pattern that characterises individualism. And yet, it is precisely money that helps "overcome the malice of separation" (Holbach [555]). [p270] Fyodor Dostoevsky called money "embodied freedom," and the poet August Graf von Platen exclaims:

> But one thing you grant, heavenly money, which few, who possess you,
> Understand to possess, understand to enjoy, what is this one thing? Freedom.[556]

The respected English economist A. Marshall refers to money as a benchmark of motives for action, not only for the driving force of economic action but also for other goals of human endeavour.

The replacement of in-kind-disbursements with monetary-disbursements, as seen in the replacement of natural rent and especially

---

[555] [tn] Paul-Henri Thiry, Baron d'Holbach (1726-1789) was a French-German philosopher and author during the Enlightenment period. He was known for his atheistic and materialistic views and was a prominent figure in the intellectual circles of his time.

[556] [tn] In simpler language: "Heavenly money, there's something special that you bestow upon a few who possess you, understand how to possess you, and know how to enjoy you. What is that one thing? It is freedom."

natural wages with monetary payments, has often been viewed as a liberation from burdensome ties. However, such liberation actually represents a new form of bondage: **the binding to the fate of money**.

The provision of in-kind-disbursement guarantees the fulfilment of a specific demand under all circumstances. Monetary payments cannot provide such a guarantee. As history has shown, the transition from in-kind-disbursement to monetary-disbursement has occurred everywhere, resulting in a whole range of associated problems stemming from this well-defined situation.

One can consider the development of money-usage as a specific example of the biogenetic fundamental law, by observing the expression of successive stages in social history in the successive uses of money. These stages are characterised by the development of functions, the transformation of functions, and ultimately, the de-functionalisation (*Entfunktionalisierung*) of money.

In summary, it can be said that the original function of money as a societal means of recognition leads to its use as a means of payment and a means of exchange. The expansion and ongoing development of money-usage, its rampant spread, as well as its occasional decline, are linked to the development of the subjective purchasing power of money. [p271] The purchasing power of money becomes the essence of monetary existence.

For money-usage, **the law of habit** (*Gesetz der Gewohnheit*), **the law of transmission** (*Gesetz der Übertragung*), **and the law of recovery** (*Gesetz der Genesung*) apply. The law of habit refers to the increasing willingness to repeat a process, in this case, the monetary usage of specific goods, corresponding to the number of repetitions. The law of transmission refers to the tendency to expand the scope of a method or technique to ever wider application areas, as seen in money-usage through the expansion of the subjective and objective purchasing power of money. The law of recovery, when applied to the monetary framework, suggests that the social body has a tendency to restore or eliminate diseased money.

In other words, the worse money becomes, the stronger the tendency to eliminate it or restore its health, akin to an anti-Gresham's law: the worse money gets, the more it is pushed out or efforts are made to restore its health.

Money is inconceivable without society; it is purely a societal phenomenon, an outcome of the social process. When people occasionally speak of society being undermined by money, in social-economic terms (not ethical considerations), they mean that money dissolves the original economic organisations, which were family associations, within which the entire economic life, the production of goods, their distribution, and consumption, took place. However, such a perspective overlooks that money here, as often, is merely a means that accompanies and certainly facilitates and promotes development but is not a factor that produces or causes it.

[p272] If Theodor Mommsen referred to writing and the coin as "those among the numerous means of civilisation that bring together and bind people and nations in an incomparably powerful way,"[557] here it can be unequivocally said "money," instead of "coin."

Just as money emerges from a specific mentality of socially organised individuals and certain forms of social co-living, its usage brings about a profound transformation of this mentality and these forms of co-living. This is associated with a piece of human education, just as it is with the usage of certain material goods, where reasonable use requires education. In an economic order where money holds the status it does in ours, there is always the danger that the means of exchange becomes an intoxicant, so that the harsh words of Boisguillebert, "Money becomes the executioner of all things, it declares war on all of humanity" (*L'argent devient le bourreau de toutes les choses, il déclare la guerre à tout le genre humain*),[558]

---

[557] Mommsen (ibid.:246).

[558] [tn] Boisguilbert (1707). Pierre Le Pesant de Boisguilbert (1646-1714) was a

become understandable. From this, however, arises the educational task that arises in every social order with respect to money-usage and money-expending.

The emergence of money is an example of how social institutions do not owe their origin to enlightened egoism and rational desire for advantage, but rather, they arise from innate drives and tendencies that are common to all humans and have their roots extending back to pre-human existence. Therefore, the statement that money is not the creation of a single nation is also understandable. It is a contribution to the cultural possession of humanity, which we do not owe to a single nation or race, but it belongs to those numerous cultural-goods that are found independently of space and race among different peoples. What Emil du Bois-Reymond[559] says about the first tools, "not just by one, only once, and only in one place, but by many, repeatedly, and at various points on the earth, they were invented," applies, if we say "emerged" instead of "invented," to money as well, which is, in a certain way, a tool. [p273] It is hardly an overstatement to venture that a significant portion of societal development can only be comprehended by examining the respective function of money in human society. One only half understands the essence of money and its societal significance, and that means not at all if one only looks at its role in the present, overlooks its development from the past and does not recognise its changes that point to the future. In any case, it is certain that an understanding of the specific function of money can significantly illuminate the course of societal development, and this holds particularly true for the stage commonly referred to as capitalism.

French lawmaker and a Jansenist, one of the inventors of the notion of an economic market.

[559] Emil du Bois-Reymond (1818-1896) was a pioneering German physiologist and physicist known for his foundational contributions to electrophysiology and his exploration of the electrical properties of nerve and muscle tissues in the 19th century.

Capitalism is not just a form of economic order but the shaper and carrier of the entire societal existence of a particular historical epoch; money always serves as a social means of relationship, but nowhere does its power to shape societal relationships and transform existing ones become more evident than in capitalist economies.

Money is a means of communication, much like language; today, its primary purpose is to facilitate understanding of the value of things, particularly the value relationships of economical entities.

However, it is not just an economical means of communication but also a social one.

K. Knies expresses this idea as follows:

> Money, like the tones of music, speaks a universally comprehensible language, understandable to every societal stratum and in every country. It tells the farmer, the miner, and the lumberjack as well as the artisan, the manufacturer, the merchant, the washerwoman as well as the lady of the court, what they can enjoy from the necessities and the splendours of the earthly world when they come into possession of money.[560]

However, this list does not exhaust the domain of influence by money as a social means of communication. The social communication-force (*Verständigungskraft*) that money holds extends much further, as has been demonstrated in various contexts. [⁋274] Money, as has been previously explained, does not originate in the world of economical entities. The display of money (*Geldzurschaustellung*), its distribution, and money-destruction — these original uses of money — are expressions of social facts and social situations, and thus, with them statements about social fact-situations (*Sachverhalte*) Bridal-money, penance-money, and feud-money — the main uses of primitive money — are means of

---

[560] Knies (ibid.:444).

communication and tools for organising social relationships.[561] Likewise, exchange-money is a social means of communication, the use of which signifies more than merely facilitating the exchange of economical goods. This has also been demonstrated. Thus, money, at every stage of its development, serves as a means of communication.

The peculiarity of this means of communication is that it is often criticised for obscuring the true situation of things, as expressed in the commonly used phrase money-veil (*Geldschleier*). However, the image of a money-veil is misleading and inaccurate. Money is not something that lies like a veil on or above the economy, which could be removed without changing the economy itself, but it is the bloodstream that circulates through the economic body, giving it life. Money is by no means a mere symbol, and its use or non-use does not simply represent the advantage or loss of a certain convenience; rather, it is an essential element and a factor in every advanced societal economy. The formation and ongoing development of the societal economy are always simultaneously the formation and ongoing development of the monetary economy. Therefore, money is not a sign of decay. Its development as a means of exchange does not signify the loss of utopian communism but rather the enrichment of human existence, the integration of the individual into a system of diverse interdependencies, and the compulsion toward a social mindset. [p275] Money is the most powerful means of overcoming intellectual and social inertial resistance (*Trägheitswiderstand*). Therefore, the beneficial consequences of its usage should be valued much more highly than the shortcomings that can be attributed to its potential misuse. In an aphorism that I have placed at the beginning of my sketch titled

---

[561] For a small region, which can serve as an example for many larger areas, C. Nooteboom provides an excellent description of the function of money in his work (Nooteboom 1940). Please refer to Section XIII, *De Sociale Beteekenis van Economische Goederen* [The Social Significance of Economic Goods] for further insight into this aspect.

"Societal Theory of Money" (*Gesellschaftliche Theorie des Geldes*)[562] this idea has been expressed with the following words:

Two things are not possible without money: the prosperity of nations and social justice.

"Two things are threatened by nothing more than by money: the prosperity of nations and social justice.

---

[562] Gerloff (1950).

References

Note: Translator's references are indicated with (*) following the authors' names.

Achilleos, Stella (2022)*, "Bodin, Jean" in Sgarbi, Marco (ed.) (2022), *Encyclopedia of Renaissance Philosophy*, Springer.

Achter, V. (1950), *Geburt der Strafe* [Birth of Punishment].

Adam, Leonhard (1923), *Nordwest-Amerikanische Indianerkunst* [Northwest American Indian Art].

Amonn, A. (1926), *Grundzüge der Volkswohlstandslehre* [Principles of the Theory of Public Welfare].

Amonn, A. (1927), *Objekt und Grundbegriff der Nationalökonomie* [Object and Foundational Concept of National Economy].

Aristotle (1872), Aristoteles' Politik: Erstes, zweites und drittes Buch mit erklärenden Zusätzen ins Deutsche Übertragen; Bernays, Jacob (tr.), Williams & Norgate.

Aristotle (1932)*, *Aristotle Politics*, Rackham, H. (tr.), The Loeb Classical Library, Harvard University Press.

Aristotle (2004)*, *The Nicomachean Ethics*, Crisp, Roger (tr.), Cambridge University Press.

Aristotle (2009)*, *The Nicomachean Ethics*, Ross, David (tr.), Oxford University Press.

Armstrong, Wallace E. (2011/1928)*, *Rossel Island: An Ethnological Study*, Cambridge University Press.

Bachofen, Johann Jakob (1861), *Das Mutterrecht* [Mother Right].

Bastable, C.F. (1888), 'Money,' in *Encyclopedia Britannica – A Dictionary Of Arts, Sciences, and General Literature*, Ninth Edition, Volume XVI, New York

Benedict, Ruth (1949), *Patterns of Culture*, New York.

332

Birket-Smith, Kaj (1948), *Geschichte der Kultur* [History of Culture], 2nd ed., Zürich.

Bodin, J. (1568): *La Response de Maistre Jean Bodin, advocat en la Cour, au Paradoxe de Monsieur de Malestroit touchant l'encherissement de totes hoses et le moyen d'y remedier*, Paris.

Boisacq, Émile (1923), *Dictionnaire étymologique de la langue grecque : étudiée dans ses rapports avec les autres langues indo-européennes.*

Böhm-Bawerk, Eugen von (1902), *Positive Theorie des Capitales*, Innsbruck.

Böhm-Bawerk, Eugen von (1908-1911a), "Kapital," in J. Conrad, L. Elster, W. Lexis, and Edg. Loening (eds.) (1909-1911), *Handwörterbuch der Staatswissenschaften*, 3. ed., Vol. V: 777-785

Böhm-Bawerk, Eugen von (1909), *Positive Theorie des Kapitals.*

Böhm-Bawerk, Eugen von, (1908-1911b), "Geld," in J. Conrad, L. Elster, W. Lexis, and Edg. Loening (eds.) (1909-1911), Handwörterbuch der Staatswissenschaften, 3. ed.

Boisguilbert, Pierre Le Pesant de (1707), *Dissertation sur la nature des richesses, l'argent et les tributs* [Dissertation on the Nature of Wealth, Money, and Taxes]

Brandl, Felix (2015)*, *Von der Entstehung des Geldes zur Sicherung der Währung Die Theorien von Bernhard Laum und Wilhelm Gerloff zur Genese des Geldes*, Springer Gabler.

Braun, Christina von (2022)*, 'Vorwort: Der Kult als Schöpfer normierter Entgeltungsmittel,' In Laum, Bernhard, *Heiliges Geld* (2022)*, MSB Matthes & Seitz Berlin.

Budge, S. (1931), *Lehre vom Geld, I* [Theory of Money].

Budge, S. (1933), *Lehre vom Gelde*, 1. Bd., 1. HalbBd.

Burckhardt, Jacob (1898), Griechische Kulturgeschichte [Greek Cultural History], Vol IV.

Büsch, Johann Georg (1870), *Abhandlung von dem Geldsumlauf in anhaltender Rücksicht auf die Staatswirtschaft und Handlung* [Treatise on the Circulation of Money in Continuous Consideration of Political

Economy and Trade], Hamburg, 1780.

Butler, John (1855), *Travels and Adventures in the Province of Assam*, London.

Careys, H. C. (1870), *Lehrbuch der Volkswirtschaft und Sozialwissenschaft*, German edition. Karl Adler (ed.). Original title in Engllish: Careys, H. C. (1864), Manual of social science, H. C. Baird, 2nd ed.

Cassel, G. (1932), *Theoretische Sozialökonomie* [Theoretical Social Economics], 5th ed.

Chevalier, Michel (1851), *Cours d'Economie politique* [Course of Political Economy], Bruxelles.

Christen, Theophil (1920), "Zur Kritik der absoluten Währung" [Critique of Absolute Currency], in *Zeitschrift für schweizerische Statistik und Volkswirtschaft*, 56. Jhrg. (1920), S. 61 – 66.

Codrington, R. H. (1891), *The Melanesians*, Oxford.

Conrad, Johannes & Elster, Ludwig & Lexism Wilhelm Hector Richard Albrecht & Loening, Edgar (eds.) (1909), *Handwörterbuch der Staatswissenschaften* IV

Diehl, Karl (1888-9), *P. J. Proudhon: Seine Lehre und sein Leben*, 2 vols, Jena, Gustav Fischer.

Dobretsberger, J. (1946), *Das Geld im Wandel der Wirtschaft* [Money in the Changing Economy].

Duncan, J. (1848), *Travels in Western Africa in 1840 and 1846*, London

Durkheim, É. (1995/1912)*, *The Elementary Forms of Religious Life*. Fields, K. E. (tr.) Free Press.

Durkheim, Émile (1895), *Les Règles de la méthode sociologique*.

Durkheim, Émile; (1982/1895), *The Rules of Sociological Method*, Lukes S (ed.) and Halls, W.D. (tr.), Free Press.

Einzig, Paul (1949), *Primitive money: In its ethnological historical and economic aspects*.

Einzig, Paul (1966)*, *Primitive money: In its ethnological historical and economic aspects*, 2nd ed. Pergamon, Oxford.

Eleutheropulos, A. (1923), *Soziologie*, 2nd ed.

Ellwood, Charles A. (1927), *Das seelische Leben der menschlichen Gesellschaft* [The Psychic Life of Human Society].

Elster, K. (1920), *Die Seele des Geldes.*

Enderlen, L (1929), *Versuch einer Synthese. zwischen Metallismus und Nominalismus* [Attempt at a Synthesis between Metallism and Nominalism].

Fichte, Johann Gottlieb (1800), *Der geschlossene Handelsstaat* [The Closed Commercial State].

Finsch, T.O. (1914), *Südseearbeiten* [South Sea Work].

Fisher, Irving (1911), *Purchasing Power of Money.*

Fisher, Irving (1920), *Stabilising the Dollar.*

Fisher, Irving (1928), *The Money Illusion.*

Fisher, Irving (1935), *Stable Money.*

Forstmann. A. (1943), Volkswirtschaftliche Theorie des Geldes [Economic Theory of Money].

Foster, William Trufant & Catchings, Waddill (1924), Business Conditions and Currency Control.

Franz, L. (1939), *Jäger, Bauern, Händler* [Hunters, Farmers, Traders].

Frauenfelder, M. (1938), *Geld als allgemeiner Rechtsbegriff.*

Geiler, K. (1926), "Geld und Recht," *Zeitschrift für gesamte Staatswissenschaften,* Bd. 81 320

George Brown, (1911), *Melanesians and Polynesians,* London.

Gerloff, Wihlem (1940), *Die Entstehung des Geldes und die Anfänge des Geldwesens"* [The Emergence of Money and the Beginnings of Monetary Framework].

Gerloff, Wilhelm (1943)*, *Die Entstehung des Geldes und die Anfängedes Geldwesens* [The Emergence of Money and the Beginnings of Monetary Framework], 2nd ed., Klostermann, Frankfurt a. M.

Gerloff, Wilhelm (1944), "Ursprung und Sinn des Geldes," *Weltwirtsch. Archiv*, Bd. 60

Gerloff, Wilhelm (1947), *Die Kaufmacht des Geldes.*

Gerloff, Wilhelm (1948a), *Entstehung der öffentlichen Finanzwirtschaft* [The Emergence of Public Financial Administration.

Gerloff, Wilhelm (1948b), *"Ursprung und Anfänge öffentlicher Finanzwirtschaft"* [Origin and Beginnings of Public Financial Administration] in *Handbuch der Finanzwissenschaft*, 2nd edition.

Gerloff, Wilhelm (1950), *Gesellschaftliche Theorie des Geldes.*

Gesell, Silvio (1906a), *Die Verwirklichung des Rechtes auf den vollen Arbeitsertrag* [The Realisation of the Right to the Full Earnings of labour].

Gesell, Silvio (1906b)*, *Die Verwirklichung des Rechtes auf den vollen Arbeitsertrag durch die Geld- und Bodenreform.* Les Hauts Geneveys und Leipzig: Selbstverlag, in Gesammelte Werke (1988 – 2009) Band 4. Verlag für Sozialökonomie.

Gesell, Silvio (1916)*, *Die natürliche Wirtschaftsordnung durch Freiland und Freigeld.* Selbstverlag, Les Hauts Geneveys.

Gesell, Silvio (1958)*, *The Natural Economic Order*, Revised edition. London: Peter Owen.

Gesell, Silvio and Frankfurth, E. (1909), *Aktive Währungspolitik, eine neue Orientierung auf dem Gebiete der Notenemission* [Active Currency Policy, a New Orientation in the Field of Banknote Issuance], 3rd ed.

Goethe, Johann Wolfgang von (1831), *Faust. The Tragedy.* Part Two.

Graeber, David (2011),* *Debt, the first 5000 years*, Melville House Printing.

Grönbech, W. (1937), *Kultur und Religion der Germanen* [Culture and Religion of the Germans], Vol. I, O. Höfler (ed.), E. Hoffmeyer (tr).

Grönbech, W. (1939), *Kultur und Religion der Germanen* [Culture and Religion of the Germans], Vol. II, O. Höfler (ed.), E. Hoffmeyer (tr).

Gross, Herbert (1949), Manager von Morgen.

336

Gruenwaldt, O. v. (ed.) (1937), *Graf Alfred Keyserling erzählt* [Count Alfred Keyserling Narrates].

Gumpel. S. (1914), *Das Geld im bürgerlichen Recht.*

Günther, Adolf (1923), *Theorie der Sozialpolitik*" [Theory of Social Policy]

Günther, Adolf (1941), *"Eine gesellschaftliche Theorie des Geldes,"* Zeitschrift *für Nationalökonomie*, X.

Haber, Franz (1927), "Geldreformer" [Money Reformer] in *Handwörterbuch der Staatswissenschaften*, 1927, IV. Bd, 762.

Halkin, Joseph (1910), *Les Ababua, Coll. d. Monogr. ethnographiques* [The Ababua, Collection of Ethnographic Monographs], vol. VII, Bruxelles.

Hartmann, G. (1868), *Über den rechtlichen Begriff des Geldes und den Inhalt von Geldschulden*

Hauser, Hermann (1920), *Moderne Geldverbesserer* [Modern Currency Reformers].

Hegel, Georg Wilhelm Friedrich (1821), *Grundlinien der Philosophie des Rechts* [Elements of the Philosophy of Right].

Heinsohn, G. and Steiger, O. (2000). The property theory of interest and money. In *What is Money?* (2000), John Smithin (ed.), 67-100, London: Routledge.

Heinsohn, Gunnar & Steiger, Otto (2000)*, 'The Property The theory of Interest and Money,' In Smithin, John (ed.). (2000), *What is money*, Routledge.

Helfferich, K. (1910), *Das Geld* [Money].

Heller, Wolfgang (1927), *Theoretische Volkswirtschaftslehre* [Theoretical National Economics].

Helmreich, Th. (1914-1915), *Das Geldwesen in den deutschen Schutzgebieten* [The Monetary framework in the German Protectorates], Gymnasialprogramm, Fürth.

Heron, A. R. (1949), *Why Men Work*, Stanford University Press.

Heyne, M. (ed.) (1890-95), *Deutsches Wörterbuch* [German Dictionary].

Hoffmann, J. G. (1838), Die Lehre vom Gelde [The Theory of Money].

Hoffmann, J. G. (1847), "Erläuterung der Frage: Was ist Geld?" [Explanation of the Question: What Is Money?], in *Nachlaß kleiner Schriften staatswirtschaftlichen Inhalts.*

Holm, Korfiz (1932), ich – kleingeschrieben, Albert Langen Georg Müller München.

Höltker, Georg (1931), 'Männerbünde,' In Vier-kandt, Alfred (ed.) (1931) *Handwörterbuch der Soziologie*, Stuttgart.

Hoyt, Elizabeth Ellis (1926), *Primitive Trade, its Psychology and Economics.*

Huppert, W. (1938), *Die Grundlagen des Geldes* [The Foundations of Money].

Ihering, Rudolf von (1913), *Law as a Means to an End*, Issac Husik (tr.), Boston.

Ingham, Geoffrey (2004)*, *The nature of money*. Polity, Cambridge Univ. Press. (2017), 'A critique of Lawson's 'Social positioning and the nature of money.' *Cambridge Journal of Economics.* (2021), 'In defence of the nominalist ontology of money,' *Journal of Post Keynesian Economics.*

Jastrow, J. (1902), *Sozialpolitik und Verwaltungswissenschaft"* [Social Policy and Administrative Science].

Jenks, J. W. (1885), Henry C. Carey als Nationalökonom.

Jevons, W. Stanley (1875), *Money and the Mechanism of Exchange.*

Jhering, R. v. (1877), *Der Zweck im Recht* [The purpose in Law].

Jhering, Rudolph von (1877),Der Zweck im Recht [The Purpose in the Law].

Kant, Immanuel (1784), *"Idee zu einer allgemeinen Geschichte in weltbürgerlicher Absicht"* [The Idea of a Universal History on a Cosmopolital Plan], *Berlinischen Monatsschrift.*

Kant, Immanuel (1797), *Die Metaphysik der Sitten* [The Metaphysics of Morals]. Erster Teil: Metaphysische Anfangsgründe der Rechtslehre.

Kant, Immanuel (1797), *Metaphysische Anfangsgründe der Rechtslehre* [Metaphysics of Morals].

Kemmerer, E. W. (1932), *"Zur Theorie des Geld- und Kreditwesens"* [On the Theory of Money and Credit, in Meyer et al. (eds.) (1932), The Economic Theory of the Present], in *Die Wirtschaftstheorie der Gegenwart* II.

Kerényi, K. & Lanckoroński, L. M. (1841), *Der Mythos der Hellenen.*

Keynes, J.M. (1930/1971), *A Treatise on Money,* Vol. I., 2nd ed., The Collected Writings of John Maynard Keynes, Cambridge University Press.

Keynes, J.M. (1936), *The General Theory of Employment,Interest And Money,* The Collected Writings of John Maynard Keynes, Cambridge University Press.

Kleinschmitt, Edmund (1922), *Hilft uns Freigeld? : Zur Kritik der Lehre Silvio Gesells und der Freigeldbewegung* [Does Free Money Help? Critique of Silvio Gesell's Theory and the Free Money Movement].

Klöppel, P. (1887), *Gattung und Gemeinschaft* [Species and Community].

Kloss, A. (1903), *The Andamanes and Nicobares,* London.

Kluge, F. (1899), *Etymologisches Wörterbuch der deutschen Sprache* [Etymological Dictionary of the German Language].

Knapp, G. F. (1918), *Staatliche Theorie des Geldes* [The State Theory of Money].

Knapp, G. F. (1923), *Staatliche Theorie des Geldes* 4 Aufl. Osnabrück: Kraemer & Hansen GmbH. (2023/1923)* *The State Theory of Money,* Hans DG Hyun (tr.), Shoin House.

Knies, Karl (1885a), *Geld und Kredit,* 2nd ed.

Knies, Karl (1885b), *Das Geld* [Money].

Kubary, J. (1895), *Ethnogr. Beiträge zur Kenntnis des Karolinen-Archipels* [Ethnographic Contributions to the Knowledge of the Caroline Islands Archipelago], Leiden.

Kudler, Josef (1856), *Die Grundlehren der Volkswirtschaft,* 2nd ed. Wien.

Labat, J. B. (1728), *Nouvelle Relation de l'Afrique occidentale,* Paris.

Landtman, Gunnar (1909), *The primary Causes of social Inequality,* Helsingfors.

Langeluetke, H. (1925), *Tauschbank und Schwundgeld als Wege zur zinslosen Wirtschaft* [Exchange Banks and Rusting Money as Paths to an Interest-Free Economy].

Laum, B. (1929), *Über das Wesen des Münzgeldes*.

Laum, Berhard (1954/55)*, Über Ursprung und Frühgeschichte des Begriffes 'Kapital' [On the Origin and Early History of the Concept of 'Capital'], FinanzArchiv Public Finance Analysis, New Series, Bd. 15, H. 1, Mohr Siebeck GmbH & Co. KG.

Laum, Bernhard (1924), *Heliges Geld, Eine historische Untersuchung über den sakralen Ursprung des Geldes*, J. C. B. Mohr, Tübingen.

Laum, Bernhard (2022/1924)*, *Heiliges Geld*. MSB Matthes & Seitz Berlin.

Laum, Bernhard (2023/1924)*, *Sacred Money*, Hans DG Hyun (tr.), Shoin Hoouse.

Leenhardt, M. (1930), '*Notes d'Ethnologie Néo-Calédonienne*' [Notes on New Caledonian Ethnology], *Travaux et Mémoires de l'Institut d'Ethnologie* [Works and Memoirs of the Institute of Ethnology], VIII, Paris.

Lehmann, F. Rudolf (1936), 'Adoption bei schriftlosen Völkern' [Adoption among illiterate peoples], *Tagungsbericht der Ges. f. Völkerkunde*, 2. Tagung.

Lehmkuhl, P. (?), *Theologia moralis*, 7th edition.

Ljungberg, Jonas & Ögren, Anders (2018)*, "Discipline or international balance: the choice of monetary systems in Europe," *The European Journal of the History of Economic Thought*.

Lowie, R. H. (1928), 'Incorporeal Property in primitive Society,' *Yale Law Journal*, Vol. XXXVII, 551 ff. (1928).

Lowie, R. H. (1928), Incorporeal Property in primitive society. *Yale Law journal*, vol. XXXVII (1928).

Luschan, F. von, (1919), Die Altertümer von Benin.

Maass, J. (1949), *Die Geheimwissenschaft der Literatur* [The Secret Science of Literature].

Malestroit, S de (1566), *Les Paradoxes du Seigneur de Malestroit*, conseillor du Roi et Maistre ordinaire de ses comptes, sur le faict des Monnoyes presented a Sa Majeste [The Paradoxes of the Lord of Malestroit, Counselor to the King and Master in Ordinary of His Accounts, Regarding the Matter of Money Presented to His Majesty], au mois de Mars MDLXVI, Paris.

Malinowski, B. (1922), *Argonauts of the Western Pacific*.

Mansfeld, A. (1908), *Urwalddokumente* [Jungle Documents].

Marshall, Alfred (1887), "Remedies for Fluctuations in Prices," the *Contemporary Review*.

Marshall, Alfred (1920)*, *Principle of Economics*, 8th ed.

Marx, Karl (1844), *The Power of Money*, Economic and Philosophic Manuscripts of 1844.
https:www.marxists.orgarchivemarxworks1844manuscriptspower.htm

Marx, Karl (1962/1890)*, *Das Kapital - Kritik der politischen Ökonomie*, Vol. I, in Karl Marx – Friedrich Engels Werke Band 23, Dietz Verlag Berlin.

Marx, Karl (1963/1893)*, *Das Kapital - Kritik der politischen Ökonomie*, Vol. II, in Karl Marx – Friedrich Engels Werke Band 24, Dietz Verlag Berlin.

Maslow, A. H. (1943)*, "A theory of human motivation," *Psychological Review*, 50(4), 370–396.

Mauss, Mauss, (1969/1914)*, 'Les origines de la notion de monnaie,' In Communication faite à l'Institut français d'anthropologie. « Comptes-rendus des séances », II, tome I, *supplément à l'Anthropologie*, 1914, 25, pp. 14 à 19. Paris: Les Éditions de Minuit. (1923-1924)*, 'Essai sur le don. Forme et raison de l'échange dans les sociétés archaïques,' *l'Année Sociologique*, seconde série. (20021925), *The Gift: The Form and Reason for Exchange in Archaic Societies*, Halls, W. D.(tr.), Routledge.

Menger, Carl (1871), *Grundsätze der Volkswirthschaftslehre*, Vienna, Wilhelm Braumüller.

Menger, Carl (1888), "Zur Theorie des Kapitals," *Jahrbücher für Nationalökonomie und Statistik*, Vol. 51, 1888,

Menger, Carl (1909), "Geld," in *Handwörterbuch der Staatswissenschaften* (3rd edition, IV, 555 ff.); (2002/1909), Money, Yeager, Leland B. &

Streissler, Monika (trs.). in Latzer, Michael and Schmitz, Stefan W. (eds.). *Carl Menger and the Evolution of Payments Systems*, Edward Elgar.

Menger, Carl (1923), *Grundsätze der Volkswirtschaftslehre* [Principle of Economics].

Mill, J.S. (1871)*, *Principles of Political Economy*.

Mills, J.P. (1932), *The Lhota Nagas*.

Mises, Ludwig v., (1922), *Die Gemeinwirtschaft: Untersuchungen uber den Sozialismus* [The Common Economy: Investigations into Socialism].

Mises, Ludwig v., (1929), "Theorie der Preistaxen," in *Kritik des Interventionismus*, G. Fischer, Jena (originally in *Handwörterbuch der Staatswissenschaften*, 4. Aufl., VI. Bd., 1923).

Mises, Ludwig v., (1940), *Nationalokonomie, Theorie des Handelns und Wirtschaftens*.

Mommsen, Theoodr (1905), "Das Geld," *Grenzboten* XXII, Vol. 1863, in Mommsen, Theoodr (1905) *Reden und Aufsätze*.

Muhs, K. (1927), *Antimarx. Betrachtungen iber den inneren Aufbau der Marxschen Ökonomik*, [Againt Marx: Reflections on the Inner Structure of Marx's Economics], Jena.

Müller-Wismar, W. (1917), *Yap, Ergebnisse der Südsee-Expedition 1908-1910* [Yap, Results of the South Sea Expedition 1908-1910] Thilenius, G. (ed.).

Mun, Thomas (1644), *England's Treasure by Foreign Trade*.

Navratil, A. von (1906), *Wirtschaft und Recht, ein Beitrag zur Theorie der sekundären wirtschaftlichen Erscheinungen* [Economy and Law: A Contribution to the Theory of Secondary Economic Phenomena].

Neumann, F. J. (1896) 'Die Gestaltung des Preises' [The Formation of Prices], in *Handbuch der Politischen Ökonomie* [Handbook of Political Economy], 1896, Vol 1.

Nevermann, H. (1933), *Masken und Geheimbünde in Melanesien* [Masks and Secret unions in Melanesia](revised).

Nietzsche, Friedrich (1886), *Menschliches, Allzumenschliches* [Human, All-Too-Human], Zweite Abtheilung: Der Wanderer und sein Schatten.

Nooteboom, C. (1940), Oost-Soemba, een volkskundige Studie (Transactions of the Royal Institute for the Language, Land, and Ethnology of the Netherlands East Indies, Part 3), The Hague.

Nußbaum, Arthur (1925), *Das Geld in Theorie und Praxis des deutschen und ausländischen Rechtes*.

Obermaier, F. (1942), *Ukraine, Land der schwarzen Erde* [Ukraine, Land of the Black Soil].

Oncken, W. (1875), *Die Staatslehre des Aristoteles"* [The Political Theory of Aristotle], Vol. II.

Oppenheim, Kristin (1941), 'Ein Deutungsversuch neukaledonischer Münzköpfe und Geldschnüre auf Grund polynesischer Analogien' [An Interpretation Attempt of New Caledonian Coin Heads and Money Cords Based on Polynesian Analogies], *Proceedings of the Natural Research Society in Basel*, Volume LII.

Oppenheimer, Franz (1922), *System der Soziologie* [System of Sociology], Vol. 1:. Allgemeine Soziologie [General Sociology], 1. First Half-Volume, Grundlegung.

Oppenheimer, Franz (1924), "Wege zur Gemeinschaft," *Gesammelte Reden und Aufsätze*, Vol. 1, p. 399, reprinted from *Weltwirtschaftliches Archiv*, Vol. 3, Issue 1, 1914.

Pareto, Wilfred (1935/1916-7)*, Mind and Society: A Treatise on General Sociology (original title: Trattato di sociologia generale), Andrew Bongiorno (tr.).

Passow, R. (1913), *Kapitalismus, eine begrifflich-terminologische Studie*.

Patenôtre, Raymond (1932), *La crise et le drame monétaire* [The Crisis and the Monetary Drama].

Paul, H. (1896), *Deutsches Wörterbuch*.

Peitmann, Heinrich (1941), *Die privatrechtlichen Grundlagen des Geldes* [The Private Legal Foundations of Money].

Petri, Helmut (1936), 'Die Geldformen der Südsee' [currencies in the South Pacific], *Anthropos* Bd. 31, H. 12. (Jan. - Apr., 1936).

Pliny the Elder (Secundus, Gaius Plinius) (?), *Naturalis Historia* [Natural History].

Ploss, H. and Bartels, M. u. P. (1927), *Das Weib in der Natur- und Völkerkunde* [Woman in Natural History and Ethnography], Reitzenstein F. v. (rev. and ed.)

Proudhon, Pierre-Joseph (1846), Philosophie de la misère [The Philosophy of Misery].

Quiggin, A. H. (1948), *Primitive Money*, London.

Quiggin, A. H. (1949), *A Survey of Primitive Money*, London.

Regling, K. (1924), *Die antike Münze als Kunstwerk.*

Rehse, H. (1910), *Kiziba. Land und Leute. Eine Monographie* [Kiziba: Land and People. A Monograph], Stuttgart, Strecker u. Schröder.

Rist, Charles (1938), *Histoire Des Doctrines Relatives Au Crédit Et A La Monnaie Depuis John Law Jusqu'a Nos Jours* [History of the Doctrines Relating to Credit and Money from John Law to the Present Day].

Rodbertus, K. (1842), *Zur Erkenntnis unserer staatswirtschaftlichen Zustände.*

Rodbertus, Karl (1870)*, 'Zur Frage des Sachwerths des Geldes im Altertum' [On the question of the real value of money in antiquity]. *Jahrbücher für Nationalökonomie und Statistik*, XV (1870).

Roß, E. A. (1905), *Foundations of Sociology*, New York.

Sacher, von Ed. (1899), *Gesellschaftskunde als Naturwissenschaft* [Social Studies as a Natural Science].

Saitzew, M. (1941), *Der Merkantilismus.* In: *Schweizerische Wirtschaftsfragen, Festgabe für Fritz Mangold.* Bale.

Sauermann, H. (1931), *Soziologie der Wirtschaft* [Sociology of the Economy], in Dunkmann, K, Lehmann, Gerhard & Sauermann, Heinz (eds.) (1931) *Lehrbuch der Soziologie und Sozialphilosophie* [Textbook of Sociology and Social Philosophy].

Savigny Friedrich Carl von (1851)*, *Das Obligationenrecht.*

344

Schade, O. (1872-82), *Altdeutsches Wörterbuch* [Old German Dictionary], 2nd ed.

Schadee, M. C. (1915), 'Heirats- und andere usages bei den Mansela- und Nusawele-Alfuren' [Marriage and other customs among the Mansela and Nusawele Alfur people] etc., *Int. Archiv f. Ethnologie.*

Schäffle, Albert Eberhard Friedrich (1906), Abriss der Soziologie.

Scheler, Max (1828)*, *Die Stellung des Menschen im Kosmos* [The Position of Man in the Cosmos]

Schiller, Friedrich (1793), *Über Anmut und Würde* [On Grace and Dignity].

Schlosser, J. G. (1798), Aristoteles Politik und Fragment der Oeconomik, Bey Friedrich Bohn.

Schlosser, J.G. (1789), *Aristoteles' Politik und Fragment der Ökonomik* [Aristotle's Politics and Fragments of Economics]. Translated from the Greek, with notes and an analysis of the text.

Schmidt, von M. (1917), *Die Aruaken. Ein Beitrag zum Problem der Kulturverbreitung* [The Arawaks: A Contribution to the Problem of Cultural Diffusion].

Schmidt, von M. (1920), *Grundriß der ethnologischen Volkswirtschaftslehre* [Outline of Ethnological Economics], Bd. 1,

Schmidt, W. (1937), *Das Eigentum auf den ältesten Kulturstufen der Menschheit* [The Ownership on the Earliest Cultural Stages of Humanity], Vol. 1 & 2.

Schmoller, G. (1900), *Grundriß der allgemeinen Volkswirtschaftslehre* [Outline of General Economics].

Schneidewin, Max (ed.) (1893), *Cicero und Jacob Grimm Über das Alter.*

Schopenhauer, Arthur (1851), "Über die Weiber" [On Women], *Parerga und Paralipomena* [Parerga and Paralipomena].

Schrader, O. (1907), *Sprachvergleichung und Urgeschichte: Linguistisch-historische Beiträge* [Comparative Linguistics and Prehistory: Linguistic-Historical Contributions], 3rd ed.

Schultz-Ewerth, Erich und Adam, Leonhard (eds.) (1929), Das

Eingeborenenrecht. Sitten und Gewohnheitsrechte der Eingeborenen der ehemaligen deutschen Kolonien in Afrika und in der Südsee. Gesammelt in *Auftrage der damaligen Kolonialverwaltung von Beamten und Missionaren der Kolonien, geordnet und kommentiert von früheren Kolonialbeamten, Ethnologen und Juristen* [The Indigenous Law. Customs and customary laws of the indigenous peoples of the former German colonies in Africa and the South Seas. Collected on behalf of the former colonial administration by officials and missionaries of the colonies, organised and commented upon by former colonial officials, ethnologists, and jurists], 2 volumes. Stuttgart : Strecker & Schröder.

Schulze-Gävernitz, G. v. (1890), *Zum sozialen Frieden* [To Social Peace].

Schumpeter, Joseph (1970/1908), *Das Wesen und der Hauptinhalt der theoretischen Nationalökonomie* [The essence and main content of theoretical national economics], 2nd ed., Berlin.

Schurtz, H. (1897), *Entstehungsgeschichte des Geldes* [The History of the Emergence of Money], Deutsche geographische Blätter, Volume XX.

Schurtz, H. (1898), *Grundriß einer Entstehungsgeschichte des Geldes.*

Schurtz, H. (1902), *Altersklassen und Männerbünde* [Age Classes and Men's Unions].

Schwander, A. (1938), *Die Geldschuldlehre.*

Schwartz, Anna J. (2018)*, "Banking School, Currency School, Free Banking School," in *The New Palgrave Dictionary of Economics*, 3rd ed.

Seidler, E. (1894), "Die Schwankungen des Geldwertes (der Kaufkraft des Geldes) und die juristische Lehre vom Inhalt der Geldschulden," *Jahrbuch für Nationalökonomie und Statistik*, III. Folge, Bd. 7 (1894).

Sieveking, H. (1933), "Wertbeständigkeit und Recht in der Geschichte" [Stability of Value and Law in History], *Zeitschr. f. Ges. Staatswissenschaft*, 94 (1933).

Simmel, G. (1900), *Philosophie des Geldes.*

Simmel, G. (2011/1900)*, *The Philosophy of Money*. Bottomore, T, & Frisby, D. (tr.) Routledge.

Simmel. Georg (1908), *Soziologie – Untersuchungen über die Formen der*

Vergesellschaftung, Duncker & Humblot, Berlin.

Small, Albion Woodbury (1920), *General Sociology*.

Smithin, John (2018)*, Rethinking the theory of money, credit, and macroeconomics: a new statement for the twenty-first century, Lexington Books.

Sombart, W. (1902), *Der moderne Kapitalismus* [The Modern Capitalism].

Sombart, W. (1919), *Der moderne Kapitalismus* [The Modern Capitalism].

Sombart, W. (1927), *Das Wirtschaftsleben im Zeitalter des Hochkapitalismus* [The Economic Life in the Age of High Capitalism].

Sombart, W. (1969)*, *Der moderne Kapitalismus* [The Modern Capitalism], Duncker & Humblot, 3 volumes.

Somlo, F. (1909), *Der Güterverkehr in der Urgesellschaft* [Goods Exchange in Primitive Society]

Spencer, Herbert (1877)*, *The Principles of Sociology*, Vol I. 2nd ed.

Spiethoff, A. (1908) "Die Lehre vom Kapital" in the anthology *Die Entwicklung der deutschen Volkswirtschaftslehre im 19. Jh.*, 1908, Contribution IV.

Stammler, R. (1914), *Wirtschaft und Recht* [Economy and Law].

Swedberg, Richard (2005), *The Max Weber Dictionary Key Words and Central Concepts*, Sandford University Press.

Tacitus, Publius Cornelius (c. 98 AD), *Germania*. (2009), Agricola and Germany (Oxford World's Classics), Anthony Birley (tr.), Oxford University Press.

Taeuber, W. (1950), "Wirtschaft und Kultur," *Politeia*, Fribourg Suisse, vol. II, special issue,,Anno Santo."

Tarde, Gabriel (1902), *Psychologie économique*, Volume 1.

Tarschys, Daniel (1988)*, "Tributes, Tariffs, Taxes and Trade: The Changing Sources of Government Revenue," British Journal of Political Science, Vol. 18, No. 1 (Jan., 1988).

Tawney, H. (1920), *The Acquisitive Society*, Harcourt, Brace, New York.

Temple. R. C. (1899), "Beginnings of Currency," *Journal of the Royal Anthropological Institute*, XXIX.

Tessmann, G. (1913), *Die Pangwe.*

Thilenius, G. (ed.) (1929-1936), *Ergebnisse der Sudsee-Expedition 1908-1910.* II. Ethnographie: B. Mikronesien Band 2. Halbband [Results of the South Pacific-Expedition 1908-1910].

Thurnwald, R. (1922), *Psychologie des primitiven Menschen.*

Thurnwald, R. (1929), 'Papuas und Melanesier,' in Schultz-Ewerth & Adam (1929).

Thurnwald, R. (1931-34), *Die menschliche Gesellschaft in ihren ethnosoziologischen Grundlagen* [Human Society in its Ethnosociological Foundations].

Tiemann, W. (1932), *Die Geldschuld.*

Tönnies, Ferdinand (1887)*, *Gemeinschaft und Gesellschaft*" [Community and Society].

Trimborn, H. (1950), *Rechtsethnologie und orientalische Rechte* [Legal Ethnology and Oriental Laws], Deutsche Landesreferate zum III. Internat. Kongreß für Rechtsvergleichung in London.

Turgot, Anne Robert Jacques (1766), *Réflexions sur la formation et la distribution des richesses* [Reflections on the Formation and Distribution of Wealth].

Varé, D. (1931), *Der lachende Diplomat, Übersetzung aus dem Italienischen* [The Laughing Diplomat, Translation from Italian].

Veit, O. (1947), *Volkswirtschaftliche Theorie der Liquidität* [Economic Theory of Liquidity].

Veit, O. (1948), *Geldreform und Geldverfassung* [Monetary Reform and Monetary Constitution].

Vierkandt, A. (1908), *Die Stetigkeit im Kulturwandel*" [The Continuity in Cultural Change].

Vordermann, A. G. (1888), "Het Journaal van Albert Colfs" eene bijdrage to de kennis der Kleine-Soendaeilanden door ["The Journal of Albert Colfs," a contribution to the knowledge of the Lesser Sunda Islands], in Huyser, I. G. (ed.) (1931), *Nederlandisch Indie oud & niew* [Dutch East Indies Old & New].

W. Eucken, (1947), *Grundlagen der Nationalökonomie* [Foundation of National Economics].

Walras, Léon (1884), "Monnaie d'or avec billon d'argent régulateur," *Revue de Droit international* du 1er décembre.

Walras, Léon (1886), *Théorie de la Monnaie*.

Walsh, C. M. (1903), *The Fundamental Problem in Monetary Science*, New York.

Wappäus, H. (1867), *Zur Lehre von den dem Rechtsverkehr entzogenen Sachen nach römischem und heutigem Recht* ["To the theory of things excluded from legal transactions according to Roman and contemporary law].

Ward, Lester f. (1907), Reine Soziologie [Pure Sociology].

Wasserrab, K. (1903), *Soziale Fragen, Sozialpolitik und Carität"* [Social Issues, Social Policy, and Charity]

Weber, Max (1922)*, *Wirtschaft und Gesellschaft*. Tübingen.

Weber, Max (1923)*, *Wirtschaftsgeschichte: Abriss der universalen Sozial- und Wirtschaftsgeschichte*. München: Duncker & Humblot.

Weber, Max (1925), *Wirtschaft und Gesellschaft*. Tübingen.

Weber, Max (1927)*, *General Economic History*. Knight, Frank H. (tr.). The Free Press.

Weber, Max (1968/1922)*, *Economy and Society*. Roth, G. & Wittich, C. (trs.). University of California Press.

Weber, Max (2019/1922)*, *Economy and Society – A New Translation*. Tribe, K. (ed. &, tr.) Cambridge MA and London: Harvard University Press.

Weigand, L. K. (1878), *Deutsches Wörterbuch*, 3rd ed.

Weiner, Annette B. (1992)*, *Inalienable Possessions: The Paradox of Keeping-While Giving*, University of California Press.

Westermarck, Edward (1891), The History of Human Marriage.

Wheeler, C. C. (1910), *The Tribe and Intertribal Relations in Australia.*

Wiese, L. von (1921), *Einführung in die Sozialpolitik"* [Introduction to Social Policy].

Wieser, Friedrich von (1903), 'Der Geldwert und Seine geschichtlichen Veränderungen. Antritts-Vorlesung' [The Money Value and its Historical Change]. Gehalten am 26. Oktober 1903 an der Wiener Universität [Inaugural Lecture. Delivered on October 26, 1903, at the University of Vienna], *Zeitschrift für Volkswirtschaft und Sozialpolitik* Vol. 13, 1904.

Wieser, Friedrich von (1924), *Theorie der gesellschaftlichen Wirtschaft* [Social Economics].

Wieser, Friedrich von (1926), *Das Gesetz der Macht* [The Law of Power]; (1983/1926), The Law of Power, W. E. Kuhn, (tr.) University of Nebraska Press.

Wieser, Friedrich von (1929), *Gesammelte Abhandlungen* [Collected Essays].

Wieser, Friedrich von (2023/1927), Theory of Money – General Study of Moneym Hans DG Hyun (tr.). Original title: Theorie des Geldes (Allgemeine Lehre vom Gelde), In Ludwig Elster, Adolf Weber and Friedrich von Wieser (eds.), *Handwörterbuch der Staatswissenschaften,* Fourth, Completely Revised Edition, Vol. 4 (681–717), Jena Verlag Von Gustav Fischer, 1927.

Wolowski, L. F. (1870)*, *"Enquête Sur La Question Monétaire,"* in L. F. Wolowski (ed.) (1871), *L'or et L'argent,* Paris: Libraire de Guillaumin.

Zweig, Stefan (1929), Joseph Fouché.

Zweig, Stefan (1941), *Die Welt von Gestern, Erinnerungen eines Europäers* [The World of Yesterday: Memories of a European].

Zwiedineck-Südenhorst, O. von (1911), *Sozialpolitik.*

350

Translation Notes

1. Action (*Handeln*), Activity (*Handlung*) and Behaviour (*Verhalten*)

We have distinguished the following words for translation, following Max Weber's use of the term.

(1) Activity (*Handlung*) refers to the specific action or deed itself, often carrying a distinct sense of purpose or intention behind it, and Action (*Handeln*) denotes the process of taking action, and it may involve a deliberate intention or purpose behind the actions.

(2) Behaviour (*Verhalten*) encompasses an individual's overall behaviour or conduct, including their actions and reactions, without necessarily highlighting a specific intention behind each behaviour.

While action or activity (*Handlung* or *Handeln*) frequently carries a stronger sense of purpose or intention behind the action, behaviour (*Verhalten*) typically covers a person's broader behavioural patterns without necessarily emphasising specific intentions behind each behaviour.

Refer to Tribe's notes (Weber 2019:468-9) and Swedberg (2005:2).

2. Commercial-Money (*Verkehrsgeld*)

We translate '*Verkehrsgeld*' as 'commercial money' in contrast to 'state money.' According to Sombart (1919:402), "Based on the origin of its validity, we can designate it as either commercial-money (*Verkehrsgeld*) or state money (*Staatsgeld*)." Commercial-money is defined as money that derives its exchange value as a general medium of exchange from "the tacit consensus of all individuals participating in an economic society." On the other hand, if "it is the arbitrary act of legislative authority (the state) that grants that something its authoritative position," it is called 'state money.'

3. Compensation (*Entgelt*) and Renumeration (*Entgeltung*)

We distinguish between '*Entgelt*' (compensation) and '*Entgeltung*' (remuneration) in this context. *Entgelt* primarily refers to compensation, remuneration, or payment for a service, work, or performance. It is a broader term that encompasses the concept of payment or fees for various services, products, or labour. *Entgeltung* often carries the connotation of compensation or settlement in a more specific context, such as retribution, restitution, or compensation for an action, debt, or obligation. It is a narrower term that relates more to the aspect of compensating or settling something in particular.

4. Disposal and Control (*Verfügung*)

We primarily refer to Max Weber to grasp the meaning of 'disposal and control.'

According to Tribe in his notes on Weber's Economy and Society, '*Verfügung* (disposal and control)' refers to the ability of "disposal over the thing so that it can actually be employed to satisfy the need" (Weber 2019:482). It corresponds to the German equivalent of the Latin '*dispone*' — making '*Disponieren*' and '*Verfügung*' essentially synonymous terms in Latin and German (Weber 2019:210n53, Tribe's comment).

This concept may have been influenced by Carl Menger, who expressed a similar idea when he said: "A good is *verfügbar* to someone in the economic sense of the word when he is in a position to obtain it for the satisfaction of his needs. Physical or legal obstacles can stand in the way of this. The wealth of a ward of court, for example, is not at the disposition of a guardian in the above sense of the word" (Menger 1871: 70n, quoted from Tribe's comment in Weber 2019: 482).

In this book, five closely related terms are employed, each with nuanced differences. These terms are: '*Verfügungsmacht*' (power of disposal and control), '*Verfügungsgewalt*' (command of disposal and control), '*Verfügungsbefugnis*' (authority of disposal and control), '*Verfügungsberechtigung*' (permission of disposal and control), and '*Verfügungsmöglichkeit*' (capability of disposal and control).

See also Swedberg (2005:72).

5. Economy (*Wirtschaft*) and Oikonomia (*Ökonomie*), Economic (*wirtschaftlich*) and Economical (*ökonomisch*)

'*Ökonomie*' has its origin in the Greek word '*oikonomia*' (οἰκονομία),' which combines '*oikos*' (οἶκος – house) and '*nomos*' (νόμος – law, order or management). In this sense, it reflects the idea of management or administration of a household or estate. Over time, its meaning expanded to encompass broader concepts related to resource management, finance, and the operations of larger-scale organisations, including economic systems and policies. We translate '*Ökonomie*' into '*oikonomia*' to distinguish it from the more evolved concept of 'economy' (*Wirtschaft*).

We also draw a distinction between *ökonomisch* and *wirtschaftlich* in this translation. In contemporary German usage, '*ökonomisch*' relates to matters concerning the economy, economics, or economic principles. It is closely tied to the administration of resources, economies, or economic systems. '*Wirtschaftlich*,' on the contrary, tends to be more expansive, covering a broader spectrum of practical, economic, or business-related aspects. We translate *ökonomisch* as 'economical' and *wirtschaftlich* as 'economic' in order to differentiate their uses in the original text. However, it is important to note that while we use these English terms, their precise correspondence to the original German context may vary.

6. Exchange (*Tausch*) and Intercourse (*Verkehr*)

'*Verkehr*,' which can be translated as 'intercourse, traffic, interaction, commerce or transaction or trade' depending on the context, is a broad term that generally refers to the economic intercourse, distribution, or movement of goods, services, or information. It encompasses various activities related to economic intercourses among people and the movement of goods and services in a broader sense. '*Verkehr*' is not limited to economic transactions; it can also involve social intercourses.

On the other hand, '*Tausch*,' translated as 'exchange' or 'barter,' specifically refers to the act of exchanging or bartering, where one party gives goods or services in exchange for goods or services from another party.

7. Force (*Kraft*) and Power (*Macht*)

'Power' (*Macht*) is differentiated from 'force' or 'strength' (Kraft) in German. The former refers to the capability, artificially created either consciously or unconsciously, to influence others within a social relationship, while the latter pertains to the inherent force present in objects or entities.

8. *Geltung* (Validity, Recognition)

'*Geltung*' can be translated to English as 'validity,' 'worth' or 'authority' in certain contexts; however, it frequently carries the connotation of attaining social *recognition* or *significance*.

This is particularly evident in the context of human aspirations and social interactions. In the author's discussion of the goals inherent in the struggle of human life, '*Geltung*' is listed as one of these objectives. In this context, '*Geltung*' pertains to the yearning for recognition, status, or significance within society. It signifies the notion that individuals endeavour to be acknowledged or affirmed by others, signifying their own value.

9. Gens (*Geschlecht*), Clan (*Sippe*) and Tribe (*Stamme*)

We distinguish three forms of communities larger than hordes or families:

(1) A 'gens' (*Geschlecht*, pl. gentes) is a group of families based on descent from a common ancestor in the male line, sharing the same nomen (a gentile name).

(2) A 'clan' (*Sippe*) is an extended family sharing the same imaginary ancestors appearing in myths, the same totem, and, therefore, a strong sense of belonging. They may live in neighbouring villages without necessarily living in the same place.

(3) A 'tribe' (*Stamme*) is a community composed of multiple clans and differentiated from other tribes in their language and culture.

10. Gift (*Gabe*) and Present (*Geschenk*)

Geschenk (present) refers to a gift, something given voluntarily to someone as a present or token of appreciation. It often implies a positive gesture and is commonly used for occasions like birthdays, holidays, or special events. It is more closely associated with personal gifts given in celebratory or appreciative contexts, while '*Gabe*' (gift) has a wider range of meanings related to giving in general. See p. 66.

11. Gift-Exchange (*Gabentausch*), Gift-Traffic (*Gabenverkehr*)

We discern the nuanced distinction between '*Gabentausch*' (gift-exchange) and '*Gabenverkehr*' (gift-traffic) in German.

'*Gabentausch*' (gift-exchange) places a narrower emphasis on the direct act of exchanging gifts, often implying a direct interaction between two parties.

Conversely, '*Gabenverkehr*' (gift-traffic) encompasses the encompassing culture, practices, and diverse occasions associated with gift-giving. It refers to the broader concept of gifts being exchanged throughout a society or community.

12. Possession (*Besitz*) and Ownership (*Eigentum*)

There is a need to clarify the concepts of '*Besitz*' (possession) and '*Eigentum*' (ownership).

(1) The word '*Besitz*' in German is indeed a combination of two elements: '*Be-*' and '*Sitz.*' The prefix '*Be-*' is commonly used to form nouns or verbs and often conveys the notion of location or position. '*Sitz*' means 'seat' or 'place.' As a result, '*Besitz*' encompasses the concept of 'possession' or 'having a place' in the sense of owning or controlling

354

something. The term *'Besitz'* can be traced back to the Old High German word *'besizzan'* (or *'bisaz'*), which originally meant 'to occupy' or 'to possess.'

(2) In the context of *'Eigentum'* (ownership), the word *'eigen'* in German signifies 'own' or 'belonging to oneself.' It is employed to express the idea of something being under one's own control. *'Eigentum'* is closely linked to the concept of personal ownership and specifically underscores the *legally protected* right of owning something.

(3) The usual translation of *'Eigentum'* (ownership) as 'property' can be misleading, as 'property' without the connotation of 'legal protection' is better represented in German by *Besitztum*, *Vermögen*, *Eigenschaft* or *Liegenschaft*.

13. Purchasing Force (*Kaufkraft*) and Purchasing Power (*Kaufmacht*)

In German, *'Kaufkraft'* is generally translated as 'purchasing power' in English, referring to the relationship between things, such as money and objects.

On the other hand, Gerloff uses the term *'Kaufmacht'* to emphasise the normative element of money's power within the context of social relationships.

To highlight the difference between these terms, which might go unnoticed, we translate *'Kaufkraft'* as 'purchasing force' (instead of the commonly used English term 'purchasing power') while retaining 'purchasing power' for *'Kaufmacht,'* drawing on the distinction between *'Kraft'* (force) and *'Macht'* (power) in German.

14. Social (*sozial*) and Societal (*gesellschaftlich*); Societality (*Gesellschaftlichkeit*), Sociality (*Sozialität*), Sociability (*Geselligkeit*); Societalisation (*Vergesellschaftung*), Socialisation (*Socialisation*, *Vergesellung*)

'Gesellschaftlich' (societal) and *'sozial'* (social) have slightly different nuances in meaning in German.

(1) Societal (*gesellschaftlich*) has a *broader* context, including interactions, structures, and functions within society as a whole, taking into account various dimensions of social life. It refers to structural and systemic aspects of society.

(2) On the other hand, 'social' (*sozial*) tends to focus more on the interpersonal and individual aspects of social interaction, such as relationships, behaviours, and phenomena that involve people in their interactions, relationships, and roles within society. It is often used to describe the human

and personal dimensions of social life.

(3) We translate '*Gesellschaftlichkeit*' into 'societality' instead of 'sociality' to emphasise the distinction between 'social' (*sozial*) and 'societal' (*gesellschaftlich*).

The German words corresponding to 'sociality' and 'sociability' are '*Sozialität*' and '*Geselligkeit*,' respectively.

(4) We choose to translate '*Vergesellschaftung*' as 'societalisation' instead of the commonly used 'socialisation' (*Socialisation* in German) to highlight the distinction between 'social' (*sozial*) and 'societal' (*gesellschaftlich*).

On the other hand, '*Vergesellung*' (socialisation) generally refers to the socialisation or social interaction within specific social groups or institutions, such as within a company, organisation, or any particular social entity. It often implies the process of becoming part of a social group and adapting to its norms, values, and customs.

15. Tiering (*Staffelung*), Stratification (*Schichtung*) and Class Formation

(1) Tiering (*Staffelung*) refers to the idea that society is organised like tiers or levels, with each level having a distinct position or rank. It is a way of categorising people based on their social standing, but the categories are not necessarily rigid or hierarchical.

(2) Stratification (*Schichtung*) suggests a layered or stratified structure, where society is divided into distinct social strata or layers. Each stratum may have different access to resources, opportunities, and privileges, creating social inequalities, but there is a certain mobility across the stratum.

(3) Genuine class formation implies the creation of real and distinct social classes. In a class-based society, people are grouped into classes based on shared characteristics, such as economic or social status. These classes can be more clearly defined and often come with specific rights, privileges, or restrictions.

16. Usage (*Gebrauch*) and Use (*Verwendung*); Money-Usage (*Geldgebrauch*), Money-Expending (Geldverwendung)

(1) While both terms involve the act of employing or making use of something, '*Gebrauch*' (usage) tends to be broader, encompassing customary or practical usage, while '*Verwendung*' (use) emphasises the specific and purposeful application of something.

(2) We also distinguish between '*Geldgebrauch*' (money-usage) and '*Geldverwendung*' (money-expending), with the latter emphasising the act of spending money, while the former

encompasses the broader spectrum of money's application, extending beyond mere spending.

17. Voluntary Gift (*Dargabe*), Contribution (*Hergabe*) and Levy (*Abgabe*)

According to Gerloff, there are stages of transition in the nature of 'giving' from *Dargabe*, through *Hergabe*, to *Abgabe* (Tarschys 1988:3).

While nuances are challenging to capture in English, we roughly translate these terms as a voluntary gift, contribution, and levy, respectively.

Index (Name)

Index (Subject)

396

404

410